RED FUNNEL 150

Celebrating one hundred and fifty years of
the Southampton Isle of Wight and South of England
Royal Mail Steam Packet Company Limited

The Original Isle of Wight Ferries

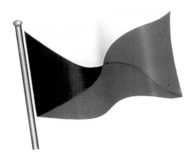

Blue to mast,
Green to fly,
Red on deck,
White on high.

The colours of the company house flag derive from the names of the original vessels in the fleet when the company was formed in 1861; namely SAPPHIRE, EMERALD, RUBY and PEARL, and is best remembered by this time-honoured mnemonic.

RED JET 4 arrived from Tasmania and ran successful trials on 14 May 2003. During the day she circled the Isle of Wight and this publicity photograph was taken as she passed the Needles at the western end of the Solent.   RED FUNNEL ARCHIVES

RED FUNNEL 150

Celebrating one hundred and fifty years of
the Southampton Isle of Wight and South of England
Royal Mail Steam Packet Company Limited

The Original Isle of Wight Ferries

BY
KEITH ADAMS

PUBLISHER:
RICHARD DANIELSON

2010

DEDICATIONS

I dedicate this book to my father, Ron Adams (1919 – 1989).

And also

To all employees of Red Funnel, past and present,
sea going and on shore, without whom there would be no story to tell.

Published in 2010 by Richard Danielson, 20 Banks Howe, Onchan, Isle of Man. IM3 2ET

ISBN 978-0-9513155-5-2

Design and image preparation by Richard Danielson.
Printing and text origination by Bridson & Horrox Limited,
Hills Meadow, Douglas, Isle of Man. IM1 5EB

CONTENTS

Dust jacket front:
Small photographs, from top left, STIRLING CASTLE, LORD ELGIN, PRINCESS HELENA, BOURNEMOUTH QUEEN, PRINCESS ELIZABETH, BALMORAL, MEDINA, CARISBROOKE CASTLE, NETLEY CASTLE, SHEARWATER 2, BALMORAL.

Main image: Returning to Southampton from the Isle of Wight, RED JET 4 hurries past a well-loaded RED EAGLE on 12 July 2006.　　　　　　　　　　　　　　　　　　　　RICHARD DANIELSON

Dedications page: This original artwork remains in the Red Funnel archives. It was used in the 1937 annual guide Red Funnel Stuff as the heading to the introduction by E P Leigh-Bennet. The subject is a 1930s general view of the Royal Pier, Southampton showing six Red Funnel steamers.

Dust jacket back:
Top left: The pristine-looking SOLENT QUEEN (I) with white funnels, and foremast dressed for an unknown special occasion.　　　　　　　　　　　　　　KEITH ABRAHAM COLLECTION

Bottom left: It is not difficult to see how the handsome LORNA DOONE (I) became a firm favourite amongst Red Funnel's excursion passengers.　　　　　　　　　　　　　　RED FUNNEL ARCHIVES

Right: The Ailsa-built, stately looking BOURNEMOUTH QUEEN on the inside berth at Ryde Pier.
　　　　　　　　　　　　　　　　　ALAN BROWN – KEITH ADAMS COLLECTION

CHAIRMAN'S FOREWORD

It is a great privilege to be Chairman of Red Funnel as we celebrate the 150th anniversary of the Company's incorporation. The full name of the Company is the Southampton Isle of Wight and South of England Royal Mail Steam Packet Company Limited, the longest name on the English register of companies. In 1935 the board took the decision to use the name Red Funnel, a more manageable mouthful reflecting the distinctive livery of the Company's ships.

Red Funnel and its predecessors have actually been running services between Southampton and Cowes since 1820. At every stage in Red Funnel's development the Company has taken the latest technology of the time and used it for the benefit of the travelling public. Wooden hulls gave way to iron in the 1860's and steel was first used in 1891. In the early days, steam propulsion reigned supreme, with occasional help from a foresail, but the Company's first diesel ship, *Medina*, was built in 1931 in the middle of the great economic depression.

Our first vessel used primarily for carrying vehicles, *Her Majesty*, was converted in 1927 and we experimented with a high speed service to the Island as early as 1933. Today we have built on these early principles, using the very latest technology for our hi-speed *Red Jet* catamarans and our vehicle ferries, right through to our online booking systems, our onboard Wi-Fi and use of mobile technology, all to create a seamless customer journey.

For 150 years we have played a proud role in our nation's story and Red Funnel ships were called on to serve our country in both World Wars. During the Great War, four of our ships served in the Mediterranean, two of them becoming war losses there. In the Second World War our tugs were under military control and many of the ships were taken over by the Admiralty, serving in roles far removed from their peacetime duties. Our then newest ship, *Gracie Fields*, was lost at Dunkirk and *Her Majesty* was sunk in an air raid at Southampton. Two favourite paddle steamers, *Lorna Doone* and *Balmoral*, the latter famous for her pre-war cross channel excursions to Cherbourg, were used as floating anti-aircraft batteries and by 1945 were too damaged for civilian use. It is to the greatest credit of our staff and crews that, despite being in the thick of it, they maintained the passage service to Cowes in the most adverse of conditions.

Since the 1950's, Red Funnel has concentrated on the vehicle ferry service to Cowes, having recognized early on the impact that the motor car would have on the once traditional excursion trade. Our *Red Jet* high speed catamarans now link with Southampton and its countrywide rail services, connecting Cowes to London with an integrated ferry, bus and train service in a little over two hours.

The business has developed from its traditional beginning as a ferry service to a fully integrated travel, transport and leisure company. We have evolved with the needs of our stakeholders and have progressed our vitally important role in the tourism industry on the Isle of Wight. We have become "destination marketers", offering everything from complete holiday packages to festival tickets and car hire. We are also a major provider of logistics and haulage solutions nationwide from the Island.

None of the Company's achievements happen without a team effort and I pay grateful tribute to the loyalty and skills of my fellow directors, all our staff and suppliers.

But I am particularly thankful for the loyal support of our millions of individual and commercial customers, without whom this business would not exist. We will continue to strive to meet their changing needs, whilst providing a safe and enjoyable place for our staff to work.

Last but by no means least, I thank the author of this book, Keith Adams, and his publisher Richard Danielson, for their magnificent efforts in recording our Company's history in *Red Funnel 150*. The profit from their endeavours will benefit *Balmoral*, Red Funnel's flagship from 1949 to 1968, which continues to operate as support ship to the preserved paddle steamer *Waverley*. Red Funnel is pleased to help Keith and Richard and we offer our best wishes for the continued success of *Balmoral*.

Here's to another 150 years!

James Cooper
Red Funnel Group Chairman
September 2010

Standing from left:
Shirley Anderson, Human Resources Director; John Rayner, Freight and Distribution Director; Jonathan Green, Sales and Marketing Director; Murray Carter, Group Operations Director; Paul Winter, Chief Financial Officer.

Seated from left:
James Cooper, Chairman; James Fulford, Chief Executive Officer; Kenton Bradbury, Non-Executive Director.

Keith Edwards, Group Technical and Quality Director, is not in the photograph.

INTRODUCTION

I was three years old when I made my first sailing on a Red Funnel ship. My father took me from Southampton to Cowes on *Vecta* and we returned on *Medina*. Two years later, in 1958, he took me on the last scheduled sailing of Red Funnel's last paddle steamer *Princess Elizabeth*. These trips were the start of my interest in the workings of Red Funnel and coastal and lake passenger vessels around the United Kingdom and Europe. When Dad retired he began writing about the Red Funnel vessels. Bert Moody offered his own notes and typed the original manuscripts of the book that was to become *Red Funnel and Before*. It was published in 1986, conveniently commemorating 125 years of the company's operation. The book's title was a play on the fact that the company's vessels had only carried red painted funnels since 1936.

Sadly, Dad died in 1989. Over the years I received many appreciative comments about *Red Funnel and Before* and his book led me into contact with maritime writer and publisher Richard Danielson when he was writing his own splendid work *The Honourable Balmoral – Her Peers and Piers*, produced by him in 1999 for *Balmoral's* 50th anniversary. We began a regular correspondence and exchange of photographs. Richard planted the seeds for this book by periodically reminding me of Red Funnel's 150 year anniversary in 2011 and generously suggesting that I should update my father's earlier work. Having agreed to accept the task, Richard re established his earlier contact with Hazel Nicholson, one time Red Funnel company secretary. This led to official recognition of the proposed book by the company and, most importantly, access to the archives which Hazel has so carefully maintained both as a company officer and subsequently during her retirement. Without access to, and the quality of, the Red Funnel archives, this book would be very different. It has been a personal delight to handle the original hand written minute books from 1861 and many important documents and splendid official photographs covering the company's long history. For many years it was believed that much of the early company records had been lost, their subsequent availability has added greatly to the fascinating story.

I have received free access to Red Funnel's official minute books from incorporation in 1861 through to 1997. The subsequent years include commercially sensitive matters and these are reported from public sources, mainly the company's own website, maritime press reports and from *Cruising Monthly*. Whoever writes Red Funnel's 175th anniversary publication will have the pleasure of delving into the background detail for that period.

ACKNOWLEDGEMENTS

Any book of this nature cannot be compiled without the help and assistance of others.

I have used my father's book *Red Funnel and Before*, as both my inspiration and for most of the historical text and facts concerning the ships whose history was already complete when it was published in 1986. Sadly, *Red Funnel and Before* is now long since out of print so *Red Funnel 150* will also help fill the space left in its absence.

My especial thanks go to Hazel Nicholson, archivist of the company archives, for her encouragement, and Red Funnel's then managing director, Tom Docherty, for his initial agreement to the project in May 2008. Marketing director, Jonathan Green and his colleagues have always been ready to help, despite pressing demands on their time, and it is Jonathan's departmental budget that has allowed the book to be produced in its present form. I also thank Caroline Taylor, personal assistant to the directors, for her tolerance in dealing with my many requests when already busy dealing with her own work. Additionally, thank you to everyone at the Bugle Street offices for their ready smiles and words of welcome when I arrived and disappeared into the basement archives for more research.

Having provided the initial impetus, I am delighted that Richard Danielson accepted my request that he take the role of publisher. Richard's personal knowledge and interest in Red Funnel and his practical experience of image restoration and publishing has been absolutely invaluable. He has also dealt with the scanning, reproduction, initial and final selection of the photographs that contribute so much to the work. Where the original photographer is known this is credited, but other images are from collections and are globally acknowledged. Apart from my own and Richard's personal collections, the following have trawled their records in response to specific and general requests – Keith Abraham; Norman Bird; Ivan Bovey; Pat and June Bushell; Richard Clammer; Terry Creswell; Barry Eagles; Tony Horn; Don Jones; Peter Lamb; Tom Lee curator of the Paddle Steamer Picture Gallery www.freespace.virgin.net/tomlee/index has found several rare images for us to use; Bert Moody; Pat Murrell; Iain Quinn and Edwin Wilmshurst. Andrew Gladwell, curator of the PSPS archives www.heritagesteamers.co.uk has produced some superb images of the early steamers as well as encouraging the whole project from its inception. English Heritage www.english-heritage.org.uk has been particularly helpful in allowing publication of the Aerofilm photographs from the 1930s which are now under their care. Susan Hill at Southampton City Archives has been of great assistance to Richard Danielson in his researches. Tim Cooper, Greg Child, David Jones and Ray Perkins have provided detailed information from their own archives and researches. Norman Bird and Geoffrey Hamer have checked facts on the after lives of the 'Castle' ferries in Italian and Croatian waters. Myra Allen, editor of *Paddle Wheels*; and George Boswell, editor of *Cruising Monthly*, have willingly included appeals for photographs and information in their journals and circulated the flyers for advance subscribers' copies of the book.

I am especially indebted to my proof readers, Keith Abraham, Don Jones and Bert Moody. All three were involved in assisting my father in the production of *Red Funnel and Before* and I am delighted they agreed to use their expertise in helping with this work. Their input has greatly improved the present text in every way. Don has both a personal and professional interest in the company and his knowledge about Red Funnel is enormous. Richard Danielson has also made many welcome and practical suggestions, both as ship historian and publisher. The intention throughout has been to provide accurate information, but I take full responsibility for errors that remain. Many other friends and fellow enthusiasts; particularly those who are often to be found aboard *Balmoral* and the paddle steamer *Waverley*, have contributed to this work by their encouragement and offering help and information. My thanks to you all, without you it would not have happened.

Lastly, I especially thank my wife Jill; my daughters, Jennie and Debbie and their husbands Pratap and Nic, for encouraging me with this project, their professional advice and assistance and, above all, for their benign tolerance of my transport interests.

Keith Adams
Milford on Sea
September 2010

NORRIS CASTLE passes HMY BRITANNIA as she enters the river Medina during Cowes Week. Traditionally the ferries are dressed overall during the first week in August when the Cowes yacht clubs host a week of sailing competitions. The 'Week' has been part of the British sporting calendar since 1826. It is said to be the longest running regatta in the world.
RED FUNNEL ARCHIVES

1861 - 1898

The beginnings of today's Red Funnel Group emerged out of competition on the Southampton to Cowes packet service. In April 1861 it became known to the existing operators that a new company, with brand new vessels, was about to upset their established routine.

Until then the service had been operated by a group of ships, separately owned by many different individuals. Over the years they had formed themselves into two groups and had co-operated on the route. The Island, Cowes-based business was The Isle of Wight Royal Mail Steam Packet Company, which operated the vessels *Ruby*, *Medina*, *Pearl* and *Queen*. The mainland, Southampton business was known as The Isle of Wight Steam Packet Company. They operated *Gem* and *Emerald* and had just built a new ship, *Sapphire*, in 1860.

The opposition came from a new concern, named the Southampton, Isle of Wight & Portsmouth Improved Steamboat Company (the Improved Co). This newcomer was formed in 1860 and had two brand new saloon steamers *Lord of the Isles* and *Lady of the Lake*. The Improved Co issued a timetable indicating that their *Lord of the Isles* would be confined to the Southampton - Cowes service. Additionally, it was reported that the newcomers had secured a lease on the Fountain Pier at Cowes, thus giving them preferential berthing facilities.

This news galvanised the existing operators into action. Under the chairmanship of Andrew Lamb, a Committee of Management of the Isle of Wight Steam Packet Company was established. The new committee first met on 9 April 1861. Later, Mr Lamb suggested a meeting with the directors of the new operators and on 31 July he reported back about his long meeting with Messrs Pinnock and Bird, directors' of the Improved Co. He was

assured that there would be no fare cutting and no touting for business at the piers. This assurance may have been given with the best of intentions, but it was not honoured for long.

Andrew Lamb set about his new business with gusto. He realised his organisation needed a new pier of its own at Cowes and set in motion a plan to arrange this. He needed a fleet of ships that was reliable and run in a co-ordinated manner. He had to persuade his members, previously sailing on their own account, to combine into a united front if they were to compete sensibly with the newcomers.

On 7 August, with Mr Lamb in the chair, it was agreed to appoint a board of directors and minutes of the meeting note that the short-lived committee of management then ceased to exist. Draft documents were prepared to incorporate a company with the name of the Southampton Isle of Wight and South of England Royal Mail Steam Packet Company Limited. There was to be an initial issue of 4,000 shares, each with a nominal value of £10, giving a total capital of £40,000.

The new company was formally registered at Companies House on 10 September 1861 and the vessels of the two original concerns began sailing for their new owner on 29 September 1861. Shortly afterwards fares were reduced, no doubt to exert pressure on the Improved Co which had to follow suit.

At their meeting on 17 March 1862 the valuations of the first vessels were agreed as follows; *Medina* £3,200; *Sapphire* £4,800; *Queen* £2,240; *Emerald* £2,880; *Ruby* £1,280; *Pearl* £1,280; and *Gem* £640. The total value of the fleet was £16,320 and 1,632 shares in Red Funnel were issued to the original owners in exchange for their vessels being transferred to the new company.

In May 1862 the Improved Co approached with a wish to increase fares, presumably because the competition driving fares downwards was becoming untenable for them. The proposal was summarily dismissed by the Red Funnel board as 'cannot be entertained'. However the board saw benefits in linking the fares issue to the lease of the pontoon at Cowes. It also seems clear that Red Funnel were aware of financial difficulties with their competitor because opposition from the Improved Co ceased from 1 July by mutual agreement with the directors. More remunerative fares were then agreed and the hours of working were revised, the share of work and earnings being split two thirds to Red Funnel and one third to the Improved Co.

A sub-committee was set up to deal with both the Cowes pontoon and the arrangements at the Royal Pier at Southampton. G W O'Connor, in his centenary book of *Red Funnel The First Hundred Years* writes that agreement was reached with the Improved Co from 6 June 1862 that both

Taken from the Parade at Cowes, showing the Drovers Marine Hotel, later the site of Victoria Pier, an early steamer, believed to be GEM, departs for Southampton.
DON JONES
COLLECTION

companies would embark passengers at the Royal Pier in Southampton, but land passengers from Cowes at a pontoon close to the western hard at the Floating Bridge on the river Itchen. In July, Red Funnel began renting this pontoon from Alfred Barton at £200 per annum. Mr Barton's name appears subsequently when he became Red Funnel's manager at Cowes. Captain F T O'Brien, in his book *Early Solent Steamers*, explains that the Improved Co had begun using the Itchen pontoon in order to avoid paying tolls on the number of passengers passing through the Royal Pier.

In December the results for the first period's trading to 30 September 1862 were reviewed. A loss was made and it was observed that there was only room for one company to operate the passage service to Cowes. It was also noted that the Improved Co had entered the Court of Bankruptcy in October 1862, the main creditor being the Thames Iron Works & Shipbuilding Co builders of their two vessels.

In December 1863 the second year's results were noted and a profit of £4,156 recorded. A dividend of 10% was paid.

Lady of the Lake entered service on 2 May 1864, 'with the sanction of the mortgagees', indicating that the working arrangements with the Improved Co were continuing while that company was in bankruptcy. She must have operated for the summer season only as Mr Barton was involved with her laying up at the end of October.

In September the minutes record that a new pontoon was being constructed at Southampton's Royal Pier. When completed it was intended that all services would use the new facilities, ending the use of the Itchen pontoon.

At an important meeting on 20 February 1865 Mr Pinnock, of the Improved Co, proposed on behalf of himself and the other mortgagees that Red Funnel should take over the steamers *Lady of the Lake* and *Lord of the Isles*, together with the Cowes pontoon with 'their entire interest in rents and traffic of goods'. They suggested a value of £8,000 and were willing to be paid by receiving 800 shares of £10 each. The Red Funnel directors met two days later, agreed the price and were willing to pay outright rather than by the issue of shares. However, when the final documentation was completed in July, 800 shares were issued and it appears Mr Pinnock also received a cheque for £2,000 in connection with the pontoon at Cowes.

In December 1865 a new vessel was required and tenders were received from John White of Cowes, with engines from Day & Co at Northam, Southampton. The cost of the vessel was £7,200 and she was to be named *Vectis*. In July 1866 the directors returned to John White for a small paddle boat costing £330 '50 feet long, 11 feet beam, drawing 2 feet and of 10 horse power', this was the small ferry *Precursor* (I) for use between Cowes and East Cowes.

The results for the year ended 30 September 1866

LORNA DOONE calls at Swanage Pier on 27 August 1937. This rare Dufaycolour image shows how immaculate the fleet was kept in the 1930s. Cosens' VICTORIA lies at the other side of the Pier.
SIDNEY PERRIER – PADDLE STEAMER PICTURE GALLERY

were less satisfactory than the previous two years. The reasons given were the countrywide money crisis, a cattle plague and the presence of cholera, combined with very wet weather.

Pearl was now regarded as being worn out and was sold by public auction. In 1868 Red Funnel acquired the lease, from the Cowes Steam Ferry Company Limited, to run the chain ferry floating bridge between Cowes and East Cowes. In the annual report for 1868, the purchase is referred to and the reason given for the acquisition was to prevent competition. The dividend was set at 7%, compared to 6% in the previous year.

There now appears to have been a quieter period in the company's history. The 1869 annual report refers to more evening and excursion sailings and the payment of an interim dividend, the total payment remaining at 7%. The floating bridge traffic was fully up to expectations. In 1870 traffic was regarded as satisfactory. Red Funnel experimented with an increased service between Cowes and Southsea during the summer, but it was not remunerative and was discontinued. In 1871 a new, larger, launch was ordered from J Samuel White for the Cowes to East Cowes ferry. This was *Princess Louise*, which was to have an exceptionally long life with Red Funnel, surviving until becoming a war time loss in 1944. At the annual meeting on 2 January 1872, referring to the year ended 30 September 1871, the shareholders were informed of *Emerald's* disposal and that *Ruby* was to follow in 1872.

Their replacement in the fleet was to be a new vessel from the Barclay, Curle & Co shipyard on the river Clyde which had produced 'considerably the lowest tender'. *Southampton* was launched on 21 May 1872 and started a 16 year relationship with the Barclay, Curle yard, which produced several vessels which all gave long service. *Southampton* was the prototype for the company's future ships.

The following year signalled a continuation in the modernisation of the fleet. *Sapphire* was disposed of and *Queen* was also for sale, but a buyer had not come forward by the time of the annual meeting on 6 January 1874. The price of coal was reported to be very high and the dividend was reduced to 5%.

At the annual meeting on 4 January 1876, news was given of two new steamers under construction. *Carisbrooke* and *Prince Leopold* were sisters from the Barclay, Curle yard. The dividend that year was 6%, but business must have been reasonable despite the commercial depression of the time. The following year's report notes that the two new ships cost £17,540 and, apart from a loan of £2,500 all had been paid from trading receipts. *Queen* had eventually been sold. Additionally, new boilers and extensive repairs were being made to *Lord of the Isles* and *Vectis* was also being reboilered and fitted with compound engines. Compounding the engines was expected to produce an economy in fuel consumption. The expectation was realised, as the

This early photograph, taken from the seaward end of Southampton's Royal Pier, shows VECTIS at the lay-by berth with SOUTHAMPTON behind her. Note the railway wagons being unloaded, the railway tracks on the Pier were damaged during World War I and the service was never resumed.
RED FUNNEL ARCHIVES

meeting on 1 January 1878 confirmed a reduction in coal used. The dividend returned to 6%, having been 5% for the year ended 30 September 1876 and 6% for 1874 and 1875.

In 1878 the dividend increased to 7%, but competition was expected from Portsmouth where the London and South Western and London, Brighton and South Coast Railways had given joint notice of their intention to seek parliamentary powers to operate steamers on the Solent. The Red Funnel directors assured their shareholders that the move would receive their watchful attention. After opening their new station at Portsmouth Harbour on 2 October 1876, the Joint Railway Committee had started work in 1878, building a railway line from Ryde St Johns Road to Ryde Esplanade, by tunnelling under the town. Work on the new steamer pier at Ryde was also progressing and the railway terminus at the pier head opened on 12 July 1880.

The annual meeting on 6 January 1880 confirmed that another new steamer had been ordered from Barclay, Curle. She would be called *Princess Beatrice* and be ready in time for the 1880 summer season.

On 4 January 1881 the shareholders were informed that a new 21 year lease for the Cowes to East Cowes ferry had been signed. As part of the agreement a new chain ferry was to be provided and this addition was presently out to tender. It was built by Napier & Company at Southampton and towed to Cowes on 25 January

1882. The accounts for the year ended 30 September 1880 were the first to include a balance sheet as part of the annual report.

At the next year's meeting on 3 January 1882, the death of Red Funnel's highly esteemed first chairman, Andrew Lamb, was reported. He had come to Southampton in the 1840's with the Peninsular and Oriental Steam Navigation Company (P&O) when that company had just ordered two new vessels to commence their regular services to Egypt and India. In P&O's 150th anniversary book Mr Lamb was referred to as their 'Celebrated Superintendent Engineer'. In Red Funnel's centenary book he was described as a man of integrity, vision and a considerable personality. His legacy lives on, with Red Funnel continuing to provide the regular services to the Isle of Wight that he began in 1861, and P&O now a division of the Carnival cruise organisation.

The dividend remained at 6% for the year ended 30 September 1881. On 2 January 1883 shareholders were told of further plans to modernise the fleet. *Medina* had been disposed of and a new vessel, *Princess Helena*, was on order for delivery in time for the 1883 season. She was launched on 22 June, completed remarkably quickly, and entered service in July.

Gem left the fleet in late 1883. The board were concerned about ideas for a subway to be built under the river Medina at Cowes. Shareholders were told that the company would oppose the

The horse drawn carriages await custom in the yard at Fountain Pier Cowes. Two of the Barclay, Curle sisterships lie at the pontoon.
TIM COOPER
COLLECTION

plans as they would be against the company's interest. Nothing more was heard of the idea and at the annual meeting in January 1885 the arrival of a new launch, *Medina* (II), in November 1884, was confirmed. She took the place of *Precursor* (I) which had been sold.

Further important announcements were also confirmed. Another new steamer, *Her Majesty*, was being built for the 1885 season. In a different line of activity, with effect from 1 January 1885, Red Funnel acquired the Southampton New Steam Towing Company Limited. The deal included the tugs owned by the company, the goodwill and a cash asset of £3,400. The subsequent development of the towage business is outlined in a separate chapter of this book. Regardless of these heavy expenditures the dividend to shareholders remained at 6%.

Despite the generally poor trading conditions, the naval fleet review in 1887 produced another satisfactory financial result. Fleet changes continued with *Lady of the Lake* being disposed of due to her being worn out and unfit for further service. *Vectis* took her place as the cargo ship while a new steamer, to be called *Princess of Wales*, had been ordered. It was intended that she be known simply as *The Princess*. On shore, the freehold of the pier and stores at East Cowes were acquired.

Red Funnel's new steamer, *Princess of Wales*, was lost in a collision whilst running trials on the Clyde on 16 June 1888. The directors were fortunate in quickly chartering the *Bangor Castle* which made her first sailing from Southampton on 26 June 1888. At the next annual meeting on 5 January 1889, shareholders were informed that no financial loss had been incurred, as *Princess of Wales* had not been handed over at the time of her sinking. Barclay, Curle was already building a replacement vessel and this was expected to enter service in May 1889. Work on the rest of the fleet had included new boilers for *Prince Leopold* and *Carisbrooke*. The dividend continued at 6%.

Solent Queen arrived at Southampton, from the Clyde, on 18 May 1889 in time to take her place in the summer excursion timetables. There was another naval review and traffic was said to be very satisfactory.

The next passenger ship was ordered from local builders, the Southampton Naval Works on the river Itchen at Woolston for delivery in 1891. *Prince of Wales* was not a success on trials and alterations were required in order to increase her speed.

No new passenger steamers were ordered between 1892 and 1895, but *Princess Helena* received a new boiler and both *Prince Leopold* and *Carisbrooke* were redecked. On 13 February 1896 *Her Majesty* was sunk in a collision with the American liner *Paris*. Immediate steps were

LORNA DOONE joined the Red Funnel fleet at Southampton in 1898. Previously she had operated for Bristol Channel owner John Gunn. This photograph shows her as originally built, in the river Avon, approaching Bristol.
RED FUNNEL
ARCHIVES

taken to order a new ship and Barclay, Curle had *Duchess of York* launched on 28 May and running local trials at Stokes Bay on 4 July. In fact, *Her Majesty* was rapidly repaired and returned to service in January 1897.

At the annual meeting in January 1898 the shareholders were told that arrangements had been made with the Southsea Clarence Pier Company to operate a local service between Southsea and Ryde. Mr A W White, secretary of the Clarence Pier Company became a director of Red Funnel. In just a few years Mr White would become chairman of the board. In the same year Mr L T Wilkins became Red Funnel's traffic manager in addition to his existing duties as manager at Cowes.

During 1897 excursion traffic had been severely affected by the arrival of competition from Bristol Channel operator P & A Campbell Limited. Red Funnel was determined to order a new ship, but due to industrial problems in the engineering industry, it was impossible to have a new vessel ready in time for the 1898 season. Red Funnel then intended to charter, but their choice of *Lorna Doone* was found to be only available for sale. A deal was completed and she arrived in Southampton on 1 April 1898. Meanwhile, at Portsmouth, the service from Southsea to Ryde became a joint arrangement with the railway steamers from 1 July 1898.

THE ENIGMA OF *VICTORIA*

Readers familiar with the author's father's book *Red Funnel and Before* will note the omission of paddle steamer *Victoria* in this book.

When *Red Funnel and Before* was being compiled there was a debate as to whether *Victoria*, a steamer from the Joint Railway fleet at Portsmouth, ever joined the Red Funnel fleet at Southampton. It was unclear why Red Funnel would have wanted this 18 year old double-ended vessel in their fleet, but the official registers said she was sold to them in 1899.

On this basis *Victoria* was included in the fleet list. However, research for *Red Funnel 150* has shown no mention in the Red Funnel records of the ship ever having been purchased or chartered by them.

The author has reviewed the directors' minute books and fixed asset registers of that era and these confirm that *Victoria* never came to Red Funnel at Southampton. On that basis the ship has been excluded from the fleet list and one must assume that the official registers cannot always be relied upon – unless of course someone knows differently.

A common sight during spring was steamers at the lay-by berth at the Royal Pier. QUEEN and LORNA DOONE are preparing for the season. The photograph can be dated as between 1901 and 1906.
RED FUNNEL ARCHIVES

1899 - 1929

On 11 September 1899 the board met and considered the desirability of ordering one or two new steamers. Eventually, it was agreed that just one vessel was required and it was to be

'in every way up to date and capable of carrying 750 passengers outside the Isle of Wight, to be somewhat on the lines of *Duchess of Fife* but with a cross Channel passenger certificate. The steamer to be delivered at Southampton not later than 1 May 1900'

Duchess of Fife was the main excursion steamer operated by the Joint Railway Committee fleet from Portsmouth. The necessity for the cross Channel certificate was the recent arrival at Southampton of P & A Campbell Limited (Campbell's) which operated their modern paddle steamer *Cambria* in direct competition to Red Funnel. *Cambria* was both up to date, fast, and could sail to Cherbourg via Bournemouth or the Isle of Wight piers. Her arrival certainly upset the *status quo* on the South Coast.

One week later tenders had been received from several companies, one of whom made a suggestion about the directors' requirements. Hutson & Co recommended that 'an improved *Cambria*' was required. Hutson's were telegraphed that day about earliest delivery dates. On 20 September, just two days later, Mr Hutson presented himself at the board meeting in Southampton with Mr Scott, manager of S McKnight & Co of Ayr. The proposed new steamer was fully discussed at a suggested cost of £27,500. On 25 September Hutson's were telegraphed, provisionally accepting their contract.

The steamer *Southampton* was now regarded as surplus to requirements. She was offered to both Messrs Cosens and Messrs Napier & Son, but neither of the parties wished to purchase.

On 6 March 1900 it was resolved that the new steamer be called *Balmoral*. The ship's hull had been subcontracted to the McKnight yard at Ayr. The work was delayed by strikes of the shipyard workers, but she was launched on 14 May and towed to Glasgow three days later for her machinery to be installed.

At Southampton, the Red Funnel manager Mr Wilkins had met with Mr Mitchell of Campbell's to try and reach agreement about the fares to be charged for excursions. Another request had been received from the Bournemouth and South Coast Steam Packets Limited for Red Funnel to purchase their assets. The proposal to buy this company's business was deferred.

Balmoral's first sailing, for directors and guests, took place on 17 July and is described under the individual ship history section. Hutson's were clearly very interested to know how their vessel was performing against the competition. They telegraphed Red Funnel on 23 July to enquire

about '*Balmoral's* ability to beat *Cambria*'. The company secretary was instructed to reply that *Balmoral* 'was somewhat the faster of the two'.

In the autumn the question of another set of boilers for *Lorna Doone* arose. The Board of Trade had become involved in the shortcomings of her Haythorn boilers and it was agreed to meet with them and ensure that the replacements met with their requirements. It was not until January 1901 that a tender from Day, Summers was accepted. More straightforward, was the new boiler and funnel for *Her Majesty*, this was ordered from Mordey Carney (Southampton) Ltd. In December, 86 shares in the Portsmouth Victoria Pier Company were acquired. Four of the existing directors resigned and were replaced by four from the Red Funnel board. This transaction secured the berthing arrangements for the company's ships at Portsmouth.

Autumn board meetings were concerned with further investment in the fleet, particularly with new boilers for *Solent Queen* and designs being reviewed for another new steamer. The Barclay, Curle yard on the Clyde won the tender for the ship to be known as *Queen* (II). She arrived in Southampton on 8 June 1902, in good time to take part in excursions to the Coronation Fleet Review on 28 June.

The author was intrigued to find in the board minutes a comprehensive abstract of a meeting on 21 July 1903 between the Red Funnel chairman, Mr A W White and Captain Alexander Campbell. There are notes of an arrangement 'which is to be carried out honourably and without opening for after dispute'. Broadly, Brighton was to become the home of Campbell's south coast operations. They might operate from Sussex into the Solent and Isle of Wight area, but restrict the sale of tickets from piers within that area. For its part, Red Funnel agreed 'not to interfere with the traffic from Brighton'.

Most records of P & A Campbell history indicate that the company pulled out of Southampton, at the end of the 1902 season, because they saw better commercial prospects in Sussex. In March 1902 they had purchased the Brighton, Worthing and South Coast Steamboat Co and took over their *Princess May* and the magnificent steamer *Brighton Queen* which went to Bristol for overhaul in the winter of 1902/03. *Cambria* stayed on the Bristol Channel in 1903 and helped fight the local competition which had arisen from the Barry Railway steamers. E C B Thornton in his book *South Coast Pleasure Steamers* relates that *Brighton Queen* left Bristol for Bournemouth and Southampton on 20 May 1903. She was temporarily based at Southampton, possibly until coaling facilities were organised at Newhaven, when she moved to Sussex. If this was the case, why was an operating agreement between

Rivals.

Campbell's CAMBRIA.
RICHARD DANIELSON
COLLECTION

BALMORAL (I).
H A ALLEN
COLLECTION

Campbell's and Red Funnel needed in July 1903? There might be a clue in Mr Thornton recording that Campbell's second steamer on the Brighton station, *Glen Rosa*, arrived from the Bristol Channel and began sailing on 22 July 1903, the day after the meeting between Mr White and Captain Campbell. Did Red Funnel intend to start sailing from the Sussex Piers in earnest and was this why Campbell's sent a second ship to Sussex and then came to an agreement with Red Funnel? In October 1903 the Mayor of Worthing wrote enquiring if Red Funnel would be prepared to operate from his town – there is no record of the reply, but it may be assumed this was regarded as being Campbell territory.

In July 1905 the brokers, H E Moss, wrote enquiring about steamers for sale. *Prince Leopold* and *Carisbrooke* were offered to them and other brokers. Negotiations commenced with Mr R R Collard of Newhaven and these were satisfactorily concluded in October with both ships sold for £1,450.

The directors now desired a new steamer for the 1906 season and sought tenders. Thornycroft's tender was accepted at £19,500, against Day, Summers at £21,500. This steamer was to be *Princess Royal*. As detailed in the ship history, she was unsatisfactory and only ran in public service for two weeks. There followed numerous meetings with Thornycroft's, her builders, and considerations of her failings. In November 1906

there was a supplementary agreement for *Princess Royal* to be lengthened, the work was carried out and further trials took place in March 1907. These were still unsatisfactory and in April Thornycroft's admitted defeat and suggested terms of repayment to Red Funnel.

As soon as it was clear in April 1907 that *Princess Royal* was not going to re-enter the fleet, the company secretary went to Leith to inspect *Stirling Castle*. His report to the board on 29 April was satisfactory and it was agreed an offer of £8,000 be made, and that this could be increased to £10,000 if required. The secretary returned to Leith on 13 May, agreed the price at £8,750 and watched the ship leave for Southampton at 16:20. She arrived at her new home port on the morning of 15 May.

In January 1908, with the *Princess Royal* saga drawing to a conclusion, the directors returned to Hutson's for a new vessel, to become *Bournemouth Queen*. The building of the ship was subcontracted to Ailsa Shipbuilding at Troon and she was launched in an unfinished state on 18 May. Industrial disputes are nothing new and a strike in the yard caused her to be one month behind schedule. The Red Funnel chairman offered a bonus if she could be completed speedily. Eventually she ran satisfactory trials on 7 July and arrived at Southampton 15 July.

At their meeting on 28 September 1908 the directors returned to their informal discussions

This delightful study shows an immaculate PRINCESS HELENA ready to sail for Cowes from the pontoon at Southampton's Royal Pier around 1908. Behind her, at Berth 1, lies SOLENT QUEEN (her two funnels just showing above the pontoon dolphin) with HER MAJESTY and PRINCESS BEATRICE alongside her. In the far background is another two funneled steamer, QUEEN, moored stern in to the lay-by berths. Close examination suggests that HER MAJESTY and PRINCESS BEATRICE are drying a foresail on their foremasts.
PSPS ARCHIVES

ATALANTA.

RAPIDE.

ST. TUDNO (II).

The above three vessels were amongst those managed by Red Funnel during the First World War.
All: RICHARD DANIELSON COLLECTION

about purchasing the assets of the Bournemouth and South Coast Steam Packet Ltd. This time it was agreed that, subject to inspection of their vessel *Lord Elgin* and a freehold property in Poole, they would offer £6,500. Things must have been satisfactory for the contract was sealed and exchanged on 21 October 1908. Their other vessel, *Prince Eddie*, was not intended to remain in the fleet and was quickly sold to Captain Stanney and Mr G E Mears, in February 1909, for £800.

At their meetings in April and May the directors considered funnel colours. Firstly it was agreed that all ships, including the tugs, but excepting *Balmoral* and *Lorna Doone*, would have their funnels painted red with a black top. In April this decision was reversed with funnel colours remaining buff, apart from *Balmoral* and *Lorna Doone* being white, and the steamers on the Bournemouth station which would have red funnels with black tops.

In July it was agreed that official company guide books would be sold on the ships. They were made available for pursers to buy at 2d each and then sold to the public for 3d, providing a very good incentive for the purser to make as many sales as possible.

Red Funnel ships began calling at South Parade pier in June. However, the low water problems at this pier soon became apparent when *Lorna Doone* twice dragged on the shingle at low tide and damaged her keel plates. *Queen* had also touched bottom, but had not been damaged.

In October 1910 the decision was made to convert *Lord Elgin* to a cargo steamer. Her place in the passenger fleet would be taken by a new vessel ordered from Day, Summers to be called *Princess Mary*.

In February 1912 the Admiralty wrote asking how soon tugs could be made available in the event of hostilities. The reply offered two of 'the best' tugs at £50 per day excluding coal, the charge would be reduced to £44 if the Government provided crews. *Princess Mary* and *Queen* were also offered at £70 per day including coal.

The loss of the liner *Titanic* was keenly felt throughout the port of Southampton. In April 1912, Red Funnel made a donation of £105 to the fund for the relief of sufferers. The disaster affected all shipping companies and Red Funnel's Mr Brodie met with the Board of Trade to discuss life saving appliances. Copper tanks were ordered for *Lorna Doone*, *Queen* and *Stirling Castle* in order to convert the existing deck seats into buoyancy apparatus. They were to be painted black and labelled 'Buoyant Seats'. Also, lists of life belts were to be placed on each ship detailing the numbers carried and where they were stored. The senior officers on board were instructed to make themselves familiar with these matters.

The official company guide books had proved very popular and supplies were nearly exhausted, so enquiries were made about a new edition for the 1913 season. A further 5,000 copies were subsequently produced.

During the Great War there were several vessels operating from Southampton that had been called up from other shipping companies. The Admiralty asked if Red Funnel would manage some of these ships for a fee of 5% of all related expenditure. Among those involved were the Glasgow and South Western Railway paddle steamers *Jupiter* and *Glen Sannox*, together with their turbine steamer *Atalanta*. The Belgian cross Channel ships were also involved with trooping duties and their *Princesse Clementine* (II), *Princesse Henriette*, *Rapide* and *Leopold 11* all came under Red Funnel management. Another notable vessel included in these war time arrangements was the former Liverpool and North Wales Steamship Company's famous paddle steamer *St. Tudno* (II). This vessel had been operating from Southampton since autumn 1912, for Hamburg-Amerika Line, as a tender to the German liners, and was seized on the outbreak of war.

At Southampton, *Lorna Doone*, *Queen*, *Princess Mary* and *Princess Helena* were in use as patrol boats in 1915. Subsequently *Lorna Doone*, *Bournemouth Queen*, *Queen*, *Princess Mary*, *Stirling Castle* and *Duchess of York* were requisitioned. The Admiralty was keen to appropriate *Lorna Doone* entirely and attempted to agree a price. However, Red Funnel did not want to part with the steamer if it could possibly be avoided. Eventually, agreement was reached on the rate for her hire. In 1917 *Her Majesty* and *Princess Beatrice* were also taken over by the Admiralty. Unhappily, *Stirling Castle* and *Princess Mary* did not return from War Service.

In order to replace their war losses Red Funnel looked at the Thames steamer *Woolwich Belle*. They paid half the cost of dry docking and survey of the vessel, but were only prepared to purchase if she could definitely obtain a Steam III passenger certificate for four years. Presumably no assurance was forthcoming as *Woolwich Belle*, after two seasons sailing from the Sussex Coast as *Queen of the South*, eventually joined the fleet of the New Medway Steam Packet Company until 1933.

In February 1919 the opportunity arose to acquire the freehold at Fountain Pier, Cowes and the purchase was completed in May 1920. During that period the Anglo Gulf West Indies Petroleum Corporation Limited (AGWI, later to become Esso Petroleum) was starting its refinery works between Beacon and Ashlett Creek in Southampton Water.

In a surprising piece of correspondence, Campbell's wrote in August 1920 asking if they could charter *Balmoral* for the rest of the season and requesting Red Funnel's charges. Unfortunately there is no information as to why Campbell's wanted Red Funnel's crack vessel, but there is no record of any reply and *Balmoral* remained at Southampton.

In February 1924 there was a national dock strike and the local shipyard workers also went on strike including those at Platform Wharf. For a time the packet service was curtailed. The board minutes throughout that period have constant reference to discussions about wages.

In July 1926, director Mr J Smith died and Sir John E Thornycroft, managing director of the local shipyard bearing his family name, was appointed to the board in his place. Soon afterwards tenders were received for a new vessel, similar to *Princess Mary*, but the minutes record that Sir John took no part in these deliberations. The order for a new paddle steamer, to be called *Princess Elizabeth*, went to Day, Summers who built a conventional steamer based on their *Princess Mary* of 1911. However, *Princess Elizabeth* might have been very different indeed. Before confirming the order, Red Funnel's chairman, Mr C G Sharp, travelled to Switzerland to examine the new Sulzer Uniflow

engine installed in the Lake Geneva paddle steamer *Helvetie*. Also considered were diesel-electric paddle propulsion and, most intriguing of all, paddles driven by geared steam turbines. The only reference the author can find to the latter form of propulsion is in F Burtt's book *Cross Channel and Coastal Paddle Steamers* where he refers to European river tugs called *Zurich* and *Le Rhone*.

Looking to the future, plans to convert a paddle steamer for the carriage of cars were discussed. Thornycroft's advised in June 1927 and produced the specifications for *Her Majesty's* subsequent alterations. *Her Majesty* was now 42 years old and the decision was a stopgap move in view of the Southern Railway's decision to build a second purpose-built, diesel, drive-through vessel, *Wootton*, to join her sister *Fishbourne*, for operation on their Portsmouth to Fishbourne route in 1928.

The first board meeting of 1930 considered employing motor vessels on the regular passage service. Plans and details were discussed at length and it was agreed that the ships should have a speed of not less than 13 knots. A new era of car carrying diesel ferries was about to commence.

Taken from one of the steamers, this photograph shows how the pontoon at Fountain Pier Cowes looked in the 1920s after the creation of the Southern Railway in 1923.
RICHARD DANIELSON COLLECTION

PRINCESS ELIZABETH arrives at Bournemouth.

LORNA DOONE leaves Southampton and later passes the Needles lighthouse on her way into the Solent.

Left:
SOLENT QUEEN (I) lies at Clarence Pier, Southsea.

Right:
BALMORAL (I) arrives at Brighton's West Pier.

All: RED FUNNEL
ARCHIVES

Left:
LORNA DOONE leaves the Red Funnel berth at the western end of Ryde Pier.

Right:
PRINCESS ELIZABETH arrives at Ryde Pier.

Left:
PRINCESS ELIZABETH lies at Shanklin Pier.

Right:
VECTA arrives at Sandown Pier.

VECTA manoeuvres at Ryde. Ahead of her is the Southern Railway paddle steamer WHIPPINGHAM, and on the other side of the pier is one of the sisters PORTSDOWN or MERSTONE.

All: RED FUNNEL
ARCHIVES

1930 - 1944

At their February 1930 meeting the directors approved plans from Thornycroft's for their first diesel vessel. *Medina* (III) was to be a steel twin screw motor ship of speed not less than 12 knots. For many regular travellers it was to seem that she rarely reached 12 knots, for her lack of speed was to be a recurring issue over the years. Writing in the Thornycroft Centenary book *100 years of Specialised Shipbuilding and Engineering* Mr K C Barnaby noted that Sir John E Thornycroft took a personal interest in the design and building of *Medina*. Sir John had a house at Bembridge on the Island and was a regular traveller on the ships throughout the year. In a time of shipbuilding depression she was the only vessel launched from his firm's Woolston yard in 1931.

The summer weather in 1930 left much to be desired and a policy for refunding fares when Red Funnel's cross Channel sailings were abandoned after setting off was agreed. Passengers could use their ticket on a future sailing or could receive a refund less pier tolls. Additionally, *Balmoral* suffered from persistent boiler trouble that year and was withdrawn after 20 August.

Industrial problems loomed in the coal industry and a significant order of 1,000 tons of coal was made in November. At a special meeting on 30 December 1930, Mr S J Procter, the manager and secretary of Alexandra Towing and Mr Stark their local manager, attended to discuss 'various matters relating to towage work in the port of Southampton'. This was the first mention of the regular discussions that were to take place between the main towage providers in Southampton.

The weather in 1931 was no better than the previous year. The directors specially discussed the receipts from the full summer sailings between Ryde and Southsea and agreed that in future years the service should not commence until 1 June, unless Whitsun was earlier. Taken with the severe recession and financial crisis, things were gloomy financially and, after lengthy discussion, the directors decreed that shareholders would not receive a dividend for that year. A 10% cut in salaries was made from January 1932.

The shipping industry remained depressed and this severely affected the towage department receipts. A small dividend of 2% was paid for the year ended 30 September 1932.

The steamer *Princess Beatrice* went for scrap in spring 1933. The new manager, Mr Sharp, had fresh ideas and his negotiations with the British Power Boat Company resulted in *Island Enterprise* starting a high speed service that summer. Fuller details of this historic decision and its subsequent development are dealt with in the 'High Speed' section elsewhere in this book.

The chairman noted in his annual report that the summer weather had been exceptionally fine and sunny, although excursion takings had been light until early August after which receipts had been good until the middle of September. A dividend of 4% was paid to shareholders.

Conditions continued to improve in 1934, with favourable weather and the dividend now increased to 5%. On board the excursion ships, modern refrigeration plants were fitted on *Balmoral* (I), *Lorna Doone* (I) and *Bournemouth Queen*. These units kept beverages cool in the bar. Financial matters further improved during 1935 with the pay cuts made in 1932 partially restored this year, with the balance in 1936. The French liner *Normandie* entered service in summer 1935 and caused widespread interest. Red Funnel provided tender facilities when she anchored at the Motherbank off Ryde.

There was a Royal Naval Review at Spithead, commemorating the silver jubilee of King George IV, in July 1935 and this benefited the excursion trade. At the end of August the directors resolved to order a new vessel from Thornycroft's. Surprisingly, they reverted to a paddle steamer, similar to the 1927 *Princess Elizabeth*, but with some alterations. Initially, they considered having her car deck aft (as in the later *Balmoral* (II) of 1949) but it was felt this would not be practical in working the pontoon at Cowes. The new steamer's name was decided at the directors meeting of 25 November 1935, in a huge departure from the traditional naming policy she was to be called *Gracie Fields*.

Around this time Red Funnel clearly gained an eye for public relations. Having named their new

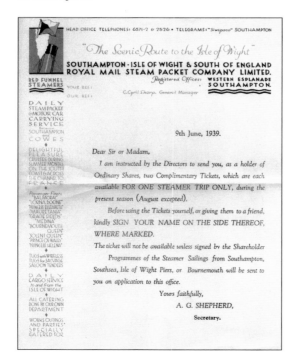

In the late 1930s Red Funnel adopted a bold and colourful letter heading for their correspondence.
RED FUNNEL ARCHIVES

Taken on 27 May 1936, the occasion of QUEEN MARY's maiden voyage to New York from Southampton, the Royal Pier is a hive of activity. The photograph is taken from BOURNEMOUTH QUEEN, in the background are MAURETANIA (ex-QUEEN), LORNA DOONE and PRINCESS ELIZABETH. On the left is Cosens' MONARCH.

Cunard's QUEEN MARY leaves Southampton on her maiden voyage to New York, 27 May 1936. CALSHOT is seen with LORNA DOONE. CALSHOT has been fitted with a taller funnel, but still has open rails amidships. Both: TIM COOPER COLLECTION

steamer after a popular singer, a 'celebrity' in 21st century parlance, they set about making the most of it. The board minutes note that after the steamer's launch on 8 April a lunch was to be held at the South Western Hotel when the press and commercial friends of the company were guests 'for the purpose of propaganda'. Just before this event, a publicity agent, Mr W M Frankish, was retained from 1 April 1936 at £50 per annum. Miss Fields was to be offered a trip at no charge, apart from normal catering tariff; she would be free to invite guests.

A new company guidebook was produced, published by F G Warne Limited. The *South Coast Guide* of 1936 cost 6d and had a black and white photograph of *Balmoral* on the cover, with the lower part of her funnel printed in red. This was clearly the start of the change to the company being referred to publicly as Red Funnel. The 1937 guide book was published as *Red Funnel Stuff*, sub titled The Story of Red Funnel Steamers. In his opening words the manager, Mr C C Sharp, referred to the change in funnel colour and the new short title by which the company would be known in future.

1936 also saw the entry into service of *Queen Mary*. She and *Normandie* competed to win the Blue Riband award for the fastest crossing of the North Atlantic. Every arrival of these new ocean liners was met with great public interest. Excursion sailings to view these events did well and mitigated against some poor weather in July and September. In his review of the financial year ended 30 September 1936, the chairman was optimistic and reminded shareholders that the cost of *Gracie Fields* had been defrayed out of cash resources. The annual dividend rose to 6%.

In the boardroom, plans were afoot for another new vessel, this time moving away from steam and using the most modern technology of the time. At their meeting on 9 November 1936 the directors discussed Voith Schneider propulsion units. It was agreed that the chairman, Mr Sharp the manager, and three others should visit the Voith factory in Heidenheim and also see the equipment in use on Lake Constance.

Alan Brown, in his book *Lymington – The Sound of Success*, relates that Cyril Sharp served in the Royal Flying Corps during World War 1. He had been shot down behind enemy lines, seriously injured and then brought back to good health in a local hospital. During the visit to Heidenheim he learned that his Voith host, Gunther Franz, had been a flyer in the Austrian Air Force and had also been brought down and hospitalised. The two men apparently got on well and the whole visit was very relaxed, with the Red Funnel party also greatly impressed with the performance of the ships on Lake Constance.

By spring 1937 provisional drawings of the new vessel were being reviewed by the naval architect and Thornycroft's were comparing the efficiencies of conventional propellers with Voith Schneider units. At their meeting on 26 April 1937 the board resolved to place an order with Thornycroft's for the new vessel which was to become *Vecta*. The estimated cost was £62,000 and the positive cash situation was such that £45,000 could be paid up front and Thornycroft's offered Red Funnel a 4% reduction on cost for the early payment.

The 1937 season was helped by the Coronation Naval Review and with generally good weather, earnings were good. A new motor launch, *Norris Castle* (I), was ordered from Clare Lallows, Cowes for the Cowes to East Cowes ferry service. The board were so pleased with the new guide book *Red Funnel Stuff* that the publicity agent, Mr Frankish, was awarded a bonus of 30 guineas (£31.50) for his efforts.

In November 1937 it was agreed to cease operating *Island Enterprise* and she was to be sold at the best possible price.

The 1938 summer weather was not good, but excursion traffic held up well. At Bournemouth, *Corfe Castle* (previously named *Mauretania* and *Queen*) had developed terminal boiler problems and in October the board were concerned about arrangements for the 1939 season. The options were to fit new boilers, or sell her and replace with a second-hand steamer. Within a few days *Queen of Kent* was inspected and a decision made

On 27 March 1936 QUEEN MARY arrived at Southampton for the first time, fresh from trials on the Clyde, to use the purpose-built King George V dry dock. In attendance are CALSHOT and CANUTE. In the background, amongst other vessels dressed for the occasion, are SOLENT QUEEN and PRINCESS ELIZABETH.
RED FUNNEL ARCHIVES

not to purchase. This was a paddle steamer owned by the New Medway Steam Packet Co and recently displaced from their Thames operations by the arrival of new motor vessels. The vessel, and her sister *Queen of Thanet*, eventually came into the Red Funnel story in 1949, when they both joined the fleet at Southampton. It is interesting to speculate what would have happened in 1939 had *Queen of Kent* been purchased at that time. The Bournemouth station would have had a large, fast, oil fired paddle steamer well capable of sailing cross Channel and making long distance excursions. Instead, *Corfe Castle* was sold for scrap and the fall-back position for 1939 was to send *Princess Elizabeth* to Bournemouth for operation on the Bournemouth to Swanage service.

In the January 1939 board minutes there is an intriguing reference to a colour film being made of Southampton. Red Funnel made a contribution of £250 towards the cost. Was the film ever made? If it was, a viewing now, over 70 years later, would be most interesting.

The 1939 season continued with a worrying foreign situation growing steadily more uncertain as the months passed. There were no formal references in the minutes to preparations for War. The only mention is at a meeting on the day it was actually declared, 3 September, when amongst other business, including the sale of *Island Enterprise* for £500, it was agreed to purchase

two air raid shelters for the site of the old cellars at Bugle Street. It may be difficult now to appreciate that only 20 years had elapsed since the end of the Great War. All those of working age in 1939 would have been directly affected by the earlier hostilities – the so called War to end all Wars.

In his report for 1939, at the annual general meeting on 23 January 1940, the chairman took a pragmatic view and noted that the whole of the September 1939 holiday traffic was lost when the weather was exceptionally fine. *Vecta* had entered service in March and her superior accommodation had been much appreciated by the public, both on the passage service and excursions. At the meeting a letter to shareholders was circulated notifying that the payment of dividends, both ordinary and preference, had been deferred. The Government had requisitioned several of the paddle steamers and tugs for national service. Advances on account of hire had been received, but no scale rates had been agreed. Already several claims for valuable salvage services by the tugs had been rendered, but no settlements obtained.

It was a bad start to the year as *Gracie Fields* had been lost on service to her country on 30 May 1940. Later, *Duchess of Cornwall* sank at her moorings at Southampton during an air raid on 23/24 November and *Her Majesty* was badly damaged at Platform Wharf during another raid

A wintry scene aboard PRINCE OF WALES at Southampton. In the background are PRINCESS ELIZABETH and SOLENT QUEEN. According to HAMPSHIRE AND ISLE OF WIGHT WEATHER by Davison, Currie and Ogley, Southampton suffered very heavy snowfalls in March and December 1937 and this appears to match the photograph which shows PRINCESS ELIZABETH with her extended, cowl-topped funnel fitted in 1936, but still with no wheelhouse, which was not added until 1938.
RED FUNNEL ARCHIVES

MEDINA was the first motor passenger vessel to serve the Isle of Wight, although the Southern Railway had introduced diesel-engined car ferries on their Portsmouth to Fishbourne route in 1927. She is portrayed here in her first livery of white funnel with a black top.
RED FUNNEL
ARCHIVES

on 1/2 December. That same night the workshops and offices at the wharf were destroyed, as was the catering store at 16 Bugle Street. The leases of these properties would be given up.

Duchess of Cornwall was raised, but *Her Majesty* was to be sold as she lay, partly submerged at Platform Wharf.

A formal annual general meeting was held on 4 February 1941, but it had been impossible to complete annual accounts due to 'circumstances under which they had no control'. Dividends would continue to be deferred. The board contributed £25,000 to Southampton War Weapons Week in July 1941.

An annual general meeting was held on 3 February 1942, to satisfy Companies Act requirements, but again without annual accounts for the year ended 30 September 1941.

During 1941 all the tugs were now on Government service. The two motor launches for the Cowes to East Cowes ferry had also been taken over by the Government. The annual report for 1941 recorded that passenger and cargo services to the Isle of Wight had been maintained despite very difficult conditions, but restrictions on travel still seriously affected the company's revenue.

By March 1943 it was clear that *Vecta* was to be converted to conventional screw propulsion. Thornycroft's had advised on the issues and the board proposed that the work be carried out.

Administrative matters were still causing difficulties and the 1942 accounts were not available at formal meetings of shareholders in 1943. In July 1944 the minutes noted that the towage department records had not been touched since 30 September 1943 and if not soon attended

to would delay the 1944 accounts. Assistance was called in from the auditors.

At the annual general meeting on 27 March 1944, it was confirmed that all the tugs and four passenger vessels were still on charter to the Government. The passage service had been maintained in difficult conditions. For a period during the summer of 1943 they had been able to offer non landing trips to Cowes in connection with 'Holidays at Home'. These had been well patronised and much appreciated by the general public. Some progress had been made with the accounts and a dividend of 5% was paid.

In the summer of 1944 the crews of both the tugs and passage boats were looking for wage increases. The discussions involved the Ministry of War, and the Unions representing the crew, before matters progressed. In August the men were still not satisfied with the proposals and meetings were held with the Shipping Federation, with their Captain Clarke in attendance to help resolve matters. It was suggested that the officers might be awarded a special gift to cover the period September 1939 to September 1944.

At the annual general meeting on 5 February 1945 the chairman reviewed events and the accounts for the year ended 30 September 1944. Again the passenger and cargo services had been maintained, apart from a short period around 'D' Day. Red Funnel had acquired a property at Chapel Wharf on the river Itchen and this would be developed as a maintenance base in the future, taking the place of Platform Wharf. A dividend of 5% would be paid. None of the vessels requisitioned by the Government had yet been released.

An early morning scene at Southampton in the 1930s with PRINCESS ELIZABETH and LORNA DOONE leaving on excursions. HER MAJESTY lies at Berth 1. In the background can be seen the reclaimed land that was later to become Mayflower Park.
RED FUNNEL ARCHIVES

VECTA heads down Southampton Water for the Isle of Wight in her first season, 1939.   RED FUNNEL ARCHIVES

1945 - 1958

At the first board meeting of 1945 various gifts were made to members of staff, recognising their loyalty and efforts over six years of war.

In a review of management Captain W V J Clarke was appointed as general manager, taking up his duties from 12 February. Captain Clarke was already known to Red Funnel by helping with wage negotiations in his earlier capacity with the Shipping Federation. Before the month's end he was in Liverpool and Glasgow, with Messrs Redman and Hastings, examining the vessels *Upton* and *Paladin*. *Paladin* was purchased immediately from the Clyde Shipping Co Ltd for £5,500. In April the board approved the purchase of *Upton*, with Captain Clarke instructed to agree the lowest possible price. She arrived in Southampton during May after £15,000 had been paid to Birkenhead Corporation.

Discussions continued with ministry officials about the reconditioning costs of *Balmoral* (I) and *Lorna Doone* (I). The Government was keen to agree a lump sum, the figure of £65,000 was mentioned and Captain Clarke was encouraged to negotiate, bearing in mind the cost of hiring replacements during the repair period and the need for the vessels to be delivered to Southampton.

In July, *Duchess of Cornwall* took the first post-war excursion sailing to Ryde. She still had her war time grey upperworks, but the event was a welcome sign of normality returning.

A special meeting of the board was called in August to discuss the possible takeover of Cosens & Co Ltd (Cosens). That company's shareholders had received a circular from the Charterhouse Trust offering £15 for each £2 share. Steamer services between Bournemouth and Swanage had just reopened after temporary repairs to the piers. Despite being in competition, there had been a local working agreement with Cosens over the operations at Bournemouth for many years. The Red Funnel directors were concerned that with new owners and management at Cosens they would face a very different situation at Bournemouth. They agreed to make a counter offer of £20 for each £2 share, but only after they had met with Messrs Frowde (former managing director) and Kaile (general manager and company secretary) of Cosens. Negotiations continued through September and concluded with a controlling interest being acquired by purchasing the directors' shareholdings. In the annual report the chairman referred to a material advantage accruing to both companies.

Mr C J Sharp died on 20 December 1946. He had been associated with the company for over 50 years and had been chairman for the last 31. Mr E Redman was elected to the chair and it was agreed that Mr K C Barnaby should be invited to join the board. Mr Barnaby was the chief naval architect at Thornycroft's shipyard at Woolston. His subsequent appointment, on 6 January 1947, was to have a considerable effect on the modernisation of the company's fleet in future years.

The formal minutes of board meetings were less regular in 1947, but undoubtedly the directors kept in touch on a daily basis. Red Funnel was still pursuing second-hand replacement vessels for war time losses. Mr Redman had been to Alloa to look at *Thane of Fife*, previously the Wallasey ferry *Snowdrop*, but she was rejected on the basis of her deep draught. The board had also considered *New Royal Lady* but, before they had made a decision, she was sold to General Steam Navigation to become their *Crested Eagle*.

Serious discussions took place about future policy for new tonnage. Due to their age, and cost of refurbishment, the directors agreed that *Balmoral* and *Lorna Doone* should not be reconditioned after their war service. It was also agreed that the company's present needs would be served by an improved *Vecta*, with a Steam III passenger certificate and capable of 15 knots. Thornycroft's were to be asked to make suggestions about an intermediate type, between *Vecta* and *Medina*, to be economical and capable of the passage from Southampton to Cowes in less than one hour. However, nothing more was heard about this intermediate type. *Medina's* slowness was clearly becoming an issue, because it was resolved to consider new engines for her, although it was not until 1953 before this work was actually carried out.

At the same meeting on 27 October Captain Clarke reported that a former part of the famous 'D' day Mulberry Harbour could be purchased from the Ministry for use at East Cowes as a buffer pontoon facilitating bow loading of a suitable ship. Southampton Harbour Board was proposing to install a similar pontoon adjacent to the Royal Pier. This was part of a plan to alter a landing craft for Red Funnel's motor vehicle service with the future prospect of adaptation for use on the cargo service. Thornycroft's had estimated £30,000 to carry out the conversion. Early photographs show landing at East Cowes directly onto the concrete slipway, so the pontoon idea was not taken forward at the Island terminus. At their first meeting in the new year, 2 February 1948, the directors agreed to the latest proposals from Thornycroft's and instructed them to proceed with the new vessel that was to become *Balmoral* (II). Contracts were submitted by Thornycroft's on 15 March and these were approved and ordered to be signed and sealed.

By the end of the month the equipment needed to operate the motor vehicle service by *Norris Castle* (II) was purchased. At the annual meeting on 3 May the chairman confirmed that *Norris Castle* would be in service that year. He noted that petrol was still rationed and until supplies were restored the ship would not be of full use to the public or to the company. She entered service in July and established the vehicle service that was to be the lifeblood of the company in future years. In August, *Solent Queen* (I) had to be withdrawn with terminal boiler problems. Her place in the fleet was swiftly filled by the purchase of *Robina*. In December 1948 an offer of £10 preference shares was made to existing shareholders. The offer was over-subscribed and 10,000 shares were issued. At the director's meeting that month, the board confirmed that Captain Clarke was to approach Esso and discuss the building and

The residents of East Cowes turn out to welcome NORRIS CASTLE on the historic occasion of her first service arrival on 23 July 1948.
RED FUNNEL ARCHIVES

The Royal Pier looks crowded with promenaders as VECTA prepares for another sailing to Cowes. Behind her NORRIS CASTLE rests at Berth 1.
RED FUNNEL ARCHIVES

management of additional tugs for the refinery complex that was being completed at Fawley on Southampton Water. This was the first reference to the provision of towage services at the refinery that was to last until 1993. The directors also considered the purchase of the paddle steamers *Queen of Thanet* and *Queen of Kent* from the New Medway Steam Packet Co Ltd. Captain Clarke was permitted to negotiate for their purchase up to £30,000. If successful, they were to become *Solent Queen* (II) and *Lorna Doone* (II) respectively. Clearly things went to plan and both ships were at Southampton in January 1949 being refitted.

1949 was a quieter year for acquisitions and disposals. *Solent Queen* (II) and *Lorna Doone* (II) duly entered the excursion fleet and went down well with the travelling public. Meanwhile *Balmoral* (II) had been building and was launched by the chairman's wife on 27 June. The purchase of the two elderly paddle steamers, together with *Upton* and *Robina*, and the controlling interest in Cosens, suggested that Red Funnel could be both financially stretched and also have enough vessels in the fleet to provide the necessary services. Consideration was given to selling *Balmoral* (II) before she entered service. The idea provoked the intervention of Thornycroft's senior management who argued strongly that Red Funnel's future lay with modern vessels and that the elderly fleet should be replaced as quickly as possible. The chairmen of both companies were involved in the discussion, together with Mr Barnaby, who also sat on both boards. Happily, *Balmoral* (II) was not sold, but the discussions about the old fleet had clearly set the shareholders thinking, culminating in an acrimonious annual meeting in May 1952.

The new decade opened with a poor excursion season. The chairman lamented that the 1950 season was the worst in the company's history. The weather had been bad and there was an outbreak of polio on the Isle of Wight. This had affected what little traffic was on offer, resulting in earnings being very seriously affected. In view of the disappointing results, the directors were unable to recommend a dividend on the ordinary shares. The only brightness in the annual report was the completion of extensive alterations to the premises at East Cowes. These enabled *Norris Castle* to deal with vehicles directly over her ramp, thus making the handling of heavy and awkward traffic less difficult.

Clearly the poor season in 1950 had affected the outlook for 1951. Early in the year the board set up a subcommittee to consider the cost of repairs to the company's vessels and also the running of excursion services, with a view to containing expenses as much as possible. Unfortunately the author has found no further specific references to the views of this committee, but it is very likely that they approved of the changes that were to come. Arrangements at Bournemouth for 1951 were agreed with the general manager of Cosens, Mr Kaile. *Consul* would open the season at Easter, with *Lorna Doone* (II) commencing at Whitsun. *Bournemouth Queen* would be retained at Southampton and *Upton* would not be used unless traffic necessitated. An enquiry had been received about the availability of *Robina* and the board approved her sale if the proceeds reached £8,000. However, the ship eventually left the company in 1953.

By May 1951 there were further problems. *Solent Queen* (II) was undergoing load line survey and the surveyor insisted on certain repairs, but would only grant her a passenger certificate for one year. The directors agreed to the work being done, but intended to contest the one year certificate. However, within a few days she had been severely damaged by fire. So extensive was the devastation that she would never sail again. *Lorna Doone* (II) was brought back from Bournemouth to take her sister's place at Southampton. Apart from Easter 1952, there would never again be a Red Funnel vessel stationed at Bournemouth.

Mr Barnaby was clearly most concerned about the course of events and specifically recorded that he was against either *Upton* or *Robina* being placed in service. His colleagues later confirmed this view on 4 June when it was agreed that 'under no circumstances' were these vessels to be put into service. Work was only to be done on them if labour was available and it was required for an inspection by a prospective purchaser.

Behind the united front of the board there had been differences of opinion. Broadly, this stemmed from arguments over the correct course of action to rebuild the company after the end of the recent war. On the one hand there was an understandable desire to get back to the pre-war size of fleet and wide range of excursion sailings. The new, and differing, view was that these times were past and the future lay with towage, the passage service to Cowes, and the carrying of vehicles by economical diesel ships. If these vessels could be used profitably on excursion work that was acceptable, but it would not be the main thrust of the business. The general manager, Captain Clarke, was clearly in the former camp. After considerable negotiation, and with legal

advice having been taken by both parties, the board agreed the financial terms of his resignation at their meeting on 5 November 1951. He would leave on 31 March 1952.

The new general manager was a railwayman, Mr C Warren Payne. At age 44 he was the personal assistant to Mr Biddle, general manager of Southampton Docks, formerly owned by the Southern Railway and nationalised on 1 January 1948 as part of the British Transport Commission. However, before Mr Payne could start work there was a public skirmish over the manner of his predecessor's departure. At the annual meeting on 26 May at the Polygon Hotel the shareholders were divided. One group supported the old school and were keen for Captain Clarke to be offered a directorship. The others were vociferous in their condemnation of the last four years, citing 'investment in a subsidiary that did not pay (Cosens), in ships that did not work, or did not pay, or were laid-up, or had now gone for scrap'. An anonymous letter had been sent to shareholders and there were questions about who had provided the list of names and addresses. The letter was personal and referred to Sir John Thornycroft taking his motor car to the Island. It was alleged that he took up a space on the ship that could be used by a paying motorist. The suggestion was strongly rebutted by the chairman who replied that Sir John was meticulous in not taking his car on a sailing when space could be used by fare paying passengers. 'If shareholders knew the money he had saved the company by his influence and contacts, they would be surprised.'

In the mid-1950s the photographer departs from the Royal Pier by paddle steamer, leaving a crowded BOURNEMOUTH QUEEN and MEDINA to follow him down Southampton Water. ALAN BROWN – KEITH ADAMS COLLECTION

At Thornycroft's Northam yard NORRIS CASTLE is undergoing refit on 21 October 1959. Originally intended to temporarily extend her certificate for six months, the overhaul included substantial work on the hull, which enabled her to remain in service until OSBORNE CASTLE's arrival in 1962. Next to her is PRINCESS ELIZABETH, already sold for further service with Torbay Steamers.
CAPTAIN P D JONES
DON JONES
COLLECTION

In other annual meeting reports the directors were normally unanimously re-elected. At this meeting those present voted against the reappointment of Sir John and Mr Barnaby. It was only with the proxy votes held by the chairman that they were re-elected.

Significantly, just two days later, the board met and agreed that further efforts be made to dispose of *Upton* and also that *Princess Helena*, withdrawn from passenger service in 1949 and retained as spare cargo vessel, be sold for scrap. *Lorna Doone* (II) had already been disposed of to the breakers in February, the costs of putting the vessel through survey having been found uneconomical.

Attention turned to detailed matters and *Medina* had new upholstered settees installed, her saloon painted cream and generally 'brightened up'. Most welcome to the regular traveller was the decision to purchase new Crossley diesel engines to be installed at her refit early in 1953. Mr Barnaby was asked to consider whether the cargo service operated by *Lord Elgin* could be taken over by *Norris Castle*.

Commercially, it was agreed to invite coach operators to Southampton in September and entertain them for the day. This excursion became an annual event for many years, much appreciated by the coach companies and also enjoyed by the Red Funnel office staff who attended to act as hosts. On the coach operators excursion of 26 September 1960 *Balmoral* disembarked her passengers at Yarmouth for their coach ride to Cowes. *Balmoral* proceeded to Cowes, arriving early and lay alongside Victoria Pier until moving to Fountain Pier at departure time. In doing so she became the last Red Funnel ship to use Victoria Pier as the pier was demolished a few months later.

By December 1952 there was still no interest in *Upton* and it was agreed she should be sold for scrap. In 1953 *Robina*, unused since September 1949, was also finally disposed of for scrap. Thus the last of the post-war second-hand passenger

ship acquisitions had left the fleet. Ventnor pier re opened and the Royal Naval Fleet Review in June, to celebrate the Coronation of Queen Elizabeth, brought extra revenue to the excursion trade. Things were clearly improving on the financial front as the annual meeting on 18 May 1953 approved a bonus dividend of 5%, bringing the total for that year to 10%. Dividends were to remain at 10% for several years.

1954 began with discussion about the future of *Lord Elgin*. Mr Payne reported that her engines were in bad condition. It was agreed that various repairs be carried out and the ship patched up to enable her to continue to the end of the year.

In November, the company's stockbrokers discussed the issue of new shares and were of the view that Red Funnel was on an 'upward trend'. It was agreed to increase the company's borrowing powers, needed for replacement and new tonnage.

The weather during the 1955 summer season was good and this reflected the positive tone of the annual report for that year. The report itself was printed in a more modern format and noted that through motor coach and steamer bookings had contributed to greater numbers on the passage service and also excursions. *Norris Castle* was now providing a regular vehicle cargo service. Loaded lorries were able to deliver on the Island and then return to the mainland the same day.

Lord Elgin finally completed her service with the company and sailed under her own steam to Pollock, Brown & Co at Northam to be scrapped on 13 May 1955.

After the good weather of 1955, the 1956 season was to be exceptionally poor. Carryings on the Southampton – Cowes passage service held up, but the excursion traffic suffered badly. Despite an hourly service on summer Saturdays it was not possible to take all the cars on offer, it was noted that a similar situation pertained on the railway operated routes to the Island.

At the board meeting on 30 July Mr Payne was given authority to look into the workings at the company's Chapel yard. He reported back on 27 August and it was agreed that the company should cease maintaining its own fleet. From 1 January 1957, repair work would be carried out by Thornycroft's, the wharf at Chapel would be sold and the workforce discharged. The chairman reported at the next annual general meeting that these changes enabled considerable economies to be made.

The poor results from excursion sailings in 1956 actively exercised the minds of the directors. The bad weather had severely affected Cosens and that subsidiary's results were regarded as being unsatisfactory. The view was expressed that it was increasingly uncertain whether pleasure steamers could any longer be operated remuneratively and the advisability of discontinuing them completely was carefully considered.

The bad season also had its effect on the Sussex coast where Campbell's had announced their intention not to operate paddle steamers on the south coast in 1957. The Town Clerk at Brighton and the operators of Eastbourne Pier both wrote to Red Funnel in the autumn of 1956 asking if the company would consider operating from their resorts in 1957. The formal response was that no change was anticipated to the present timetables and the company did not have the necessary vessels to run in those districts. Subsequently, Campbell's chartered the small motor vessel *Crested Eagle* for South Coast service in 1957, but the service was unsuccessful and not repeated. Interestingly Ron Adams recorded, in his personal notes, that Red Funnel directors inspected *Crested Eagle* at Shanklin Pier, with a view to possible purchase for Cosens' fleet. However, their view was that the engines were in poor condition and would need to be replaced. No official record of this inspection has been discovered.

The operation of the cargo service had last been examined in 1955 when *Lord Elgin* was withdrawn. It was now felt that an efficient cargo service could not be operated with the existing antiquated terminal facilities. The view was that the service could be discontinued without adverse financial effects. From 1 January 1957 the carriage of normal cargo would cease and vehicular traffic would be concentrated on. At Cowes, the three lorries used for deliveries would be sold.

The cost of maintaining *Norris Castle* was becoming a concern and the board noted that she would be slipped for survey on 31 October 1956, if there were any exceptional costs a special board meeting would be called.

The board meetings in 1957 included important decisions about the future direction of the business.

The directors considered a general purpose vessel to replace *Norris Castle* and other vessels. Drawings were produced by Thornycroft's and orders placed for the passenger/vehicle ferry that was to become *Carisbrooke Castle*. To assist in financing the new vessels, a further 10,400 £10 shares were issued and a ship mortgage of £155,000 taken up.

Bournemouth Queen was withdrawn from 30 August 1957. At the October board meeting, her running costs and earnings were reviewed concluding that she was an uneconomic proposition. All useful articles were to be removed before her disposal. Her deck seats were earmarked for use on *Carisbrooke Castle*. However, the Board of Trade forbade this plan. Some of them were cut vertically in two, painted grey and used in the waiting room at the Cowes terminal.

In his review of the 1957 season, at the annual general meeting on 2 June 1958, the chairman outlined the board's intentions to develop activities with a progressive programme for the company's future prosperity. This would involve the modernisation of the fleet and elimination of vessels uneconomic to operate and unsuitable for present day requirements. It would include a realistic reorganisation of excursion services and a review of all management and administrative procedures to ensure utmost efficiency and strict control of operating and maintenance costs. Chapel Wharf had been sold and the new maintenance arrangements with Thornycroft's had reduced the time vessels were out of service for overhaul with resultant increase in earning capacity.

The proposals signalled the end of paddle steamer operation. *Bournemouth Queen* had already been sold and *Princess Elizabeth* was to be withdrawn when the new *Carisbrooke Castle* was commissioned in time for the summer service in 1959. *Carisbrooke Castle* was to be the first of a class (the 'Castle class') of four similar vehicle-carrying ferries all of which were named after local stately homes and castles.

CARISBROOKE CASTLE is seen unloading in this quiet scene at the reconstructed East Cowes terminal in 1966. The slipway had been enlarged and re-aligned to ease berthing, together with replacement of the offices and waiting room. A pontoon and bridge had been installed to enable foot passengers to embark without walking over the vehicle ramp.
RED FUNNEL
ARCHIVES

1959 - 1984

1958 started with discussions about the changes needed to the slipway at East Cowes to accommodate *Carisbrooke Castle*.

At the board meeting of 23 May a suggestion that *Princess Elizabeth* be disposed of to Cosens' was debated. The proposal was regarded as being impractical as the Board of Trade would require restoration of the lapsed Steam III passenger certificate. On 25 July it was agreed that *Princess Elizabeth* be laid-up from 6 September. It was not until 6 July 1959 that her fate was decided when the minutes record, with the specific agreement of the chairman, her sale to Torbay Blue Cruises for £4,000. Either the name was recorded inaccurately or the organization later changed to become known as Torbay Steamers Ltd.

Her place in the fleet was taken by *Carisbrooke Castle*. The launch in November was attended by the BBC and ITV, she ran trials in April 1959 and was handed over on 12 May 1959. Despite the possibility of *Norris Castle* being withdrawn at the end of the season, minor repairs were agreed to enable a six month extension to her passenger safety certificate. These minor repairs turned into some substantial work on the ship's hull in October 1959.

The financial results were improving and the dividend rose to 15% in 1958, from 12% in 1957. There was a further increase to 20% in 1959, with a special payment of 35% for the year ended 31 December 1960, to celebrate the company's centenary.

Modern technology continued to assist operations with Pye VHF radio equipment being fitted to *Carisbrooke Castle* and *Medina* during 1959, specifically to help in foggy conditions by enabling communication with Southampton Harbour Board port operations centre at Calshot. Despite some initial teething problems with levels of vibration, *Carisbrooke Castle* was deemed a great success and the chairman's report for 1959 referred to a large increase in passengers, cars and commercial vehicles being carried. The company's strengthened financial position allowed further steps to be taken in the modernisation of the fleet.

On 15 September 1961 a banquet took place at the Polygon Hotel in Southampton to celebrate the centenary of the company's formation. The chairman, Mr Redman, presided over the proceedings and Mr G W Powell, managing director of Esso Petroleum was chief guest and proposed the toast to the Southampton Isle of Wight and South of England Royal Mail Steam Packet Company Ltd. The MP for Southampton Test replied, as did the chairman of Alexandra Towing, Mr Bicket, who noted that his company and Red Funnel had enjoyed 42 years of the closest cooperation and friendship. Mr Redman paid a 'warm tribute to his fellow directors, the executive officers and staff', he especially mentioned the valued services of Mr C W Payne, general manager; Mr A H Levy, company secretary; Cmdr H B Samways, marine superintendent and Mr H Brundritt, tug superintendent.

Mr G W O'Connor was commissioned to write a centenary book and this was dispatched to shareholders on 1 February 1962 and made available for public purchase at 10s 6d (52.5p).

In the boardroom the directors were concerned by an application, from the firm of Starways Limited, for licences to operate hovercraft in the Southampton and Bournemouth areas. The subsequent trials and tribulations of operating high speed craft are dealt with in a separate section of this book.

At the October meeting the board considered plans from Thornycroft's for the vessel which was to become *Osborne Castle*. *Norris Castle* and *Medina* were already in the hands of selling agents with delivery from May 1962.

At their meeting on 28 November 1960 the directors stood in respect for the passing of Sir John E Thornycroft. He had served the Red Funnel board for 34 years, since 1926. The close relationship with the Thornycroft organization would continue as Mr John W Thornycroft CBE was appointed to fill the vacancy. He was the third generation of the Thornycroft family business and would later be followed by Mr Timothy E P Thornycroft. Timothy, known by many as Tim, would later become managing director of Red Funnel.

At Southampton, extra land had been acquired in Bugle Street and plans to extend the existing office were approved. The building work commenced in June 1961 and resulted for the first time in everybody being accommodated in one building.

Having undertaken her sea trials in February *Osborne Castle* was handed over on 6 March, entering service on Monday 19 March 1962. *Norris Castle* had been withdrawn the previous Friday. *Norris Castle* was still on the market but was later sold to Greece and left Southampton on 27 May 1962.

After reasonable weather in 1961, adverse conditions affected the excursion services in 1962.

On 26 October 1962 the board minutes record that the directors considered new liveries for the fleet. The general manager produced paintings of *Balmoral* with her hull painted in various colours. Unfortunately these paintings are no longer in the company records, but only one possibility interested the directors. Thornycroft's were to be asked to quote for scraping off *Balmoral's* black

hull paint and replacing it with a shade of green. However, the chairman clearly felt this was a step too far, as his recommendation to retain the existing colour scheme was accepted at the next meeting in November. It was to be 1992 before *Balmoral* briefly carried a green hull when operating for the *Waverley* organisation.

The final board meeting of the year, 21 December 1962, was the first to be held in the new board room constructed at 12 Bugle Street. The minutes of this meeting were the last to be hand written in bound ledgers, future minutes were typed and stored in Twinlock-style binders.

On 1 January 1963 the formal registered office of the company was moved from Western Esplanade to 12 Bugle Street, where it remains today.

The annual report noted increases in passengers, motor cars and commercial vehicles carried. Even the excursion business had improved, despite generally unfavourable weather. However, the chairman noted a slight decrease in the general shipping using Southampton which reduced the income from towage services. The shareholders dividend was 17.5%.

The premises at East Cowes had been refurbished and revised services to Cowes and East Cowes commenced on 1 January 1964. Meanwhile, at Southampton, defects had been discovered in the piles supporting the Royal Pier. Southampton

Harbour Board immediately applied a weight limit of 10 tons to vehicles using the pier.

At Weymouth, Campbell's sent their paddle steamer *Bristol Queen* to Cosens for overhaul during the winter of 1962/63. Clearly Red Funnel were keen to pursue engineering work for their subsidiary as they approached Campbell's to also carry out work on their *Cardiff Queen*. A meeting was arranged with the chairman of Campbell's in the autumn to discuss their overhaul requirements. In the end Campbell's reported that it was too expensive to send a ship to Weymouth that year.

At their meeting on 21 April 1964 the directors considered financial resources and their priorities for a new tug or vehicle ferry. The outcome was an order with Thornycroft's for a new ferry to be delivered at the end of 1965. It would be generally similar to *Osborne Castle* and replace *Vecta*. At their July meeting the directors agreed the name of the new vessel; the ferry would be *Cowes Castle*.

At their meeting on 18 September 1964, the board noted that Cosens had received enquiries from Mr H Bolson's firm, Crosons, about *Embassy*. If she was disposed of Cosens would continue as marine and general engineers. Mr Bolson agreed to make an offer by 21 December 1964, but there is no further mention of his interest and *Embassy*

Hydrofoil SHEARWATER, as delivered, in her original Red Funnel Seaflight livery.

SHEARWATER 2 arrived in Cowes Roads on 20 July 1970. Still boarded up, she is lowered into Solent waters for the first time. The two propellers are clearly seen, later hydrofoils were all single screw.

The saloon of SHEARWATER looks rather utilitarian compared to the opulence of ISLAND ENTERPRISE on page 55.

RED FUNNEL ARCHIVES

continued sailing for two more seasons.

However, relations with Mr Bolson must have been cordial because at the board meeting on 26 March 1965 it was agreed that *Vecta* would be offered for sale and both Crosons' and Campbell's would be informed. Delivery would be mid-September. The eventual sale agreement to Campbell's included provision for *Vecta* to have initial alterations and two refits carried out by Cosens at Weymouth. The splendid builder's model of the ship, previously on display at the Cowes office, was presented to Southampton Maritime Museum.

Cowes Castle entered service on 21 December 1965 having completed sea trials earlier that month. Her vehicle ramps were one foot longer than her two sisters, in order to help dispense with the 'slip boards' used at certain states of the tide to prevent vehicles grounding when manoeuvring on and off the ship.

Work had been underway reconstructing the East Cowes terminal. At their meeting on 29 April 1966 the board noted the unusual sailing of *Balmoral* to East Cowes on 5 May 'to test the new berthing arrangements'. The nature of the test, and why *Balmoral* was to carry it out, was not explained. However, Don Jones confirms that Captain Tom Kane berthed the ship at East Cowes that day, stern in towards the shore at slack water. It was rumoured locally that the visit was connected with a plan to convert *Balmoral* to a stern loading car ferry, but no other reference has been found to confirm or deny this possibility.

The chairman mentioned the forthcoming annual general meeting on 20 May and confirmed he would be reporting on board changes, together with commenting on hovercraft and hydrofoils. During the summer of 1966 the port of Southampton was severely affected by the national seamen's strike. Thankfully, the passage boats were unaffected and ironically towage income increased due to the moving of dead ships from berth to berth within the docks.

Reclamation of land next to the Royal Pier enabled the terminal to be improved and the extra space eased congestion of vehicles waiting to board the ferries.

Fewer passengers had used the Southampton-based excursion services during 1966, but as these were now operated solely by *Balmoral* the financial results were regarded as satisfactory. Cosens were concerned that the Board of Trade were asking for extensive work on *Embassy's* hull before issuing a passenger certificate for 1967. An enquiry had been received through a broker offering £10,000 for her future static use as a club. The minutes recorded the directors' reluctance to discontinue the excursion sailings. Their intention was to retain *Embassy* for about two years. However, they agreed to consider her

SHEARWATER 2 arrives at Southampton on 20 July 1971, with the chimney of the old Marchwood power station in the background.
BARRY EAGLES

sale if a firm offer of £10,000 was received. A later update from the general manager at Cosens resulted in agreement that *Embassy* be scrapped. Mr Bolson was to be informed of the decision. The author is intrigued by the board's apparent desire to keep *Embassy* in service for another two years, could there have been a plan to replace her in due course with *Balmoral*? She was certainly in much better condition than the recently departed *Vecta* and could have maintained excursions under the Cosens' houseflag for many more years.

At Southampton, the directors met on 30 June 1967 and noted continued demand for vehicles crossing to the Island. Consideration was being given to a 'Castle' type ship, but with accommodation for only 150 passengers and greater space for commercial vehicles. It was likely that *Balmoral* would be surplus to requirements within two years.

By October matters were clearer. The pier at Ventnor would not be useable in 1968 as the local council were unwilling to fund repairs. Sandown and Shanklin piers would be available, but Clarence Pier at Southsea was also under threat of closure. *Balmoral* was only used on the passage service on peak Saturdays and so 1968 would see the last excursions and she would be surplus from the end of that summer season.

The order for *Norris Castle* (III) was placed on 6 October 1967. On the towage side Red Funnel still regarded business as encouraging in the long term, although they expected difficulties in the next few years. Cunard had announced the withdrawal of both *Queen Mary* and *Queen Elizabeth*, reducing work in the port. Other shipping companies were also reducing their fleets.

Mr K C Barnaby, a Red Funnel director since 1947 and the architect of much of the new fleet, died on 22 March 1968. He had also been a director at Thornycroft's, where he had been their naval architect since 1924, until his retirement in 1955. His place at the Red Funnel boardroom table was taken by Mr C W Payne, general manager since 1952.

Changes were also underway on shore. Cdr Samways retired early, to be replaced as group engineering manager by Mr T E P Thornycroft, presently works manager at Vosper Thornycroft's Northam repair yard. Commercially, the chairman of Vectis Shipping had written suggesting amalgamation of his business with Red Funnel. Talks proceeded and just under one year later formal documents were signed for the acquisition of Vectis Shipping and Vectis Roadways.

Norris Castle was launched on 8 August. Her sea trials were delayed by labour disputes, but the handover took place on 6 December with a press trip on 10 December.

Mr James Hill was made an executive director from 1 January 1970. In a sign of the times

SHEARWATER is off service as SHEARWATER 2 loads passengers at the pontoon with CARISBROOKE CASTLE and OSBORNE CASTLE in the background on 20 July 1971.
BARRY EAGLES

Mr C W Payne now took the title managing director. He had formerly been known as director and general manager. In the office the accounts and payroll functions were partly mechanised by the acquisition of a National Cash Register accounting machine for £3,000.

The first moves towards a further new ferry were discussed in June 1970. It was recognised that *Carisbrooke Castle* had a limited deadweight capacity. It would be ideal to replace her with a vessel with the passenger capacity of *Cowes Castle*, but the commercial capacity of the new *Norris Castle*. In July a meeting was arranged with Mr S Dale, formerly shipbuilding director at Thornycroft's, to consider his appointment as consultant naval architect and technical advisor. The outcome was a two year contract to produce a feasibility study. In practice Mr Dale's remit was to range over many operational areas of Red Funnel in the next few years.

Within a couple of months he was reporting on the possibility of a drive-through vessel, using linkspans. His opinion was that a through-loading vessel would give a better rate of return, but dealing with foot passengers would need special consideration. By autumn the board were seriously considering a replacement for *Carisbrooke Castle*, to be delivered in June 1973. Plans for the new ferry progressed. The cheapest tender was received from Ryton Marine and the chairman visited their yard at Wallsend on Tyne. He was impressed with both the facilities and management. Everyone was well aware that Ryton Marine had not built a double-ended vessel of this type previously, but with a £250,000 difference between their tender and Bolson's, the

next lowest, it was agreed to go forward with Ryton's.

In 1972, two new directors joined the board. In February, from outside Red Funnel, came Mr G A H Jones MBE, a director of Powell Duffryn and a member of the Council of Shipping. In May, Mr Timothy Thornycroft, the group's technical manager, was appointed to take the place of Mr W G Probert who had died on 4 April.

Other potential projects were investigated around this time. British Rail Sealink was moving its Channel Island freight services from Weymouth and Southampton to Portsmouth. Red Funnel investigated a new freight service from Southampton to the Islands. Market research was carried out and that possibility was abandoned, to be replaced by ideas for a roll-on, roll-off service to Jersey which also came to nothing. News was received that the Raglan Trust, owners of the Bournemouth – Swanage Motor Road and Ferry Company, who operate the chain ferry across the entrance to Poole Harbour, were interested in selling their investment. Red Funnel were most interested in this, but unfortunately the Raglan Trust then decided not to sell.

Only three months before his planned retirement Mr C W Payne, the group managing director, died on 12 April 1973. The board met the following day and stood in silence. The following announcement was sent to all department heads and posted on all notice boards:

'It is announced with great regret that Mr C Warren Payne died yesterday evening. The board wish to place on record their great appreciation of all he has done for this company during the past twenty years. The outstanding devotion and

OSBORNE CASTLE prepares to sail from Berth B on 20 July 1971. CARISBROOKE CASTLE and the hydrofoil fleet lie at Berth A.
BARRY EAGLES

enthusiasm that he showed for the interests of the group and for all associated with it will long be remembered with gratitude.'

The notice was signed by those directors present; A E L Hill, G A H Jones, Sir Robert H Hobart, J W Thornycroft, J R L Hill and T E P Thornycroft. Subsequently, James Hill became group managing director and Dennis Archdeacon joined the board, whilst retaining his duties of company secretary and group financial controller. Tim Thornycroft was a contender for the role of group managing director, but the minutes record that in view of the importance of his duties as head of the group's engineering matters, it was felt he should not be asked to undertake any other major responsibility.

Returning to commercial matters, Ryton Marine had got themselves into severe financial difficulties, culminating in the appointment of a receiver and manager on 3 October 1973. Details are included in the ship's history section, but Mr Dale estimated another £140,000 of work was required to complete *Netley Castle*.

During April 1974 the local haulier, Hills of Southampton, went into liquidation. They had held shares in Red Funnel and these passed to Barings Bank. Barings now held 28% of the Red Funnel Group, they gave an assurance that they would continue to hold the shares unless they found another investor approved by the Red Funnel board.

In July 1974 the board looked at the Truckline ferry operation from Poole to Cherbourg, but decided not to become involved.

Office accounting arrangements now moved to a Burroughs electronic accounting machine. This was due for delivery in March 1975 at a cost of £16,000.

In early 1975 Mr Dale was awarded a five year consultancy agreement with Red Funnel. He reported that both Ferguson and Ailsa shipyards on the Clyde were interested in building new ships. Both could produce a vessel for early 1977 if an order was placed by summer 1975. It was agreed that nothing be done until Seaspeed vacated their Solent site at Cowes. The 'Solent site' lay between Thetis Wharf and Shepards Wharf and had formerly been the yard of Sounders – Roe. In June Mr Dale suggested that *Norris Castle* and *Cowes Castle* could be converted to drive-through operation and lengthened by about 30 feet. The Dutch company Boele could deal with the first in January 1976. If the conversions were carried out, the two vessels, together with *Netley Castle*, would provide a better return on capital employed. The board agreed to his proposals. Also looking forward, the board agreed to try and acquire Shepards Wharf, Thetis Wharf and the BHC Solent site to provide flexibility in planning the next major review of services which might take place around 1982.

Mr Ledger Hill retired as chairman from 31 October 1975 and Mr G A H Jones took his place. Cosens celebrated its centenary in 1976 and tug tender *Calshot* (II) provided a cruise in the Solent for its staff and their families on 10 June.

SHEARWATER 3 waits in the spare hydrofoil berth, while OSBORNE CASTLE departs for the Island. The bridge of NETLEY CASTLE can be seen at Berth B and one of the tug fleet moves up to the Western Docks, on 5 April 1975.
KEITH ADAMS

In November it was agreed that Mr Dale would join the board as a non-executive director from 1 January 1977. Before the 1977 annual general meeting Mr J W Thornycroft indicated his wish to stand down and make way for a new appointment having served on the board since 1961.

The old subject of investigating a shorter route for the car/commercial traffic was looked at again in 1977 this time from Hill Head, close to Lee-on-the-Solent, to Cowes. Financial outlay would be considerable, with extra fast craft needed for the passenger service from Southampton and new terminal facilities on the mainland. Against this would be the ongoing reduction in costs and the possibility of a more frequent service using fewer vessels. However, for the right financial return there would need to be an immediate increase in vehicle traffic, this was unlikely and the project was not taken further.

1978 started with a shake-up in the board room. Managing director, James Hill, wrote resigning from 21 December 1977. The subsequent press announcement stated that 'with the agreement of the company Mr J R L Hill is resigning all his appointments with the Red Funnel Group from 31 December 1977'. The new managing director was to be Mr T E P Thornycroft. Mr Thornycroft's appointment coincided with a decision to move some overhaul work away from his old family firm, now Vosper Thornycroft. *Norris Castle* went to Husband's yard at Marchwood for refit for the first time. He also inherited a change in catering arrangements on board the ships. Three outside caterers and a consortium of Red Funnel stewards had been asked to tender for a

franchaise. The contract was awarded to the stewards, under the name of Solent View Catering, and they brought back the serving of cooked breakfasts on board the ferries.

In February 1979, Mr H Barkham contacted Red Funnel, in accordance with an agreement made many years before, giving them first opportunity to acquire his firm of Blue Funnel Cruises. This was the trading name of his partnership with Mr W Hogg. Red Funnel did review Blue Funnel Cruise's accounts and established that a considerable mortgage was secured on the vessels *Island Scene* and *Solent Scene*. In view of the level of profits generated it was decided not to proceed further.

In January 1980 the Royal Pier was closed and a long series of discussions commenced between Red Funnel and the British Transport Docks Board (forerunners of Associated British Ports) about the use of the domed entrance building and other parts of the pier used for the ferry business. Changes in the Companies Acts required Red Funnel to register as a Public Limited Company, renaming eventually took place on 7 January 1982 with the revised official name becoming the 'Southampton Isle of Wight and South of England Royal Mail Steam Packet PLC'

Commercially, it was decided to cease the Vectis Shipping barge service from 30 October 1981 and replace it with a trailer service using the ferries. During this year the nationalised Sealink organisation was in the first stages of being privatised. Red Funnel wrote to the Minister of Transport expressing interest in the Lymington – Yarmouth route. Later, the Monopolies

Commission became involved with the whole Sealink disposal and Mr Ross, the Isle of Wight MP, weighed in with a suggestion that it would be good if European Ferries started in competition with both Sealink and Red Funnel on the Isle of Wight Services. Mr Ross was invited to Bugle Street and informed that Red Funnel made losses on its ferry business for seven months each year and already offered concessions to ferry users based on the Island. Mr Ross indicated that he had previously been unaware of these details. Red Funnel's interest in the Lymington – Yarmouth route was confirmed to the Minister in January 1983, but the whole of Sealink was eventually sold in 1984 to Sea Containers Limited, a company based in Bermuda.

At about this time Red Funnel also looked seriously at a service from Calshot to East Cowes. The advantages, and downsides, were similar to the issues previously reviewed at Hill Head. Discussions took place with officers from Hampshire County Council and New Forest District Council but it was impossible to take the matter further.

In 1983 the East Cowes terminal was redeveloped and the ships needed revised bow ramps for the new arrangements. The number of passenger vehicles using the service was declining and the board noted that this coincided with Sealink's introduction of their new ferry *St. Catherine* on the Portsmouth – Fishbourne route. A sister vessel was on her way at Portsmouth and Red Funnel reviewed its marketing policy on publicity, use of travel agents etc.

In early 1984 exploratory discussions took place with Alexandra Towing about whether they would be interested in acquiring the towage business. At the same time James Fisher sold a block of shares in Red Funnel to Alexandra Towing. The normal good relations continued between Red Funnel and Alexandra about towage operation in the port, but no change in ownership occurred.

Wrongly showing an '&' rather than the word 'and', the company's legal nameplates are displayed on the wall outside the registered office at 12 Bugle Street, Southampton on 19 January 1975.
KEITH ADAMS

1984 - 2010

The transfer of shares from James Fisher to Alexandra Towing caused a meeting to be held with Barings, the merchant bank. A questionnaire was completed calculating the price per share that might be obtained if an offer from an outsider was received to acquire Red Funnel. Barings reported that the present share price reflected the asset values, but a premium of 50% might be expected in a takeover bid, especially if the directors were forecasting improved future profits.

During this period the Red Funnel directors were actively looking at other business possibilities, both joint ventures and outright acquisitions. They looked at the business of Andrews (Shipside Services) Ltd, which had property in dockland, and also the Portsmouth Harbour Ferry Company, but that company's senior officers were not keen. Dean & Dyball Holdings Ltd, Shamrock Developments and Leading Leisure PLC were all active in local property development and talks took place with them over joint projects, some of which reached completion.

In preparing the trading budget for 1985, two scenarios were reviewed. The first showed the worst effects of the current dock strike and the second included the best income expected if two major container ship operators returned to the port. The difference in profit between the two situations was over £300,000. It had been regular practice to hold a Christmas party each year for contacts in dockland. It was usually held on one of the ships, latterly the tug tender *Calshot*. The industrial situation in Southampton docks had worsened, with no work taking place at the container terminal and a serious situation in the port generally. Red Funnel's directors agreed that it would not be appropriate to hold a party in these circumstances and the arrangements for December 1984 were cancelled. During February 1985 the dock labour disputes were settled after disruption lasting 13 weeks.

In July 1985 talks at East Cowes with the British Hovercraft Corporation (BHC) and Trinity House had failed to reach agreement about the installation of a linkspan for the ferries. Mr Dale designed an alternative engineering solution, a device known officially as the 'travelling articulated ramp', nicknamed 'The Wedge', which was placed on the slipway and adjusted by winch depending on the state of the tide.

The 125th anniversary of the company was reached in September 1986. Various ways of celebrating the occasion were discussed. The possibility of updating the Centenary book *The First Hundred Years* was considered, but not taken forward and eventually it was agreed not to mark the occasion in any way, although the 1986 timetable did declare '125th Anniversary'.

The board were mindful that the succession of directors needed to be urgently addressed, including a new chairman when Mr Jones retired. Mr Michael Wilkinson, a director of Powell Duffryn and Mr Christopher Bland, chairman of Hovertravel, were approached and both subsequently joined the board.

A slightly modified livery was applied to *Cowes Castle* in autumn 1985 when a horizontal red line was painted on the hull and the topsides became magnolia, the effect being found satisfactory. The 'travelling articulated ramp' entered service at East Cowes in February 1986 and worked very well with the newly extended ramps on the ships. Mr Dale was congratulated on his design and for supervising the construction process.

Meetings with the estate surveyor from Associated British Ports (ABP) continued about possibilities for the Southampton Terminal. ABP were reluctant to offer a lease of 125 years due to possible plans for a leisure area from Berth 101 in the western docks to Ocean Village. Interestingly, over 20 years later, plans are still being discussed for the development of parts of this area, but nothing has changed very much on the ground.

SHEARWATER 6 lies at the Gosport ferry pontoon at Portsmouth Harbour, loading for the 12:50 crossing to Cowes on 12 October 1991. GOSPORT QUEEN crosses from Gosport.
DON JONES

Talks continued with ABP, about the area of the old railway tracks that ran between the eastern and western docks, parallel to the road outside the Royal Pier. Leading Leisure PLC was putting forward commercial plans for the whole area and suggested that Red Funnel and Southern Newspapers become financially involved. The financial commitment would have been huge and Red Funnel looked for much more information before taking any involvement. In 1987 there was also conflict between ABP, the City Council and the free trade zone about development in the area of Berth 101.

At their meeting on 27 February 1987 the board considered the ramifications of Vosper Ship Repairers entering administration and the future of their yard and slipway at Northam. Red Funnel eventually made a joint offer with Dean & Dyball to acquire the premises. The offer was unsuccessful and the yard went to Halmatic, however Thew Engineering organised access to numbers 6 and 7 dry docks with financial assistance from the City of Southampton.

In April 1987 the fleet replacement policy was considered. The existing fleet was expected to give good service for some years, but a study would be undertaken of the economics of bringing in a new vessel, to cover design, capacity and financial costs. A new ferry was expected to cost about £5M at this time.

The company secretary was asked to investigate having Red Funnel's share price quoted in the *Financial Times*. The company was aware of a number of nominee holdings of its shares and the secretary was encouraged to use his discretion in sharing information with beneficial owners about significant share transfers.

Mr Wilkinson became deputy chairman on 2 September, subsequently taking over as chairman when Mr Jones retired on 1 January 1988.

With the benefit of hindsight, movements were taking place in some of the shareholdings in the company. Local brokers, Cobbold Roach, reported that they were unable to buy or sell shares at 'normal' market prices. It was apparent that some market makers were buying-up shares at high prices, at which Cobbold Roach were reluctant to deal. Barings recommended a change in brokers to Phillips and Drew. After discussions over fees, they were appointed national brokers, with Cobbold Roach still involved locally.

A new company secretary and financial director was appointed in February 1988. Roger Shepherd joined Red Funnel from Sealink UK where had had been financial director.

At their meeting on 29 July 1988 the directors reviewed the business plan for the three years to 1991. The plan identified priorities to increase the rate of change; improve the company's image; consider the next generation of high speed craft and a new ferry; and revise arrangements at the Southampton and East Cowes terminals. The first action was to appoint Rayner Advertising as marketing and public relations agents to advise on corporate image. The 1989 budget process was also underway with a note that individual departments should expect to be under increased scrutiny during the process.

In the autumn Rayner Advertising reported about rationalising signs at the Southampton Terminal, developing a 'house style' and proposing a new livery for the ferries and hydrofoils. Red Funnel timetables were considered erratic, with a need to adopt regular 'clock face' times in the way that Sealink operated.

In the secretarial department it was noted that some shares had changed hands at 535p. This price prompted a joint meeting between Mr Shepherd and Phillips and Drew, with Barings to discuss strategy in case of a takeover approach. A list of shareholders was prepared as at 1 October and out of a total of 735 shareholders, 26% held exactly 2,400 shares, the number required to secure a shareholder's free pass.

On 16 December 1988 Hazel Nicholson was appointed assistant to the company secretary. Miss Nicholson had joined Red Funnel in 1952 and was later to become company secretary in 1990 and, after retirement in 1998 take on the role of archivist of the company's records.

ABP had continued discussions about the leases of the Royal Pier site and were now willing to discuss a longer lease. The board minutes record that the terminal area was now regarded more as a development site and not part of the port.

Further investment opportunities presented themselves in early 1989. The business of Grays Transport, a privately owned haulage business in Andover, was for sale and Ocean Sound was looking at a new radio franchise for the Isle of Wight. Both possibilities were followed up, but only the transport acquisition reached completion. Red Funnel set up a new subsidiary, Grays Transport Ltd, into which the business previously owned by Peter Gray was transferred. Things were moving ahead with plans for the ferry terminals. At East Cowes, Westland had offered some land next to the existing terminal, but at a price greater than Red Funnel was prepared to pay. Plans for the Cowes terminal were approved to seek planning permission with a view to completion in Easter 1990. In the office, computerisation of tickets and reservations was being explored.

Norris Castle was now operating in the new livery, incorporating a red hull, however plans were afoot for her replacement. Inclining tests had been completed, but loading on-board was often difficult and sometimes commercial vehicles had to be taken off to correct her trim.

RED JET 3 is shown building at FBM's yard at Cowes on 13 May 1998.
DON JONES

Seen entering the river Medina, RED JET 3 is launched on 16 June 1998.
DON JONES

With the prospect of a new ferry the possibility of a four ship service was considered, but eventually the decision was made to withdraw *Norris Castle* and continue with three ships. An announcement of the proposed new ship, and her expected entry into service in January 1991 was made at the annual general meeting on 10 May 1989. The chairman commented that despite many changes at the company, ferries were at the heart of Red Funnel and he intended to keep that heart beating strongly.

Burness Corlett and Partners (BCP), naval architects, had produced plans for the new ferry. The lack of a linkspan at East Cowes and continued use of the slipway meant that Voith Schneider propulsion units would be vulnerable to grounding. Two versions of the new ship were prepared, the first based on similar propulsion arrangements to *Netley Castle* and the second using Voith propulsion, if planning permission for a linkspan was granted in time. However, tendering procedures were about to be delayed due to other events.

Without prior warning, on 23 June 1989, Sally UK Holdings Limited (Sally) made a bid to acquire control of Red Funnel. In their offer document they argued that Red Funnel would soon face competition on its ferry operations and that without more dynamic management, earnings would drop and the value of shares decrease. They offered 205p for each ordinary share, which they suggested was a premium of 12% over the middle market quotation for Red Funnel ordinary shares the previous day. Shareholders would retain any rights to fare concessions or free travel.

The response of the board was immediate and emphatic. Advice was taken from the company's merchant bankers, Barings, and the Red Funnel chairman, Michael Wilkinson, wrote to shareholders the following day. The letter confirmed that the directors considered the proposed offer unwelcome and that it was wholly inadequate in value. Proposals had been announced for a new ferry and, with the recent acquisition of Grays Transport, there were excellent prospects for the future as an independent company.

Sally's next move was a letter, dated 11 July addressed to Red Funnel shareholders, from their chairman Michael Kingshott. It was a long letter and argued Sally's case from a number of angles. Firstly, it cited what it described as poor financial performance – profits of £1.71M in 1988 being £300,000 less than in 1986. Secondly, it talked about future uncertainty, Cowes Express were about to compete on the high speed service and the four hydrofoils were becoming outdated. No new ferry had been ordered in 15 years and Cosens' engineering prospects were deteriorating. The 'Sally Solution' to these perceived issues was that their 'dynamic executive management' would improve Red Funnel's prospects and Sally's Ramsgate – Dunkirk ferry operations would be transferred to Red Funnel. They reported that in six years operating from Ramsgate they had demonstrated impressive growth and a reputation for quality.

There was no mention of financial performance and Sally's own financial details, tucked away in the letter, indicated cumulative losses between 1984 and 1988 of £6.9M. This was despite management and charter fees from their holding company, totalling £3.5M, being waived. Their 1988 balance sheet was only solvent because assets had been revalued upwards by over £10M. When starting from nothing, any 'growth' is high in percentage terms. This was hardly an impressive record.

Unsurprisingly, the Red Funnel directors seized on these details and sent a printed document to shareholders on 25 July 1989. There were three slogans backed up by comment and statistics:

- Red Funnel is a company with a future and a strategy that works

- Sally has a management that has failed and a strategy that looks doomed
- Don't let Sally save itself at your expense

They argued that Red Funnel shareholders had received good dividends and that the share price had outperformed the *Financial Times* all share index by 44%. The document's summary was;

- Sally need us – We (Red Funnel) do not need them.

Also, it was pointed out that Sally's operation was likely to be devastated by the opening of the Channel Tunnel and the proposed ending of duty-free sales on cross Channel ferries.

Sally's response was to increase their offer to 236p for each Red Funnel ordinary share.

Red Funnel directors wrote again to their shareholders on 30 August 1989, this document's punch line was:

- Sally has a management that has failed and a strategy that looks doomed, by trying to buy Red Funnel on the cheap, it is trying to save itself at your expense – Don't let it.

Behind the scenes, time was running out for Sally and Associated British Ports Holdings PLC (ABP) was taking an active interest in proceedings. They entered the market on 22 August and began buying Red Funnel ordinary shares at 240p. By 30 August they owned 183,500 shares representing about 11% of the issued ordinary shares.

Talks took place and on 30 August ABP published an offer document for Red Funnel shares that enjoyed the recommendation of the Red Funnel directors. ABP were offering 260p in cash, or ABP shares valuing Red Funnel shares at 281p. Shareholders who qualified for travel concessions at 31 August would retain the right to similar concessions for his or her lifetime. Sally could not, or did not wish to, match the ABP price and their offer lapsed.

The logic behind ABP's move was outlined in their document, which recorded three reasons for the offer. Firstly, ABP were committed to the continuing prosperity and development of the port of Southampton and an efficient ferry service to the Isle of Wight was an important part of that vision. Secondly, the Royal Pier site occupied by Red Funnel had potential for property development. The site was held under a series of leases from ABP and the merger of interests would more easily facilitate that development, including improvements to the ferry terminal. Thirdly, Red Funnel's towage business would usefully complement ABP's services to its customers in the port.

During these tumultuous two months 'normal service' had continued with the Cowes terminal plans receiving planning permission and naval architects BCP had been busy with the specifications and arrangements for tenders for

the new ferry which was now expected in service in May 1991. BCP were also working on the new fast craft whilst FBM Marine were asked to look into a new fast car ferry and these details are noted in the High Speed section of this book.

During August 1989 plans were circulated in Southampton for a rapid transport system and 10/12 potential subscribers wishing to invest £20,000 in a feasibility study were needed. Red Funnel were potential subscribers, and Schroders were expected to produce an initial report in September, but nothing more was noted in the board minutes and Southampton still awaits its rapid transport system in 2010.

At two board meetings on 20 October the formal changes in ownership of the company were recorded. At 10:00 it was noted that 78% of shareholders had accepted the ABP offer. The board welcomed three new directors from ABP, they were Messrs C S Bradley, A S Kent and C W Orange. At 10:15 a second meeting commenced when Mr Wilkinson resigned as chairman and Mr Bradley took his place. Items noted that day included the ordering of two new catamarans and the possibility of a high speed passenger/car ferry with a designated terminal outside of Southampton. BCP reported on a draft specification for a new conventional ferry and confirmed that if ordered by January 1990 it could be in service for the 1991 summer season. A new computerised system of ticketing and reservations had gone live as planned.

Tendering documentation for the new ferry was dispatched on 1 December 1989 for a double-ended passenger vehicle ferry with two options: a) four combined rudder propeller/units, and b) twin Voith Schneider propulsion units. Tenders closed on 9 February and seven bona fide tenders were received. BCP were requested to ask each tenderer to give the price of a second vessel based on option a).

An issue that would cause much work within the company, and become the subject of local press comment, was the attention of the Office of Fair Trading (OFT). During the takeover bid someone had contacted the OFT complaining about excessive fares on Isle of Wight services. The OFT had subsequently written to Red Funnel and Sealink (to become known as Wightlink from November 1990) requesting further information about their arrangements, including details of capital employed. The latter was an irritation for Red Funnel. As the average age of the 'Castle' car ferries was old, their written-down value in the accounts was low. Thus the calculated return on capital employed was high compared to Wightlink which had a more modern fleet. It had to be explained to the OFT that when future new vessels were taken into account a more modest return would be disclosed. One important side

SHEARWATER 3 passes Cunard's QUEEN ELIZABETH 2 as NEW FORESTER heads for Hythe on the ferry service.
KEITH ADAMS

effect of the OFT enquiry was that the board felt unable to commit to a new ferry until the outcome was known.

At the board meeting of 22 February 1990 concern was expressed over the lack of ship repairers in Southampton. With the closure of the Northam yard there was no slipway capable of taking *Netley Castle*. The nearest commercial possibilities were Gravesend or Falmouth. Talks would be held with the Naval dockyard at Portsmouth, but there were problems with their system of overhead costing procedure.

At Southampton, ABP now completely owned the Town Quay site and plans were for the pier to be demolished, some land reclaimed, and a new ferry terminal constructed. The new terminal at Cowes was well advanced and the island MP, Barry Field, would formally open it on 8 June 1990. In a commercial change, the name of the Grays Transport Ltd operation was changed to Andover Transport Ltd.

There were now a series of departures from the board room after the installation of ABP as new owners. Mr Tim Thornycroft attended his last board meeting on 27 June 1990 before resigning as managing director at the end of the month. This marked the end of an association since 1926

between Red Funnel, the Thornycroft family and the shipbuilding and repair yards bearing their name. Mr Alistair Whyte took over as managing director from 1 July 1990. Mr Roger Shepherd also resigned as financial director and company secretary, from 2 October Hazel Nicholson became the new company secretary. Mr Michael Wilkinson, chairman during the Sally takeover bid, attended his last board meeting on 3 December 1990.

The OFT wrote to Wightlink and Red Funnel in December 1990 informing the companies that they were now involving the Monopolies and Merger Commission, due to the perceived lack of opportunity for new operators to enter the Isle of Wight ferry market. The OFT was not expected to report until early 1992, which caused further delay in committing to new ferries.

However, new tonnage was needed urgently so planning continued and options were reviewed. Red Funnel investigated the 'Superflex' ferries that had been built speculatively and were now available for sale. They also looked at second-hand ferries operating in the Straits of Messina and British Columbia, but none of these possibilities was found to be suitable. An open mind was being kept about mainland terminals and in December 1990 Red Funnel began investigating land around the Fawley power station as a possible new vehicle terminal.

An important timetable change took place from 27 April 1991 when the vehicle ferries stopped calling at (West) Cowes and ran directly to East Cowes. There was considerable local concern, particularly about the reliability of the service from Cowes in foggy conditions. Assurances were given that, unlike the hydrofoils, the new 'Red Jet' catamarans would have a similar operating ability in fog as the ferries. Every effort was made to ensure that island residents knew about the changes. From 15 April a big leaflet drop was organised by the marketing department and a bus toured the Island with a jazz band on board and badges for children. This was the first major campaign organised in-house to increase Red Funnel's market share and improve the visibility of the company. Olive Glass had been appointed marketing director in December 1990 and her department replaced the outside agency, Rayner Advertising. *Red Jet 1* entered service on 6 April and immediately met with approval from passengers. It was very helpful for publicity purposes that the craft was locally built in Cowes. At Fawley power station, the New Forest district plan restricted planning possibilities and Red Funnel had objected to the relevant parts of the plan.

After a meeting with the Monopolies and Mergers Commission on 17 July a preliminary report was received in September. The Commission was coming to the view that there was no monopoly situation in favour of Red Funnel, but they did have concerns over Wightlink's situation and its owner, Sea Containers Ltd. The managing director immediately began approaching shipyards for designs and possible delivery dates for new vehicle ferries. Cochrane's shipbuilders of Selby prepared outlines of a revised Wightlink ferry *St. Faith* for consideration.

The marketing campaign continued with the launch of 'Sailaway Breaks', featuring package holidays to the Island, targeting families in peak periods and senior citizens off-peak. Other promotions included cheap fares for drivers and their cars travelling under 'Nightflyer' arrangements, while shoppers could travel on the high speed service off-peak as 'Shopper Hoppers'.

At their meeting on 28 November 1991 the directors agreed to look at the ferry *St. Helga* then operating at Sicily which was available for charter or sale. In early 1992 the possibilities of a Fawley vehicle terminal progressed a stage further when National Power agreed to support Red Funnel at the local planning enquiry. It also became clear that Sally Line had approached National Power in September 1991 about this

site, but it had not been pursued.

In March 1992 the Monopolies and Mergers Commission agreed that there was no monopoly situation with Red Funnel and that the company had never operated against the public interest. The directors now needed to make a decision about the new ferry, if it was to be in service for the 1994 season. The naval architects, Burness Corlett and Partners (BCP), were engaged to prepare specifications and tender documents and these were ready by 15 May. Tenders from eleven interested shipbuilders were opened on 3 July and a short-list prepared for detailed assessment.

The good news was that the price was likely to be no more than £8M, indicating a keen market. Thoughts turned to names of the new vessels and at this stage it was agreed that the 'class' should have a common theme, perhaps incorporating the names of the early steamers *Pearl*, *Ruby*, *Sapphire* and *Emerald*.

At the board meeting on 11 September 1992 it was agreed to purchase two new ships and proceed with a refurbishment at the terminals. The first vessel would be due in March 1994, with the second arriving one year later. The formal contract was signed with Ferguson Shipbuilders Ltd of Port Glasgow on 8 October. The yard was very competitive, both on price and in the efficiency of its operations. The company secretary was asked to investigate possible names for the new ships.

Consulting engineers were appointed to devise a linkspan for East Cowes and advise on matters at Southampton. By December the East Cowes possibilities had been narrowed down to two schemes, but a final decision was needed by May 1993. The Southampton layby berth was likely to be at the Town Quay.

Immediately, a marketing strategy was produced. The signs were good, as Red Funnel had already increased its market share in all areas except commercial vehicles, carrying record numbers of cars and high speed passengers in 1992. However, Wightlink were reducing rates to help their position in the marketplace. It was a time of recession and Wightlink made the decision to lay up their Fishbourne – Portsmouth vehicle ferry *St. Helen* at the end of 1992.

She was offered for charter, a move that generated interest from Stena-Sealink who announced their wish to compete on the Isle of Wight services. Stena-Sealink had no terminals of their own, Wightlink refused to charter their vessel to them, and after a year or so their interest waned. When economic conditions improved, *St. Helen* was brought back into service by Wightlink for the 1994 summer season.

The possible names of the new ferries were chosen, in order of preference, as *Red Falcon*, *Red Kestrel* and *Red Osprey*. The name *Red*

Two views of NORRIS CASTLE (III). RED FUNNEL ARCHIVES

Kestrel was not available and the other two names were allocated to Red Funnel. The board noted on 16 March 1993 that it would be difficult to keep *Norris Castle* and *Cowes Castle* going until the arrival of the new ships. Their engines were old and it was now difficult to obtain spares with nothing being available off-the-shelf. However, the old ferries did carry on and Red Funnel's marketing department was delighted to report that for the first time the company had a 30% share of the total market. Special attention was now being paid to car traffic levels to ensure that the extra capacity of the new ferries would be filled.

Progress was also being made in other areas. At Bugle Street, numbers 11-15, premises across the road from the main offices, had four parties interested in their purchase and sealed bids were due by 31 July, although the eventual final exchange of contracts did not occur until 23 March 1994.

In September 1993 a firm of outside consultants carried out consumer research into the cross Solent ferry trade. In their summary they described Red Funnel as being a warm and friendly company, but old fashioned. Wightlink were perceived to be a clean, bright, modern company, but lacking in soul. Whatever the interpretation of market research, Red Funnel's ferries were about to become the most modern on the Solent.

The launch of the company's first new ferry since 1973 took place on 18 October 1993. The Southampton participants travelled by coach to Heathrow for their flight to Glasgow. *Red Falcon's* launch was a success in every way and the event received a mention on the front page of the Times newspaper. Ferguson's shipyard expected to have her ready for service at Easter 1994. The yard had received a new order from Caledonian MacBrayne and was keen to deliver *Red Osprey* four months earlier than planned, in October 1994.

The new arrangements required at East Cowes had passed the various planning hurdles and ABP's heavy lift crane was used to move the new linkspan from Cowes to East Cowes over the weekend of 26/27 February 1994. The first vessel to use the new facility was *Cowes Castle* at 06:30 on the Monday morning. She had only a short period left in service as *Red Falcon* was already on her delivery voyage from the Clyde. In a very exciting few days, *Cowes Castle* made her final crossing on Monday 21 March, with *Red Falcon* commencing service and providing 'hospitality week' from that day. Happily the new vessel operated reliably and passenger feedback was very good.

By September traffic growth had continued to rise and arrangements were in progress for the naming ceremony of *Red Osprey* at Fountain Pontoon,

Cowes on 19 October. Ferguson's were keen to build a third ship and offered to hold their 1992 tender price if an order was forthcoming. The Red Funnel board prepared a paper for ABP Holdings PLC concerning the issue. It had been intended that *Netley Castle* would remain in service as the third ship, until 2003, undergoing work to comply with new regulations coming into force in 1996. However, the full potential of the three ship service could not be realised until *Netley Castle* was replaced. ABP were asked to authorise the ordering of a new ferry in 1995 rather than 2002 as previously envisaged. The proposal to build *Red Eagle* was agreed and negotiations with the builders allowed an extension of the accommodation area and 30 new seats all within the contract price.

The contract with Compass Catering ended in February 1995 and the opportunity was taken to bring the catering operation back in-house. The dormant subsidiary company Grays Transport Ltd, changed its name to Masthead Services Ltd to operate the new catering division. The new arrangements began on 11 March 1995, when the traditional post of purser was replaced by the On Board Service Officer.

The Royal Pier Gatehouse at Southampton returned to Red Funnel control when the lease to European Leisure ended early. The fence behind the building was removed which allowed space for another 50 cars in the marshalling area. The ongoing review of other potential cross Solent terminal sites continued, but in 1996 the preferred alternative site was Ensign Park at Hamble.

The Orkney and Shetland ferry contracts to the mainland were coming up for reassessment and Red Funnel asked the Scottish Office for them to be included on the tender list. This was granted but the later requests for information, together with a feeling that they were most unlikely to win the contract, led to a decision not to takes matters further. There was an interesting enquiry from Swiss bankers, on behalf of the Turkish Government, about running a service across the Bosphorus with *Netley Castle* and the two remaining *Shearwater* hydrofoils. The directors agreed that all avenues should be considered, but that their preference was for a bareboat charter or an outright sale. No positive offers had been received for *Netley Castle* and costings were considered for using her as a relief freight vessel during the overhaul season.

With the new 'Raptor' ferries (the fleet now referred to in this way due to their naming after birds of prey) well established it was important to have back-up facilities in place for emergencies. Berth 25 in the Eastern Docks at Southampton was modified to be used by the ferries for standby and contingency purposes. At East Cowes, a design for back-up lifting arrangements was put in place in case the hydraulic systems operating the linkspan failed.

On 21 November 1996 the board considered replacement vessels. Provisional arrangements had been in place to finance a fourth new ferry, but these were replaced with plans for a new tug and a further high speed craft in 1997.

The 'Raptor' ferries performed very well during the rough weather of the 1996/97 winter. The local radio station, Radio Solent, was persuaded to give details of the cross Solent services that were still running and not just those routes that had been cancelled in bad weather.

An updated market research document suggested that Red Funnel and Wightlink operations were now similar in many respects, but that Wightlink had better facilities that allowed them greater efficiency in loading. Red Funnel's directors had been constantly aware of the shortcomings of their terminals for many years, particularly the available space for marshalling at East Cowes. In 1997 negotiations were underway to purchase two shops and a public house with potential for demolition. The Isle of Wight authorities were in favour of Red Funnel reclaiming an area to the seaward side of the breakwater at East Cowes for use as a completely new terminal, but this would require approaches to the EEC for funding

assistance. A new building at the existing East Cowes terminal was opened in July 1997 by Red Funnel director Mr Bland, in his capacity as Lord Lieutenant of the Isle of Wight.

In November 1997 Red Funnel received accreditation for achieving the International Safety Management code for shipboard safety and pollution management in respect of the ferries, high speed and company safety systems.

In 1998 the company published *Red Funnel – a Pictorial History* a small booklet priced at £4.95. It was compiled by Michael Archbold, at that time a member of the public relations firm, Arcadia PR & Design, used by Red Funnel.

In June 1999 Red Funnel announced the winning of a safety award from the British Safety Council and the gold award of the Royal Society of the Prevention of Accidents. Only companies with below average accident rates are eligible for the British Safety Council awards.

In 2000 it was reported that investigations were underway to alter the 'Raptor' ferries so that commercial vehicles could be carried under the deployed moveable mezzanine decks. At that time height restrictions meant that only cars could fit under them. The initial idea was to raise the upper deck to increase the headroom. However, without any other change the level of the ramps

RED FALCON sails around the stern of QUEEN ELIZABETH 2 outward bound for Norway, on 24 July 2007. In the right background is the river Itchen, where many of Red Funnel's ferries and tugs were built and maintained.
RICHARD
DANIELSON

ALI CAT moored in front of the distinctive pier buildings at Dunoon. Red Funnel chartered this vessel from Isle of Wight operator Solent & Wightline Cruises in autumn 2002 and then chartered her on to Cowal Ferries Limited (Caledonian MacBrayne) for use primarily on their Dunoon to Gourock route. At June 2010, ALI CAT is still in service on the Clyde under extensions to the original agreements. However the Scottish Government has started an open tender procedure for the whole route, so ALI CAT's future on the Clyde must be uncertain.
CHARLES
McCROSSAN

up to the mezzanine decks would become unacceptably steep. The next proposal was to install a fixed upper car deck and utilise twin level loading. BCP carried out a feasibility study and found that to carry the additional cargo deadweight, it was necessary to lengthen the vessels. BCP then prepared the details of the conversion design, specification and tender documentation. Tenders were opened on 5 July 2002 and contract negotiations concluded with Gdansk ship repair yard 'Remontowa' for the conversion of two ships with an option for the third vessel.

Rumours circulated in August 2000 that ABP were looking to sell Red Funnel, to raise about £80M and concentrate on their core business of port operation. The Japanese company Nomura was thought to be a potential buyer, but a management buyout was also a possibility. In December 2000 it was announced that the new owner was J P Morgan Partners, the private equity arm of J P Morgan Chase, the investment bank. The bank said they would see what improvements could be made and would also investigate the possibility of a fourth ferry.

Traffic levels were good and having extended the three boat service through the autumn to Christmas in earlier years, a shuttle service was proposed for 2002. It began on 15 February and provided an approximately 50 minute frequency of service, the maximum that could be operated with three vessels. Commercially the alterations may have been helpful, but to the average

passenger, used to 'clockface' departure times, the changes were not appreciated. The three ships had their on-board shops removed during the overhaul season because the facilities had not met commercial expectations.

During 2002 Red Funnel continued their major project to increase the vehicle capacity of the 'Raptor' ferries. The project required the reconstruction of the East Cowes terminal and the conversion of the first two ships was then delayed by one year until planning and permission for the new double deck linkpsans was granted. In November 2003 Red Funnel publicly announced the £7M investment in the 'Raptor' ferries. Each ship would go to Poland to be lengthened by 9.6m and heightened by 2.8m. The alterations enabled the creation of an extra vehicle deck, increasing capacity by approximately 70 cars. While the ships were away a second-hand Norwegian ferry, renamed *Bergen Castle*, was purchased to provide back-up and temporary capacity. The new upper car deck on the 'Raptors' needed redesigned linkspan facilities at both terminals. While the work was progressing at Southampton the ferries temporarily used Berth 25 in the Eastern Docks and a bus connection was provided from the Royal Pier.

With future extra capacity available on the converted ferries, the welcome decision was made to revert to an hourly service in 2004.

In July 2004 it was announced that a management buyout had taken place. The Bank of Scotland provided a £60M debt and equity package to fund the deal which allowed the management team to hold 51% of the shares. As part of the arrangements the new non-executive chairman was Gavin Simonds, chairman of fashion retailer Peacocks and former managing director of Inter-Continental Hotels. In his opening statement he described the management team as 'outstanding' and said the business had 'rock solid earnings'.

Soon after the management buyout, the directors of the new holding company, Red Funnel Group (Holdings) Ltd, announced the merging of the boards of Vectis Transport and Red Funnel into Red Funnel Ferries Ltd, thus ending the separate directors meetings of the transport and haulage entities.

In November 2004 the East Cowes terminal issue came to public attention once more. In an updated development of the 1997 ideas, the new possibility was to see the Red Funnel vehicle terminal, and that of the 'Red Jets', moved onto reclaimed land from the Solent off East Cowes. This time many local residents objected, fearing a blot on the landscape and the disadvantages to passengers, and traders, of foot passengers not being able to stroll into Cowes. The Solent Protection Society was also against the proposals. Early 2006 saw the South East England Development Agency, known as SEEDA, publish a plan to redevelop the town of East Cowes. Both Red Funnel and East Cowes District Council opposed these ideas, which would have reduced the size of the existing ferry parking and marshalling area.

In March 2007, it was reported that the management team and joint owner Halifax Bank of Scotland (HBOS) were considering selling the business as a going concern. The value reported in the press was £200M. Negotiations reached a conclusion when the majority of shares in the business were sold to Infracapital – the investment arm of the Prudential Group. Red Funnel's managing director, commercial director and financial director joined the board of the new holding company and senior management continued to hold a minority stake in the business. The Prudential Group are part owners of ABP, which directly owned Red Funnel between 1989 and 2000.

In summer 2007, business publications in the Isle of Wight suggested that Infracapital intended to introduce new tonnage over the next 5/6 years. A new *Red Jet* would join the fleet to replace *Red Jets 1* and *2* and *Red Kestrel* would follow enabling a three ship service to be maintained through the overhaul season. *Red Jet 5* joined the fleet in 2009, but economic conditions will require a longer wait for the new ferry. In June 2008 exceptionally high fuel costs and environmental concerns prompted the withdrawal of two round trips on the high speed service at 11:45 and 12:45 from Southampton until 30 March 2009. The two ferry, 90 minute frequency ferry service commenced on 31 October 2009 for the winter timetable, until 25 March 2010, indicating that the national economic downturn is having its effect on traffic. However, the recurring story of Red Funnel through its 150 years is of survival through tough economic conditions and ambitious plans when the recovery comes.

Red Funnel became involved in a market study into Isle of Wight ferry services by the Office of Fair Trading (OFT) in 2009. Local politicians had encouraged a petition about fares on the Island ferry routes and a two month consultation followed. Both Red Funnel and Wightlink publically offered assistance to enquiries and the OFT quickly announced that it would not refer the market to the Competition Commission. In its summary the OFT study concluded that average fare prices had risen at around the same rate as the Retail Price Index and that overall fares were not obviously out of line with other European commercial ferry services. There was some scope for improved communication between the operators and their customers and Red Funnel now provide a 'service status' area on their website which details the actual positions of ferries and the high speed craft and is updated every 90 seconds. The information can also be accessed by mobile phones and portable computers.

Red Funnel had two of its ferry fleet on excursion duty to bid farewell to the Cunard liner *Queen Elizabeth 2* when she left Southampton for the last time on 11 November 2008. Initially, *Red Eagle* was advertised from Southampton at 18:45, due back 22:40. However this sailing quickly sold out and *Red Falcon* was then advertised from East Cowes at 18:00 returning 21:30. *Red Jet 4* also carried out some sightseeing trips at lunchtime and during the afternoon.

It is fitting that this updated history of Red Funnel should end with mention of an excursion, taking us back to the earliest days of the company. But this is a forward-looking organisation, one of commercial management keen to embrace an opportunity for financial reward at the same time serving the populations on both sides of the Solent. In times of peace and war, prosperity or recession, Red Funnel has safely and reliably plied the waters between Southampton and the Isle of Wight and been present at all the great maritime events in local waters. The author is confident that in 2061 someone will be penning an update of the 200 year history of the Southampton Isle of Wight and South of England Royal Mail Steam Packet Company Limited – known to all as Red Funnel.

This pictorial spread shows today's Red Funnel fleet at work between Southampton and Cowes. The main service is provided to East Cowes, round the clock, seven days a week. Three large, comfortable, ro-ro passenger ferries named RED FALCON, RED OSPREY and RED EAGLE carry rolling freight, tourist coaches, lorries carrying letters and parcels, cars and passengers on an interesting cross-Solent journey lasting about an hour. During the voyage passengers will be likely to see some of the world's most famous passenger ships,

a wide variety of ocean going and coastal vessels, local ferries and leisure craft. Additionally, for foot passengers wishing to travel more quickly, three large high-speed 35-knot catamarans named RED JET 3, RED JET 4 and RED JET 5 provide a service every half-hour crossing to and from Cowes in under 25 minutes.
All: RICHARD DANIELSON

HIGH SPEED SERVICES

A fast launch service was operated from Southampton to Cowes using *Island Enterprise* between 1933 and 1938. A winter service was tried during 1933/4 and 1934/5, but after that only a summer timetable was operated.

The 1936 edition of *The South Coast Guide* described the vessel as a fast, eleven passenger, powerful, twin engined motor cruiser, affording comfort and safety to passengers in all weather. The cabin was fitted out in the manner of a luxury road motor coach of the period, toilet facilities were provided and hand baggage accommodation was available.

The crossing time was 35 minutes. The boat was capable of 30 knots, but was operated at 22 knots for comfort. Due to her exceptional manoeuvrability, *Island Enterprise* could stop within one and a half lengths from full speed and turn at right angles in five seconds. Although new for passenger work, the design was based on the RAF crash boats which had been used in all sea conditions by the British Air Ministry.

The initiative had come from the British Power Boat Company who had their works at Hythe. At a board meeting on 13 February 1933 it was agreed to accept the offer of a loan of a power boat, or boats, with a view to ascertaining their suitability or otherwise for the company's service. It was left for the general manager to sort out details of the offer. The service was advertised to commence at Whitsun. The next mention in the minutes was 11 September 1933 when it was agreed to continue with the service subject to satisfactory arrangements being agreed with Mr Scott-Paine of the British Power Boat Company. Discussions were favourable, the meeting of 6 November recording the end of the loan arrangement and the purchase of *Island Enterprise* at a price of £2,019. In April 1934 a spare engine was purchased to 'expedite repairs to the engines'. The end of the service was decided at the board meeting on 14 November 1937 when it was resolved that the boat was to be sold 'at the best possible price'. However, *Island Enterprise* did continue to operate through the 1938 summer season, finally being sold at the outbreak of World War II in September 1939.

The craft was sold to Imperial Airways and it was to be 1968 before the company again experimented with a high speed passenger service.

However, the subject of high speed craft was regularly discussed at board meetings. During Red Funnel's centenary year, 1961, there was mention in the press of Saunders-Roe (later known as Westland Aircraft) developing a hovercraft for cross Solent service. Later the same year, the directors were concerned over an application, by a firm called Starways Limited, for licences to operate hovercraft in the Southampton and Bournemouth areas. Letters of objection were sent and application forms received, from the Air Transport Licensing Board (ATLB), for Red Funnel to apply for their own operator's licence. Later it became clear that licences were only being issued for development and operational trials and so the issue was allowed to rest.

In June 1962, Southdown Motor Services applied to the ATLB to operate services on the South Coast and Red Funnel made an official objection. Despite this an experimental service did operate during summer 1964 from Eastney beach at Southsea to Appley beach between Ryde and Seaview.

Meanwhile, Westland Aircraft Limited, later to become British Hovercraft Corporation (BHC), sent an invitation for representatives of the Red Funnel board to inspect their new SRN2 hovercraft. This was taken up on 15 June and the chairman later reported that he had viewed the SRN2 that was to enter service experimentally. The estimated cost at this stage was £317,000. It is interesting to compare this with Thornycroft's quote for *Osborne Castle* which had been £357,000 in December 1960. The directors' view was that much further development was required before Red Funnel could seriously consider this form of transport.

In February 1966 Cowes Harbour Commissioners reported an approach from British Rail (Seaspeed) to operate a SRN6 hovercraft into Cowes. They were taking delivery in May, intending to commence services in June. Official enquiries were made and Mr McKenna of Seaspeed replied saying that their plans were not yet finalised. Red Funnel's chairman attended a meeting at Waterloo Station on 6 April when it was confirmed that the service would operate from Cross House Hard in Southampton. The frequency would be irregular and it was said that the operation had been requested by the Ministry of Transport to obtain experience before a larger SRN4 craft was operated across the English Channel. It was intended to charge a commercial fare, probably twice that of Red Funnel. The lease from Southampton Corporation for Cross House Hard would be for a maximum of two years.

The prospect of a competing service, funded by a nationalised industry, could not be ignored. Within one month each director had received a memorandum comparing estimated costs of hovercraft and hydrofoils with a Castle class ferry. Additionally, it became clear that Seaspeed were proposing to start on 6 July with 12 trips in each direction at a fare of 15 shillings (75p), very different from the information discussed at the meeting in April.

A very early photograph of ISLAND ENTERPRISE running trials, before her name was painted on the bow.
RED FUNNEL ARCHIVES

The saloon of ISLAND ENTERPRISE followed the luxurious style of a 1930s touring motor coach.
RED FUNNEL ARCHIVES

Another fine view of ISLAND ENTERPRISE at speed before the sign writing was completed. She later had the words 'Southampton – Isle of Wight Express' painted onto the roof of her saloon.
RED FUNNEL ARCHIVES

In November, Hovertravel Ltd wrote suggesting a possible lease of a side wall hovercraft for commercial operation, to establish seaworthiness, reliability and costs of operation on a Cowes service. This was to be the craft later known as HM2 built by Hovermarine at Southampton. A meeting took place on 1 December at which Red Funnel were informed that the first craft would be handed over in September 1967 and be ready for service in Spring 1968. Red Funnel were prepared to consider a lease, but wished to manage the operational side, with Hoverwork Limited (a subsidiary of Hovertravel) being responsible for crew and maintenance. Later it was stressed that they were not interested in running hovercraft unless they were completely suitable for their purposes. The board would continue to acquire information and watch developments, but were adamant they would not commit capital on research and development.

In April 1967 it was agreed to continue discussions with Hovertravel, but there was to be no publicity at this stage. Meanwhile at Portsmouth, Seaspeed had started running their SRN6 craft to Cowes on 23 March. Events began to move more quickly as British Rail were starting their new electric train service on the Waterloo – Southampton – Bournemouth line from 10 July. Red Funnel indicated they were considering a name for their new service and they wished it to blend in with the new image of the modern trains.

Red Funnel signed a charter agreement with Hovertravel on 21 September and registered Hoverservice Limited on 15 December 1967. This company would remain dormant, but the business name would be used. Delivery of the craft was now expected on 1 April 1968. In

HM2 No 002, undergoing trials in May 1968. Although in full Red Funnel Hoverservice livery the craft never entered public service.
TERRY CRESSWELL COLLECTION

February a leaflet was published advertising the service as starting from 1 May.

The craft, HM2 No 002, was brought out of Hovermarine's shed on 26 April carrying Red Funnel Hoverservice livery. The company announced that the new service would now start on 28 May. The craft ran trials on 9 May, however there was a further set back. Hovertravel wrote on 20 May saying the craft could not meet specification by the revised delivery date of 23

May and advising a further two months delay. A joint press release was agreed and a claim for irrecoverable expenses made.

This development was a major disappointment for the directors. The annual general meeting was being held on board *Cowes Castle* at the Royal Pier on 24 May and a celebration was intended. The chairman had to confirm the press report that Red Funnel had not accepted the HM2 hovercraft. The company would not introduce a service that did not reach its established standards of reliability. However, the HM2 was moored at the pier and shareholders were invited to inspect it after the meeting. Those who took up the invitation were able to have a ride in the machine. Hazel Nicholson recalls it being rather noisy and an unpleasantly rough experience. It was not an auspicious event.

At their meeting on 28 June the board formally noted that the HM2 had not reached specification. They had already investigated hydrofoils, particularly the Seaflight H57 and Rodriguez PT20 and agreed that a Seaflight H57 should be acquired for delivery at the earliest possible date. In July, Red Funnel wrote to Hovertravel formally cancelling their agreement. The company's first hydrofoil was to be delivered at Messina on 12 August 1968. Hindsight confirms the board's decision. Seaspeed started operating their HM2 service from Portsmouth Harbour to Ryde on 1 April 1968, the craft experienced continual technical difficulties and the Isle of Wight County Press recorded the closure of the service on Saturday 9 September 1972.

However, the Red Funnel hydrofoil service was also about to cause headaches for some years. A meeting took place with the Ministry of Transport in London on 15 October, concerning the delays in obtaining certification for the craft, which was still at Messina. Eventually, there was indication that agreement would be forthcoming and it was hoped to ship the vessel before the end of 1968. The Ministry of Transport inspection took place in Italy and the craft arrived at Southampton on 11 January, commencing initial trials later that month. In February the craft appeared from the Thornycroft yard with the name of *Shearwater*. Eventually, the public service commenced on 5 May 1969, but issues arose quickly with the Fiat engines.

The winter service had to be stopped from 21 December when the shaft bearings began to give trouble. Replacements were obtained from Italy and trials commenced with new propellers. A second craft was ordered, for delivery by 15 June 1970. There were continuing difficulties in the supply of spares and Red Funnel issued an ultimatum that if they were not forthcoming in a reasonable period then they would not accept the second craft. Eventually the refit was complete and *Shearwater* started its second season on 6 May, with an hourly service introduced from 1 July.

Messrs Payne and Hill travelled to Messina and officially accepted *Shearwater 2* on 22 June. She was shipped on 6 July arriving in Southampton on 20 July and entered service immediately. The summer passed without too many problems, but at *Shearwater's* overhaul in the autumn there was considerable concern about the state of her engines and again delay in obtaining spares. *Shearwater 2* was also in trouble and the winter service was abandoned, with a proposal to only operate from 1 May to 31 October in future.

Both craft were withdrawn on 3 October and matters came to a head in the board room during the winter. The engines on both craft were in a poor state. As *Shearwater 2* was much newer this was particularly upsetting and attempts were made for her to be taken back by the builders. The course decided on was to charter a Rodriguez RHS70 craft and use *Shearwater* as back-up. The charter was agreed and there was an option to purchase after 12 months.

Shearwater 3 ran trials in April and was accepted at Messina on 5 May 1972. She was shipped the next day, arrived in Cowes Roads as deck cargo on 20 May and running trials on 22 May. A press trip was made on 25 May and *Shearwater 3* entered public service two days later. Through the summer she was described as operating satisfactorily, whilst the older craft still received mention of various mechanical problems. All references to 'Seaflight' were removed from the original *Shearwater's* livery. In August Red Funnel announced that the new craft had been so successful that the hydrofoil service would be extended through the coming winter.

In the winter of 1972/73 the board considered developments at length. They agreed on a future plan of two RHS70 craft running a regular timetable. There was clearly a feeling that much money and time had been spent on these new-fangled craft. So far the service had lacked consistent reliability and was not making any contribution to profits. The ferries were doing well and supporting the hydrofoil service, this might be acceptable in the short term, but was undesirable going forward. There was concern over the Seaspeed operation and the wish to meet their management, at chairman level including Hovertravel, to discuss the future of high speed services to the Island.

By March 1973, *Shearwater 3* was leaking water into the engines' entablature water jackets. This was regarded as serious and Rodriguez agreed to temporary repairs and offered the use of one of their craft that had been operating on the Thames in 1972. *Fleccia di Reggio*, a PT20 craft built in 1962 yard no 074, duly arrived and operated from

16 April until she was needed back at Messina. The craft was operated by Red Funnel crew, but flew the Italian flag. She was shipped away on *Malvern Prince* from Portsmouth on 2 June 1973. At this stage a verbal order was placed for a new craft.

Shearwater 4 arrived and was in service from 21 August. For two weeks commencing 31 August a half hourly timetable was operated. This was low key and only advertised at the booking offices. The objective was to simulate the proposed full timetable that the board had previously discussed. The trial confirmed their view that such a service could not be operated with just two craft.

In March 1974 the board discussed passenger numbers carried by the high speed services from Southampton in 1973. It was noted that Seaspeed took 250,000 and Red Funnel 125,000. This left plenty of room to increase market share.

In July 1974 both of the original H57 *Shearwater* craft were sold to Pounds Marine Shipping Ltd, scrap merchants.

The managing director met with his opposite number at Seaspeed in January 1975. Seaspeed had been reviewing their Solent services and the resulting report was due shortly. However, the impression was that their Solent hovercraft services would cease later in the year. Red Funnel's reaction was to indicate they were acquiring another craft anyway and that a long period of notice was unnecessary.

The financial results for 1975 indicated that the high speed service had contributed to profits, so financial matters were looking slightly more hopeful. However there was still no real return on the capital employed in that area of the business.

By Spring 1976 it seemed clear Seaspeed were planning to end their Southampton - Cowes hovercraft service. BHC had indicated they were interested in taking on the route. They had approached Red Funnel with a view to operating from East Cowes and offering some land at Cowes known as the Solent site, previously the works of Saunders - Roe, in exchange. However, within a few months BHC had decided to charter their craft to Hovertravel and remain operating from Cowes. The technical transfer from British Rail Hovercraft Ltd (Seaspeed) to British Hovercraft Corporation (Solent Seaspeed) took place during the evening of 1 May 1976.

Meanwhile the number of passengers on the hydrofoils was rising in 1977, but the ferry traffic was lower.

Mr Bland, chairman of Hovertravel, visited the board and indicated that Bland Lines of Gibraltar would shortly be acquiring the controlling interest of Hovertravel. He suggested that their Southampton - Cowes Solent Seaspeed service did not make any money and also suggested that Red Funnel might buy the goodwill of the route.

The first SHEARWATER hydrofoil.
RED FUNNEL
ARCHIVES

Financial expectations from the high speed service were still poor, the budget for 1977 was only expecting a return on capital of 0.25%. It must have been galling for the Red Funnel directors, responsible to their shareholders, knowing that Sealink, their main competitor, was being funded by the taxpayer.

The actual running of the service with the RHS70 hydrofoils settled down and there were far fewer problems than in the early years. However in March 1978 *Shearwater 3* was undergoing annual survey, when *Shearwater 4* failed. Red Funnel chartered an HM2, No GH2058, which maintained the high speed service for about a week until *Shearwater 3* was able to return to service.

There was regular contact and discussion with Mr Bland about the Solent high speed services generally. Most of the discussion revolved around Hovertravel's finances and BHC's concern about maintaining a hovercraft service in the Solent, effectively as a showpiece for their products. In September 1978, BHC entered into a new two year agreement with Hovertravel and so the regularity of the talks about joint arrangements declined - temporarily.

Only a few months later, in September 1979, Hovertravel were voicing their concerns about high fuel costs and joint arrangements were back on the table for discussion. At this time they would have been happy for Red Funnel to acquire their share capital. Meanwhile, having agreed they really needed a third craft, Red Funnel were looking at second-hand hydrofoils available in the overseas market. After long deliberation a new RHS70 craft was ordered for delivery in spring 1980.

The directors were now firmer in their views and were confident they could offer a reliable and good hydrofoil service. Hovertravel were reliant on a subsidy from BHC to operate. It was felt that BHC would like to withdraw from the arrangement, but were loath to see the hovercraft service cease. Red Funnel's board concluded that the new hovercraft being developed would be slightly quicker, but not really suitable for Cowes due to air turbulence.

Shearwater 5 was accepted in Messina on 16 April 1980. She arrived in Cowes Roads on 4 May, was off-loaded the next day, ran trials and entered passenger service on 23 May.

That same month the managing director, and his fellow director Mr Dale, had been passengers in a new Hovermarine side wall hovercraft – the HM2 Mark IV. They noted that it provided a comfortable ride at similar speed to the hydrofoils. However, the sea had been calm and they wanted to test the craft in different sea and wind conditions. BHC was busy developing the SRN7 (later to become the AP1.88) which aimed to be quieter and faster than the SRN6. Red Funnel's chairman commented that the possibilities now required 'more than a cursory examination'.

On 14 November 1980, Mr Bland visited to advise that Hovertravel would be abandoning the Southampton – Cowes route on 24 December 1980. His business had a contract for conveying Vosper Thornycroft (VT) employees between Cowes and their works at Woolston. This had been operated by two HM2 MarkIII craft and he was looking to sell these to Red Funnel. After negotiation both craft, and a quantity of spares,

The short-lived HM2 craft are seen in this image taken on 14 March 1981, together with SHEARWATER 5 and NETLEY CASTLE. HM2 Numbers GH 2024, left, and GH 2019 joined the Red Funnel fleet in November 1980 and were sold in October 1982.
DON JONES

were purchased for £175,000. It was agreed that Hovertravel would inform its staff about the cessation on 28 November and Red Funnel would make an announcement the same day. VT agreed to the change of contract and Red Funnel would operate it with one HM2 and one hydrofoil.

In order to operate the workmen's service, Red Funnel's directors agreed to keep the HM2 craft serviceable, but to obtain quotes for a new hydrofoil. This was ordered in May 1981, for delivery in April 1982, costing approximately £680,000. After about 12 months VT agreed that their contract service could be operated by one hydrofoil and the balance of their employees would travel on the service craft. This change would save one crew in the summer months and enable the HM2s to be disposed of in due course. Brokers were informed that whilst not yet for sale, Red Funnel would be pleased to hear of any interest. Nothing was forthcoming and it was decided not to renew the Civil Aviation Authority certificates when they came up for renewal in June 1982. The craft were eventually sold in late October 1982 to a Frenchman for further use in the Caribbean.

Meanwhile *Shearwater 6* had arrived in Cowes Roads on 30 May 1982, been towed to Southampton for Department of Transport (DoT) inspection and issue of passenger certificate on 3 June, and entered service at 15:30 the following day.

The high speed service was operating satisfactorily, but carryings were disappointing. Only 105,000 passengers had transferred from Hovertravel's Southampton - Cowes service, against the expected 160,000. There was a forecast profit of around £50,000, which was still a very low return on an investment of about £1.2M in the net book value of the craft at that time. The board continued to consider the future of the operation and were mindful that the new AP1.88 craft had now begun trials and was much quieter than the SRN6, but still produced a lot of spray in Cowes harbour.

In May 1983 Mr Bland suggested that Hovertravel and Red Funnel might merge their high speed services and operate four AP1.88 craft. One could operate the Ryde service, two for Cowes with one craft for back-up. He was not keen to sell as it had taken several years to build up the present position, but some commercial arrangement might be possible.

In June 1985 Red Funnel's chairman met senior Sealink officials. Sealink had not committed to building another Solent ferry, but had ordered two catamarans for their passenger service from Portsmouth to Ryde.

At the board meeting on 31 January 1986 it was agreed that the chairman of Hovertravel, Mr Bland, should be approached about joining the

Red Funnel board of directors and asked whether he might view this as a conflict with his duties at Hovertravel. Later, Mr Bland indicated that he would be happy to become a Red Funnel director if invited. However it was not until 27 February 1987 that he was welcomed to the board as a non-executive director.

By June thought was again being given to new fast craft as the numbers of passengers using the service were rising. Quotes would be obtained for an updated *Shearwater 6*. Sealink approached Red Funnel about a joint venture agreement for a service between Cowes and Portsmouth. This would make use of their spare craft when not in use on the Ryde service. Red Funnel's view was that they did not wish to be involved and their pontoon at Cowes was already in full use.

In May 1988 the hydrofoil services were extended to provide two earlier morning departures and also later evening services. During Cowes Week, and the Southampton International Boat Show, there was virtually a 20 minute interval service all day.

The board meeting of 29 July 1988 considered the business plan for the next three years. Under 'immediate issues' was included the next generation of high speed craft and naval architects, Burness Corlett & Partners (BCP), were invited to advise on the issue. The brief was to look at craft with a capacity of 160/200 passengers, capable of maintaining the 30 minute block schedules established by the hydrofoils. BCP reported in November, when it was felt that a passenger load of around 120 was more appropriate. BCP then prepared specifications for a catamaran of that capacity. Subsequently the opportunity arose for full size trials to compare the sea keeping of a hydrofoil, *Shearwater 4*, with a 17m catamaran on 9 March 1989. The resulting view was that a catamaran of about 30 metres would give a better ride than the existing hydrofoil. A practical consideration was that if only one new craft could be afforded, this would present difficulties in balancing the timetable of calls at Cowes. If the vehicle ferries were to only call at East Cowes then the possibility of operating a connecting launch to Cowes would be considered.

From 1 September 1988 the high speed craft displayed a yellow flashing light when underway, thus distinguishing them from slower vessels. As part of the new marketing style being introduced, a new livery was applied to *Shearwater 5* in April 1989.

In May 1989 rumours were circulating in Cowes about a new rival service. A 300 seat SES (Surface Effect Ship) side wall hovercraft was part of a plan to operate from Shepards Wharf, but its mainland destination was unclear. The operation was to be known as Cowes Express.

The Red Funnel directors were now engaged in defending the hostile take-over bid from Sally Line. It was agreed that, for the first time, season tickets would be available for the hydrofoil service and quotations were needed for the new fast craft.

Tenders for the construction of a 120 passenger catamaran were opened on 21 July 1989. BCP reported that the best technical tender had come from FBM Marine at Cowes; however they were not the cheapest tender.

Surprisingly, the board also decided to investigate the possibility of a small high speed car ferry. The vessel might carry 50 cars, 350 passengers, sail at 25 knots and needed to make little wash! The investigation appears to have been taken seriously because it is mentioned in the board minutes over 16 months. A feasibility study was given to FBM Marine, which reported that the project was possible. However at the board meeting on 20 December 1990 it was agreed that this was a high-risk project, involving an untested prototype, and would not be financially viable.

At the first meeting of the new ABP controlled board on 20 October 1989 the decision was taken to order two catamarans from FBM at Cowes. The price was expected to be £3.26M with the final details to be agreed shortly, contracts later being signed on 8 November. Thought was given to names and a list of either 'Royal or strong local connection possibilities' was to be drawn up.

Cowes Express was a major irritation to Red Funnel. The new operation was offering fares at around 33% less than Red Funnel's high speed service, early analysis of the Cowes Express operation suggested that it could not make a profit on the fares being proposed. Red Funnel decided at the outset not to enter a fares war, but to mount specific offers to tempt passengers at certain times. The competition began operation on 25 May 1990, from Thetis Wharf at Cowes to the Town Quay at Southampton, but laid off staff in July when their craft was repossessed by its owners.

Red Jet 1 was launched in December without ceremony and was running trials in January 1991 and handed over on 11 March, entering service on 6 April.

Red Funnel was also looking at the possibility of operating a service from Cowes to Portsmouth, using the Portsmouth Harbour Ferry pontoon at the Harbour station. The facilities were assessed and discussions opened with Dutch shipbuilder Royal Schelde for the charter of a craft to operate the service. Further analysis indicated that the service could be operated without many problems, but it was only likely to be financially viable at peak periods. No further action was taken until Cowes Express received a new lease of life, including operating the Dutch vessel

previously being examined by Red Funnel.

The result was immediate on three fronts. The high speed service was rebranded to 'Hi-Speed' in all adverts and the media from 1 July 1991. *Red Jet 2* had been launched on 16 May, her entry into service was then pushed ahead to 28 June so as to enable a '2 Jet' service to be in place when Cowes Express recommenced on 3 July. It was also decided to go ahead with the Portsmouth service, using *Shearwaters 5* and *6*. This started on Friday 2 August, in time for Cowes Week, and was opened by Mrs Margaret Rule, chairman of the Mary Rose Trust.

By September it was clear that the Cowes Express operation and the new 'Red Jets' had produced growth of 17% in the high speed market. Part of the increase had come from passengers who were only travelling due to special low fares, such as shoppers in the middle of the day. The market had grown, but Cowes Express was carrying most of the new passengers. Red Funnel directors agreed they would carry on their special promotions, but continue to keep away from an all out price war. They did not intend to compete with the 'throw away prices' offered by Cowes Express.

However, by November the Cowes Express fleet had mechanical difficulties and no services at all were provided on three days at the end of the month. Red Funnel took the view that the competition was in the process of collapsing. Some of the extra traffic would remain and FBM Marine was asked to produce new-build proposals, whilst the world market was scoured for suitable second-hand craft to buy or charter.

The Portsmouth service had been very disappointing with low passenger numbers and forecasts that showed little prospect of future market growth. The board decided to end the service from 22 December 1991.

Red Funnel advertised a half-hourly service throughout the day during the normally quiet period between January and March 1992. However, each *Red Jet* would be overhauled in this period with one of the later *Shearwater* hydrofoils standing in. *Shearwater 3* had been lifted out of the water for dry storage at Cowes on 30 December 1991; she would not run again on the Solent.

The high speed service had lost money in 1991, mainly due to the late delivery of the 'Red Jets' and the promotions and offers made caused by the opposition. However, the Cowes Express service continued to have mechanical problems and the final services were operated by the Dutch vessel *Wight Prince* on its own. This vessel was repossessed by its owners on 26 February 1992 when the service ceased, as expected, and Red Funnel looked to continue operating a reliable service on the route. Unfortunately, no suitable back-up craft could be obtained for the 'Red Jets'

*RED JET 3 at speed
8 October 2008.*
RICHARD DANIELSON

and *Shearwaters 5* and *6* were refurbished to stand in when required. *Shearwaters 3* and *4* were mothballed ashore at Cowes.

At Southampton plans to move the operation to the Town Quay were welcomed. This provided a terminal more in keeping with the high speed image and giving greater exposure to the travelling public. The move to the new Terminal 2 took place on 20 July. The existing ferry terminal, latterly known as Berth A, now became Terminal 1.

With the faster 'Red Jets' now well settled in, the 1992 Cowes Week timetable reverted to a half hourly schedule, apart from a two hour span of 20 minute operation in the evening peak. The larger vessels coped well with the high numbers of passengers carried.

The service now settled into a steadier routine, the catamarans providing a reliable service, well liked by the travelling public.

Tenders were received on 10 September 1997 from five shipbuilders worldwide for a new fast craft. Red Funnel signed a contract with FBM on 31 October 1997 for a 190 seat catamaran for delivery in July 1998 at a cost of £2.73m.

In July 1998 *Red Jet 3* joined the fleet, allowing the timetable to be operated for the first time without a standby hydrofoil. *Shearwaters 5* and *6* were then placed on the sales list and finally withdrawn from service in the autumn.

Red Jet 3's entry into service contributed to an increase in passenger carryings of 4% during 1998.

1999 Cowes Week saw a reversion to a 20 minute high speed service with all the 'Red Jets' in service.

Passenger levels were breaking all records and investigations were made into stretching *Red Jets 1* and *2* to increase their capacity to nearer the 190 carried by *Red Jet 3*.

In June 2000 the withdrawn *Shearwater 5* was moved from Southampton to Cowes and lifted out of the water at Souters yard, formerly the yard of J Samuel White, joining *Shearwater 6*.

The quest for an extra fast craft continued when tenders from nine international yards were opened on 25 March 2002. The order for *Red Jet 4* was eventually signed on 29 May 2002. She was to cost approximately £2.68M and be built by North West Bay Ships Pty Ltd in Tasmania for delivery in May 2003. At 39 metres long she is 5 metres longer and carries 87 more passengers than *Red Jet 3*.

In September 2002 the remaining hydrofoils were sold for further service in Thailand. Their names were obliterated and they were boarded up ready for the voyage, under their own power.

On 13 February 2003 *Red Jet 1* carried out a trial berthing at the East Cowes vehicle terminal.

Red Jet 4 arrived in Southampton on 9 May and entered service on 23 June 2003. She brought the fleet strength up to four, although the two later acquisitions were rather larger than the two older craft. Her increased passenger capacity, double that of the original 'Red Jets', enabled a reduction from the 20 minute service from Cowes in the early morning, with the withdrawal of the 07:10 departure.

Red Funnel announced a very successful Cowes Week with increased high speed loadings of 10%, attributed to the greater capacity of *Red Jet 4*. During the Southampton International Boat Show

RED JET 3 heads for Cowes on 21 October 2008, passing the Coastguard tower at Calshot.
RICHARD DANIELSON

a new service was operated from Gosport to Southampton. It ran from 12 to 21 September and was opened by Seb Clover, at that time the youngest single handed sailor to cross the Atlantic Ocean.

The Gosport service was well supported and plans were made for a Christmas shopping service. Between 8 November 2003 and 4 January 2004 a four round trip service was provided on Saturdays and Sundays, increasing to six trips in December and daily pre and post Christmas week. In connection with the Cowes service, Red Funnel trialled a water taxi service, marketed as 'JetConnect' from East Cowes directly to the Cowes pontoon from 3 November 2003. It operated weekdays at commuter times from the public pontoon, but was withdrawn on 29 April 2005.

During Cowes Week 2004, Red Funnel ran a Gosport to Cowes service from 7 to 13 August. Although *Red Jet 1* carried the Gosport service banners and operated the route on the first day, most of the services were taken by *Red Jet 2*. The seasonal Southampton Boat Show Gosport service operated 11 to 19 September. Although generally operated by *Red Jet 1*, *Red Jet 3* was noted operating on the final day.

On 28 June 2005 *Red Jet 4* was present at the 'Trafalgar 200' fleet review by H M The Queen. The usual Southampton Boat Show service from Gosport operated over the period 16 to 25 September using *Red Jets 1* and *2*.

After public consultation in summer 2006 it was announced that the high speed departure times from Southampton would be changed to 15 and 45 minutes past each hour from 12 November 2006. This was the first major change in timings since the service was established in the late 1960s. The alteration was made to enable better connections with the railway service between Southampton and London Waterloo.

On 11 November 2008 *Red Jet 4* operated a number of cruises for *Queen Elizabeth 2's* last day in her home port and final evening departure. For much of that day the high speed service was in the hands of *Red Jets 1* and 2 one of the last occasions on which the two craft would be operating together in the Solent.

Specifications were drawn up during summer 2008 for a new craft, two possibilities with 190 or 275 seats were considered. However the project was not progressed.

Red Funnel was pleased to charter *Red Jet 1* to Stagecoach for a one month trial service across Torbay from 28 August 2009.

Early in 2009, knowing that foreign buyers were keen on purchasing *Red Jets 1* and 2, Red Funnel purchased a second-hand catamaran that had been designed by FBM and was a close sister to *Red Jet 3*. Operated by Bahamas Fast Ferries and named *Bo Hengy* she arrived in the Solent on 11 June. After a thorough refit at Testbank, Portchester, and becoming *Red Jet 5*, she was ready to take her place in the Cowes Week timetable in August.

Meanwhile, *Red Jets 1* and 2 had been renamed *CM Jets 1* and 2 and left the Solent on 14 May 2009 bound for St Petersburg and further service in the Caspian Sea.

SHEARWATER 2 is dressed overall during the acceptance ceremony at Messina, 22 June 1970.
RED FUNNEL
ARCHIVES

SHEARWATER

Built:	1969	Tonnage:	27.3 displacement tons
Withdrawn:	1973	Dimensions: feet	61" x 15' 4" (26' 3" over foils)
Scrapped:		metres	18.60m x 4.68m (8.0m over foils)
		Reg. Number:	336741
		Builders:	Seaflight SpA. Sicily.
		Machinery:	2 x Fiat – Carraro V12 SS diesels. 2 x 650 bhp.

The 1968 annual report noted that a new, twin screw, Seaflight H57 hydrofoil had been purchased under construction from Messina, Sicily. The craft arrived in Cowes Roads aboard *Gloria Maris* on 11 January 1969. She commenced service 5 May 1969. *Shearwater* carried 54 passengers at a maximum speed of 35 knots.

It was intended to operate a winter service. From 1 January 1970 eight round trips were advertised on weekdays and four round trips on Sundays, however problems of reliability led to this being abandoned early in the year.

When *Shearwater 3* arrived in 1972, *Shearwater* became the back-up craft and was withdrawn on the arrival of *Shearwater 4*. The craft was blocked up on her foils near No 7 drydock at Southampton and was reported sold to the ship breakers Pounds, and later to Biba Shipping Ltd, a Portsmouth firm. Further reports indicated she was sold again to Italian interests. The only firm report of her whereabouts at this time is a sighting of her aboard ex-LCT *Molpa* at Berth 37 in Southampton docks on 15 April 1976.

SHEARWATER lies at Southampton. The photograph shows the special gangway arrangement, required to keep the hull away from the pontoon and avoid the underwater foils being damaged.
RED FUNNEL
ARCHIVES

SHEARWATER 2

Built:	1970	Tonnage:	26 displacement tons
Withdrawn:	1971	Dimensions:	As for *Shearwater* (I)
Still in		Builders:	Seaflight SpA. Sicily.
service		Machinery:	2 x Fiat diesels.
named			
North Owl			

Intended to improve the reliability of the service, *Shearwater 2* was purchased and accepted at Messina on 22 June 1970. There was no formal naming ceremony, but Mrs James Hill, wife of the managing director, became the craft's 'godmother' in accordance with local custom. *Shearwater 2* arrived in Cowes Roads on board *Gloria Maris* on 20 July 1970. She entered service immediately and operated until 1971, but experienced continual mechanical problems. The craft was laid-up at Groves and Gutteridge's yard at Cowes and cannibalised in order to keep her identical sister *Shearwater* in service.

Later, it was discovered there had been a manufacturing defect which had caused this particular craft to be so unreliable. The warranty period had expired and the manufacturers were unwilling to remedy the problems.

Shearwater 2 was reported towed from Cowes to Portsmouth for scrapping on 31 July 1974. However, by 1975 she had been resold, defoiled and was in use as a workmen's ferry between Tarbert and Portavadie in Loch Fyne. She was named *North Owl* and owned by Offshore Workboats Limited of Hartley Wintney, Basingstoke. The craft was fitted with new Cummins diesel engines giving a speed of 15 knots.

SHEARWATER 3

Built:	1972	Tonnage:	31.5 displacement tons 62 gross tons
Withdrawn:	1992	Dimensions: feet	72' 10" x 15' 9" (25' 6" over foils)
		metres	22.20m x 4.80m (7.78m over foils)
		Reg. Number:	357766
		Builders:	Rodriguez, Messina. Yard number 150
		Machinery:	1 x 1,350 bhp Maybach MB 12V493 Ty 71diesel.

NOTE:
The engines of *Shearwaters 3* and *4* were interchangeable.

The unreliability of the Fiat engines on the original *Shearwater* sisters had been a source of considerable disappointment and annoyance to Red Funnel. The solution was to be well tried German Mercedes machinery installed in the single screw RHS70 hydrofoil. This was yard number 150, the first of the RHS70 type built, an updated version of the well proven PT20. *Shearwater 3* operated a press trip on 26 May 1972 and entered public service on 27 May, the first day of the summer operation. The craft immediately became the route's mainstay. The reliability of the operation improved and an identical sister was ordered.

The winter service reopened from 16 October 1972 with five round trips each day, operated by *Shearwater 3*.

When first delivered *Shearwater 3* had a black hull with red foils. However during her overhaul in the 1973/74 winter she was repainted with a red hull and blue foils to match her newer sister *Shearwater 4*.

In April 1992 she was laid-up ashore at Cowes Marine Services. Inspected by potential Greek operators in November 1992 she remained at Cowes until, with foils removed, she was towed to Southampton on 19 March 1993. *Shearwaters 3* and *4* were loaded aboard freighter *Huassafell* later that day and departed for Piraeus.

Later *Shearwater 3* was reported as working for Piraeus based operator Hermes and renamed *Nike 1*.

SHEARWATER 3 foilborn at speed. The view enables sight of the single shaft to her propeller.
RED FUNNEL
ARCHIVES

SHEARWATER 4

Built:	1973	*Tonnage:*	31.5 displacement tons
Withdrawn:	1992	*Dimensions:*	As for *Shearwater 3*
		Reg. Number:	351756
		Builders:	Rodriguez, Messina. Yard number 156
		Machinery:	1 x 1,350 bhp Maybach 12V diesel

Shearwater 4, arrived at Cowes Roads aboard *Valkenburg* on 15 August 1973. After being unloaded and towed to Southampton she quickly entered passenger service on 21 August.

The craft's career closely followed her older sister, but on 9 March 1989 she was used in trials in the Solent. These compared her sea keeping qualities with those of an Aluminium catamaran *London Broadcasting Co.*

She was laid-up ashore at Cowes in March 1992 until 19 March 1993 when she was towed to Southampton with *Shearwater 3* after sale to Greek owners.

Later *Shearwater 4* was reported as working for Piraeus based operator Hermes and renamed *Nike II.*

SHEARWATER 4 *arrives at Cowes on the 11:30 from Southampton on 10 August 1981. The hydrofoils normally used the inside berth at Cowes, on departure for Southampton they used a rope to assist canting round the end of the pontoon.*
DON JONES

SHEARWATER 5

Built:	1980	*Tonnage:*	31.5 displacement tons
Withdrawn:	1998	*Dimensions:*	As for *Shearwater 3*
		Reg. Number:	387525
		Builders:	Rodriguez, Messina. Yard number 197
		Machinery:	1 x 1,350 hp MTU V12 331 diesel.

Sea conditions off Calshot can sometimes be lively, SHEARWATER 5 *digs her bow into the swell on 24 September 1988.*
DON JONES

Shearwater 5, entered service on 23 May 1980. She was equipped with the slightly more powerful MTU diesel engine, which was also fitted to *Shearwater 6*. After *Shearwater 6* was withdrawn in 1998, she became the last of Red Funnel's hydrofoil fleet in service, until joining her sister laid-up at Cowes in June 2000.

Eventually she was sold, with *Shearwater 6*, to new owners in Thailand. The sisters were noted at Southampton on 6 September 2002 with names painted out and boarded up for the delivery voyage. Reports indicated that because of delivery costs being quoted at over £100,000 the owners decided to sail them to the Far East. By 14 November, they were reported in the Red Sea and they arrived in Thailand on 12 December. The voyage was reported to be one of the longest undertaken by a hydrofoil on its own hull. Because of the extra weight of fuel needing to be carried, large parts of the voyage could only be undertaken on the hull and not on their foils. They

were to be operated by Kon-Tiki Diving and were renamed *Colona 7* and *Colona 8*.

SHEARWATER 6

Built:	1982	*Tonnage:*	31.5 displacement tons
Withdrawn:	1998	*Dimensions:*	As for *Shearwater 3*
		Reg. Number:	700233
		Builders:	Rodriguez, Messina. Yard number 221
		Machinery:	1 x 1,287 hp V12 331 MTU diesel.

NOTE:
The engines of *Shearwaters 5* and *6* were interchangeable.

Shearwater 6 was ordered in May 1981 for delivery in spring 1982. She was yard number 221 and provided sufficient back-up for her three sisters and enabled maintenance of the increased service schedules. She effectively allowed Red Funnel to stop using the HM2 sidewall hovercraft that they had inherited with the Vosper Thornycroft workmen's service between Cowes and the firm's Woolston yard.

Shearwater 6 was the mainstay of the short-lived high speed service between Portsmouth Harbour and Cowes in late summer and autumn 1991.

When *Red Jet 3* entered service in July 1998 she took the role of back-up craft and was then taken to Cowes in November and stored ashore at FBM's yard pending sale.

She remained laid-up with *Shearwater 5* until they were put back in the water on 2 October 2001. This enabled trials to be run for potential buyers, but it was not until 22 August 2002 that a Malaysian operator bought the sisters.

Under their own power they sailed to the Far East by way of Spain, Portugal, Gibraltar, Tunisia, Malta, Crete, Egypt, Sudan, Yemen, Oman, India, Sri Lanka and Indonesia.

Subsequently a photograph appeared in *Fast Ferry International* of one of the sisters submerged after the 2004 Boxing Day Tsunami. The report indicated one craft was a total loss and one repairable. It is believed that *Shearwater 6* was written off, but that *Shearwater 5* continued in service until sold in 2009.

SHEARWATER 6, in her final livery, is at full speed off Fawley, heading towards the Island in December 1996.
BARRY EAGLES

RED JET 1

Built:	1991	*Tonnage:*	168 gross
Withdrawn:	2009	*Dimensions:*	32.5m x 8.32m
Still in		*Reg. Number:*	719584
service with		*Builders:*	FBM Marine, Cowes. Yard No 1289
Caspian		*Machinery:*	2 x 1,360 kW 2 x 1,824bhp MTU 12V
Mainport Marine			396 TE84 diesels. 2 x MJP Waterjets.

Ordered from the local yard of FBM at Cowes, builder's number 1289, *Red Jet 1*, took the high speed service into its next phase in 1991. She was the first waterjet propelled high speed vessel on the Solent. Originally she and her sister carried 120 passengers, but this was increased in 1993 by 10 and again in 1998 to a total of 138 passengers. With a maximum speed of 38.3 knots on trials, the service could be operated in 22 minutes at a cruising speed of 32.5 knots.

dignitaries and press were taken from Torquay to Brixham in 17 minutes on 28 August, with a public service commencing the following day. The charter lasted until 27 September and the vessel then returned to Southampton, arriving on 29 September. Stagecoach reported that they were delighted with the performance of *Red Jet 1* which was able to operate in weather conditions that caused other operators to cease.

In early 2009 enquiries were received for her sale

Left:
RED JET 1 leaves Southampton at 15:00 on 6 April 1991, her first sailing in public service.
DON JONES

Right:
In July 1991, RED JET 1 turns in the river Medina before berthing at the Cowes terminal.
BARRY EAGLES

None of the *Shearwater* hydrofoils had received official naming ceremonies, but after running trials in January, *Red Jet 1* was named by Lady Stuart at FBM's yard in Cowes on 15 February 1991. Her first passenger crossing was on 6 April 1991 and her addition to the fleet led to the retirement of *Shearwater 3*. Later, the arrival of *Red Jet 4* in 2003 led to her own relegation from front line service. She then generally operated at off-peak times and during the overhaul season.

In August 2008 *Red Jet 1* was taken on charter, with a Red Funnel crew, by Stagecoach to trial a high speed ferry service across Torbay. Local

which resulted in her disposal to Caspian Mainport Marine. This Cork based company, operating in the Caspian Sea, renamed her *CM Jet 1*. With her sister, she left Southampton Royal Pier on 13 May to be loaded aboard *La Rochelle*, departing for St Petersburg the next day. Following removal of the original fuel tanks aft, new deck mounted stainless steel fuel tanks were fitted both forward and aft. These were fitted to assist the craft in making their own way through the rivers and canals to the Caspian Sea and in their future service.

Seen from the boat deck of CANBERRA, outward bound for Gibraltar and the Mediterranean on 4 May 1994, RED JET 2 departs on another trip to Cowes.
RICHARD DANIELSON

RED JET 2

Built:	1991	*Tonnage:*	168 gross
Withdrawn:	2009	*Dimensions:*	32.5m x 8.32m
Still in		*Reg. Number:*	721064
service with		*Builders:*	FBM Marine, Cowes. Yard Number 1290
Caspian		*Machinery:*	2 x 1,360 KW 2 x 1824bhp MTU 12V
Mainport Marine			396 TE84 diesels. 2 x MJP Waterjets.

RED JET 2
photograph on
previous page

Originally the intention was to only build one catamaran in 1991, but the new regime under ABP ordered two craft. *Red Jet 2*, builder's number 1290, was identical to her sister and launched on 16 May 1991. She was named by Lady Mottistone at FBM's yard at Cowes on 6 June 1991.

The competition from Cowes Express caused a desire to have her in service prior to the start of the rival operation. Every effort was made to complete her early and she successfully entered service on 28 June 1991.

Together the twins provided better comfort and higher reliability in all weather conditions. Their performance in fog was much superior to the hydrofoils' due to their ability to vary their speed more easily. The hydrofoils were either up on their foils or travelling slowly on their hulls. *Red Jet 2's* arrival meant the end of the hydrofoils in regular service and *Shearwater 4* was withdrawn from service in 1992.

Both *Red Jets 1* and *2* underwent a 'mid life' upgrade in the winter of 1998/99 to bring their accommodation into line with the new *Red Jet 3*. *Red Jet 2* was sold with her sister in spring 2009 to Caspian Mainport Marine and renamed *CM Jet 2*.

RED JET 3

Built:	1998	*Tonnage:*	213 gross, 77 net.
Still in service		*Dimensions:*	32.9m x 8.32m
		Builders:	FBM Marine, Cowes. Yard No. 1439.
		Machinery:	2 x 1,500 kW, 2x2,012 bhp MTU, 12 cylinder
			12V 396TE74L diesels, 2 MJP Waterjets.

Left:
Taken from the Town Quay, looking towards Southampton's Ocean Cruise Terminal at Berth 46, RED JET 3 arrives from Cowes.
RICHARD DANIELSON

Right:
RED JET 3 swings around off Terminal 2 at Southampton before heading back to the Isle of Wight. The domed building in the background is the old Southampton Harbour Board headquarters building, built in 1925, now used as a night club.
RICHARD DANIELSON

In late 1997 Red Funnel returned to FBM for a larger catamaran. An extra 52 seats over the earlier *Red Jets 1* and *2* produced a total of 190 which helped to cope with the increasing commuter traffic. The hulls of the earlier 'Red Jets' had been built upside down in the construction shed and turned over before launching; however *Red Jet 3* was constructed in a conventional manner. The vessel had a similar hull design to the first 'Red Jets', but is two metres longer and was fitted with 'trim-tabs' helping to maintain the low wash characteristics of the design in all conditions of loading. On board, passengers had access to a drinks service, improved ventilation and a modern style of video safety announcement.

Red Jet 3, yard number 1439, was launched on 16 June 1988 and named on 7 July by Mrs 'Tree' Smith, wife of the Associated British Ports' managing director, Mr Andrew Smith. The craft undertook a publicity cruise on 14 July from Southampton to the Needles carrying invited guests. During this cruise she achieved 37.4 knots in force 4 winds. *Red Jet 3* was handed over on 17 July and entered service on 27 July, taking her place in the timetable with her earlier sisters. With her greater capacity and airline style seating, *Red Jet 3* was a favourite for use on peak hour services. In 2007 leather seats were installed in the cabin and LCD screens were added and improved space for luggage provided.

RED JET 4

Built: 2003
Still in service

Tonnage:	342 gross, 120 net.
Dimensions:	39.88m x 10.82m
Builders:	North West Bay Ships Pty. Hobart, Tasmania Yard No. 6.
Machinery:	2 x 1,740 kW,2 x 2,333 bhp MTU, 12 cylinder 12V 4000M70 diesels, 2 MJP Waterjets.

With 275 seats, and space for two wheelchairs, *Red Jet 4* has twice the passenger capacity of the first catamarans, *Red Jets 1* and *2*. Turnaround times at ports still needed to be within the existing timetable, so passenger flow was important. A large boarding ramp on the port side can be handled by one attendant. Accommodation continues to be on one deck to avoid having choke points at stairs.

Continuing the use of MJP waterjets she has more powerful engines providing a maximum speed of 41 knots when lightly loaded and 38.1 knots when full. Anti-vibration mountings separate the hull from the cabin to reduce noise and vibration. Particular care has been taken about noise levels within the passenger spaces and the wheelhouse. Vertical interceptors lift the aft section of the hull when operating at speed to reduce wash.

Red Jet 4, yard number 06, was launched on 20 February 2003 and loaded aboard the heavy lift ship *Egmondracht* at Hobart's Princess Wharf, Tasmania on 20 March 2003, sailing the following day. She arrived at Southampton on 9 May. Unloaded the next day she ran trials on 14 May, including a trip around the Isle of Wight. The craft was named by round-the-world yachtswoman Ellen MacArthur in a ceremony at Cowes Yacht Haven on 18 June 2003. The mechanism for breaking the bottle of champagne on the hull was reluctant to operate and a crew member quickly stepped forward and completed the ceremony with the aid of a hammer.

The vessel undertook special trips for Island Club Season ticket holders and Gold Card members during 19 and 20 June. On 21 June *Red Jet 4* followed the Round the Island yacht race, supported by Red Funnel, circumnavigating the Island with over 200 VIPs. She entered passenger service on 23 June 2003.

Red Jet 4 offered a big step forward in terms of ride comfort, speed and low wash. She is the fastest commercial passenger catamaran operating in the Solent.

RED JET 4 under construction in Hobart, Tasmania – 15 November 2002.
RED FUNNEL
ARCHIVES

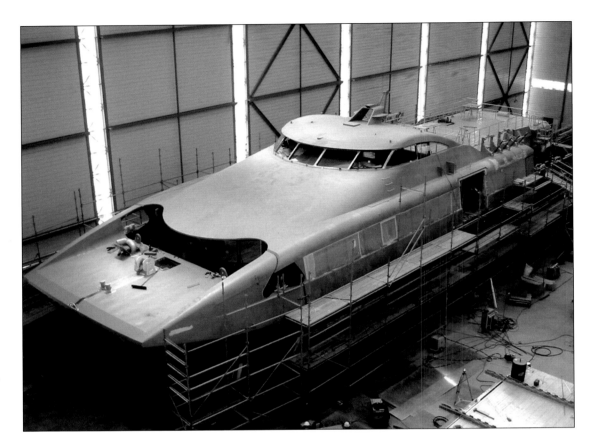

RED JET 4 under construction in Hobart, Tasmania - 15 November 2002.
RED FUNNEL ARCHIVES

RED JET 4 at speed passing RED EAGLE on 18 October 2008.
RICHARD DANIELSON

RED JET 5

Built:	1999	*Tonnage:*	209 gross, 74 net.
Acquired:	2009	*Dimensions:*	32.9m x 8.32m
Still in service		*Builders:*	Pequot River Shipworks, New London, Connecticut, USA. Yard No. PR 85.
		Machinery:	2 x 1,700 kW 2 x 2,280bhp MTU / Detroit Diesel Corporation. 12 cylinder 12V 4000 M70 diesels. 2 Ka Me Wa Waterjets.

Plans had been on the drawing board for a new high speed craft for some time, but the opportunity to purchase a near sister craft to *Red Jet 3* in spring 2009 could not be missed.

With *Red Jets 1* and *2* now too small for use at peak times, but providing essential back-up at overhaul periods and during daily maintenance, *Red Jet 5*, with 186 seats, provided the answer to a complementary fleet.

She was built in Connecticut, USA, by Pequot River Shipworks, to a design by FBM at Cowes. Built in 1999 for Bahamas Fast Ferries and named *Bo Hengy* she operated from Nassau around the islands. Bought by Red Funnel in spring 2009 she arrived in Southampton on 11 June aboard heavy lift ship *CEC Meadow*. She was towed to Portsmouth the following day for an extensive refit at Testbank, Portchester. The interior layout is based on the well tried design of *Red Jet 4* and includes air conditioning and leather seats. Business travel is crucial to the economics of the high speed service and lap top power points are available with on-board video and an 'at seat' refreshment service is provided.

Red Jet 5 was named by Olympic Gold medal winner yachtswoman and BBC sports presenter Shirley Robertson OBE. The ceremony took place at Cowes Yacht Haven on 21 July 2009. *Red Jet 5* entered service 29 July and took her place in the 20 minute service frequency during Cowes Week from 2 August 2009.

Left:
RED JET 5 shown in her original guise as BO HENGY and in the livery of Bahamas Fast Ferries.
RED FUNNEL ARCHIVES

Right:
RED JET 5 passes Trinity Landing at Cowes on 23 October 2009.
TIM COOPER

RED JET 5 on the inside berth at Cowes pontoon on 21 July 2009, the day of her naming ceremony.
RED FUNNEL ARCHIVES

PS GEM

Built:	1840	Tonnage:	87 gross, 47 net.
Acquired:	1861	Dimensions: feet	107' 6" x 14' 9"
Withdrawn:	1883	metres	32.77m x 4.5m
Scrapped:	1889	Builders:	J White, Cowes, Isle of Wight.
		Machinery:	Summers, Groves & Day, Northam, Southampton. Paddle steamer, 40 nhp.

Built for the Isle of Wight Steam Packet Company and launched on 5 September 1839, this vessel received her engines at Millbrook, Southampton.

Gem passed to Red Funnel on its formation in 1861. In 1867 she was based at Cowes for tendering American liners in Cowes Roads. By 1869 she was reported at Cowes being used for 'odd jobs' and towage work. From then on she was used for cargo work. The vessel was sold to R Pollock of Woolston, Southampton in 1884, passing to C C Duncan of Middlesbrough the following year. *Gem* was broken up in 1889.

PS RUBY

Built:	1841	Tonnage:	103 gross, 53 net.
Acquired:	1861	Dimensions: feet	114' 9" x 16' 4"
Withdrawn:	1872	metres	34.97m x 4.98m
Scrapped:	1872	Builders:	Summers, Groves & Day, Northam, Southampton.
		Machinery:	Summers, Groves & Day, Northam, Southampton. Paddle steamer, 40 nhp.

This ship was the first Island steamer built of iron and was ordered by a new concern, the South Western & Isle of Wight Steam Navigation Company, as a competitor to the existing operators on the Southampton to Cowes route. She was launched at Northam, Southampton on 14 October 1840 as *The Pride of the Waters*. However, the launching appears to be the end of the new company, as nothing more is heard of it. She was bought by the Isle of Wight Royal Mail Steam Packet Company for the Cowes to Southampton service and renamed *Ruby*. This ship was one of the earliest excursion steamers. In 1849 she made the first trip from Southampton to Swanage.

As a unit of Red Funnel from its formation in 1861, she performed cargo service prior to being withdrawn.

In September 1864 it was recorded that her outside plating was very thin, however it was recommended not to cut this out for replacement, but that she could run for sometime without danger.

It is recorded in the company's pre-war handbook, *South Coast Guide*, that *Ruby* was the first steamer to run round the Isle of Wight on an excursion. The company's guide book should have read that *Ruby* performed the first 'Round the Island' sailing after Red Funnel had been incorporated.

PS PEARL

Built:	1844	Tonnage:	64 gross, 32 net.
Acquired:	1861	Dimensions: feet	89' 8" x 13' 3"
Withdrawn:	1867	metres	27.3m x 4.03m
Scrapped:	1875	Builders:	Summers, Day & Baldock, Northam, Southampton.
		Machinery:	Summers, Day & Baldock, Northam, Southampton. Paddle steamer, 32 nhp.

Built at Northam, Southampton, *Pearl* was constructed of iron for the Cowes owned mail fleet, and was launched on 2 May 1844. She served Red Funnel from its incorporation in 1861 and was sold by public auction for £150 in 1867, finally being deleted from the register in 1875.

The Southampton Times, 28 May 1870, stated that the vessel would run during the summer between Poole, Bournemouth and Swanage, and be operated by a Mr T Rickman. However, Mr Rickman died on 24 May 1870, so it is doubtful if the sailings ever started.

PS QUEEN (1)

Built:	1848	*Tonnage:*	93 gross, 56 net.	
Acquired:	1861	*Dimensions: feet*	117' 1" x 14'	
Withdrawn:	1876	*metres*	35.69m x 4.27m	
Scrapped:	1876	*Builders:*	Summers, Day & Baldock, Northam, Southampton.	
		Machinery:	Summers, Day & Baldock, Northam, Southampton. Paddle steamer, 40 nhp.	

This ship served the Southampton to Isle of Wight service for a period of 28 years. An iron-hulled steamer, she was originally part of the Cowes owned fleet. She had alterations carried out by Summers, Day & Baldock in June 1861.

PS MEDINA (1)

Built:	1852	*Tonnage:*	104 gross, 55 net.	
Acquired:	1861	*Dimensions: feet*	120' 8" x 14' 9"	
Withdrawn:	1882	*metres*	36.78m x 4.5m	
Scrapped:	1883	*Builders:*	J White, Cowes, Isle of Wight.	
		Machinery:	Summers, Day & Baldock, Northam, Southampton. Paddle steamer, 50 nhp.	

In 1850 there was a threat of opposition to the two regular companies operating to Cowes, it being announced that a new company was being formed to build two new ships of superior size and speed. The first vessel, *Times*, was forecast as due for an early launching. No more was heard of this venture until May 1852, when it transpired that *Times* had indeed been built, her wooden hull laying engineless in the river Medina for over a year. She was then acquired by the Isle of Wight Royal Mail Steam Packet Company, engined by Summers, Day & Baldock, and renamed *Medina*. She proved to be a fast steamer and became much used on excursion work including visits to Weymouth.

Arrangements for a new boiler for *Medina* were made in October 1861 and the required pressure was to be 20 lbs per square inch. Trials were made in April 1862 when the results were regarded as very good. Plenty of steam was raised and *Medina's* engine was turning at 44 rpm on a boiler pressure of 19 lbs per square inch.

PS EMERALD

Built:	1857	*Tonnage:*	69 gross, 43 net.	
Acquired:	1861	*Dimensions: feet*	105' x 14' 1"	
Withdrawn:	1871	*metres*	32m x 4.3m	
Scrapped:		*Builders:*	Summers, Day & Co, Northam, Southampton.	
		Machinery:	Summers Day & Co, Northam, Southampton. Paddle steamer, oscillating, 32 nhp.	

Originally owned by the Isle of Wight Steam Packet Company, *Emerald* passed to Red Funnel in 1861.

The ship needed a new boiler in 1863 and a tender from C A Day & Co at Northam was accepted for £384.

An iron paddle steamer with oscillating engines, she served until 1871 when sold to Spanish owners.

This engraving, used in Red Funnel's early guides and handbooks, gives an impression of one of the early steamers.

PS SAPPHIRE

Built:	1860	Tonnage:	82 gross, 52 net.
Acquired:	1861	Dimensions: feet	120' 3" x 14' 5"
Withdrawn:	1873	metres	36.65m x 4.39m
Scrapped:		Builders:	Summers, Day & Co, Northam, Southampton.
		Machinery:	Summers, Day & Co, Northam, Southampton.
			Paddle steamer, oscillating, 40 nhp.

Launched on 5 July 1860, *Sapphire* was built to the order of the Isle of Wight Steam Packet Company and ran her trials on 17 August 1860. She was an iron-hulled vessel with two oscillating engines, and was fitted with Morgan's patent feathering paddles. On her trial, she is reported to have run to Portsmouth, from Southampton via Cowes, in 1 hour 50 minutes, under the command of Captain J Clark.

Sapphire was sold to Spanish owners in 1873, her British register being closed on 26 November 1873.

PS LORD OF THE ISLES

Built:	1861	Tonnage:	126 gross, 96 net.
Acquired:	1865	Dimensions: feet	145' x 18' 1"
Withdrawn:	1889	metres	44.2m x 5.52m
Scrapped:	1889	Builders:	Thames Ironworks & Shipbuilding Co, Blackwall.
		Machinery:	J Stewart, London
			Paddle steamer, oscillating, 60 nhp.

This steamer was the first ship built for the newly-formed opposition, the Southampton, Isle of Wight and Portsmouth Improved Steamboat Company. This competition was one of the reasons why the two already established companies amalgamated into the company known today as Red Funnel. The words 'Improved Steamboat', used in the owner's title are significant. This new iron-hulled ship was the first local steamer to have deckhouse saloons, the deck level of the saloons being recessed slightly below that of the main deck. The aft saloon had a ladies cabin attached, and both extended the full width of the hull. The forward saloon was set inboard slightly, allowing a narrow walkway for passengers along the deck. Both saloons were heated by hot water pipes and, on top of the after saloon, a promenade deck with seats and handrail was provided. *Lord of the Isles* was a very modern steamer, making a speed of 14.18 knots over the Stokes Bay measured mile. The maiden passage of this ship was on 6 May 1861, and she made her first excursion from Southampton to Bournemouth, via Cowes, on 21 May.

In May 1865 *Lord of the Isles* was acquired by Red Funnel. It appears she was off service at this time as in November the company received an enquiry to buy the ship, or her sister *Lady of the Lake*. *Lord of the Isles* was offered for £3,500 as she lay at Northam with a new boiler ready for installation. However nothing came of the enquiry and *Lord of the Isles* was later used as a cargo steamer from October 1883 until sold for breaking up in October 1889.

This artist's impression portrays LORD OF THE ISLES and LADY OF THE LAKE, the two vessels of the Southampton, Isle of Wight & Portsmouth Improved Steamboat Company.
RED FUNNEL ARCHIVES

PS LADY OF THE LAKE

Built:	1861	*Tonnage:*	104 gross, 46 net.	
Acquired:	1865	*Dimensions: feet*	147' 6" x 17' 9"	
Withdrawn:	1887	*metres*	44.96m x 5.41m	
Scrapped:	1887	*Builders:*	Thames Ironworks & Shipbuilding Co, Blackwall.	
		Machinery:	J Stewart, London	
			Paddle steamer, oscillating, 60 nhp.	

The Improved Steam Boat Company's second steamer's career was the same as her consort. Like *Lord of the Isles* she was fitted with deck saloons, but the forward saloon was peculiar, being almost oval in shape and the after saloon did not extend to the full width of the hull.

Lady of the Lake arrived at Southampton on 19 September 1861 and, after various special trips, entered passage service on 1 October. She became a cargo boat in December 1882 and was sold in October 1887.

PS VECTIS

Built:	1866	*Tonnage:*	137 gross, 87 net.	
Withdrawn:	1910	*Dimensions: feet*	150' 6" x 18' 2"	
Scrapped:	1911	*metres*	45.87m x 5.55m	
		Builders:	J White, Cowes, Isle of Wight.	
		Machinery:	Day & Co.	
			Paddle steamer, 60 nhp.	

The wooden-hulled *Vectis* was the first steamer built for Red Funnel. She was launched on 14 June 1866 by Miss Elizabeth Lamb, daughter of the chairman. When new, she was used on excursion work during the season.

As a series of new ships joined the fleet and undertook excursion work, *Vectis* was used on the packet services until 1887, when conversion into a cargo steamer took place. The 1887/8 Lloyd's Register shows her length as 140ft. 8in., with a gross tonnage of 122 and a net of 49. *Vectis* was withdrawn in 1910 and scrapped the following year.

The late Frank Burtt, in his book *Cross Channel and Coastal Paddle Steamers* states that the clipper type bow was removed in 1877 when *Vectis* was re-engined by Day, Summers & Company at Northam, Southampton, with a two cylinder compound diagonal engine of their own construction. A hurricane deck was fitted at the same time. If the illustration in *Red Funnel and Before* of a cargo steamer at the Royal Pier, Southampton is indeed the *Vectis*, then there would appear to be an error, because the ship in that illustration has a clipper bow. Further alterations were made to *Vectis* in 1888 and this may have been when the bow was altered.

Captain F T O'Brien, in his book Early Solent Steamers, refers to this image as being the oldest known photograph of an island steamer. The master stands on the starboard paddle box.

PS SOUTHAMPTON

Built:	1872	Tonnage:	203 gross, 100 net.
Withdrawn:	1902	Dimensions: feet	150' 1" x 20' 1"
Scrapped:	1915	metres	45.75m x 6.13m
		Builders:	Barclay, Curle & Co, Whiteinch, Glasgow. Yard No. 230.
		Machinery:	Barclay, Curle & Co, Whiteinch, Glasgow. Paddle steamer, compound diagonal, 84 nhp.

SOUTHAMPTON, after being fitted with a bridge and in the livery of R R Collard.
RED FUNNEL
ARCHIVES

This ship was the first of a series of new iron-hulled buildings to come from the Clyde shipbuilders and engine makers, Barclay, Curle & Company. The steamer had compound diagonal engines, a narrow deck saloon aft, open foredeck, steering wheel on the deck below the bridge, forward of the funnel, and engine room telegraphs on the sponsons. Later a plank bridge was fitted between the paddle boxes abaft the funnel.

Trials appear to have taken place in Scotland on 22 June 1872 and a preliminary trip took place from Southampton on 6 July 1872.

Photographed at Ostend whilst running for R R Collard.
AUGUST GOETHAELS
COLLECTION

During the week ending 18 June 1881, *Southampton* was chartered to operate from Bournemouth by the Bournemouth, Swanage & Poole Steam Packet Company, and the following week *Carisbrooke* undertook a similar charter.

This was to replace their steamer *Lord Elgin*, which was undergoing repairs at Southampton. During 1881 *Southampton* needed a new boiler. At the same time she was strengthened and had a lower dining saloon added, bringing her into line with the later steamers. The *Southampton Observer* for 3 June 1882 records that the main promenade deck was raised to the level of the paddle box deck and the floor of the main saloon also raised, enabling a commodious dining saloon to be provided underneath. These were substantial alterations and it would appear that she had been delivered as a raised quarter deck ship and that *Carisbrooke* introduced the deck saloon in 1876.

The ship was sold to G Power & Sons of Newhaven in 1902, passing in the following year

As sailing in North Wales as ST. ELIAN.
FRANK THORNLEY
RICHARD DANIELSON COLLECTION

to R R Collard, retaining her name but being registered at Newhaven. For Mr Collard, *Southampton* ran on the Sussex Coast, and also under the same ownership she ran short excursions between Ostend, Blankenburgh, Breskens and Flushing.

In 1907, the Liverpool & North Wales Steamship company Ltd bought the steamer to compete with ships owned by the opposition, and to serve Rhos-on-Sea, etc. Her bridge was placed forward of the funnel by the new owner, and the name *St. Elian* was bestowed. *St. Elian* served until the end of the 1914 season, and was scrapped by T W Ward Ltd at Briton Ferry in 1915.

PS CARISBROOKE

Built:	1876	*Tonnage:*	198 gross, 118 net.
Withdrawn:	1905	*Dimensions: feet*	165' 7" x 20' 1"
Scrapped:	1935	*metres*	50.47m x 6.13m
		Builders:	Barclay, Curle & Co, Whiteinch, Glasgow. Yard No. 260.
		Machinery:	Barclay, Curle & Co, Whiteinch, Glasgow. Paddle steamer, compound oscillating, 70 nhp.

Carisbrooke was launched on 26 January 1876, left Glasgow on 25 March and arrived at Southampton on 31 March after a stormy passage, sheltering at Kingstown (Dun Laoghaire).

The previous steamer, *Southampton*, had been quite a modern ship, with compound diagonal engines and funnel forward of the paddle boxes, but Red Funnel had reverted to the older style with *Carisbrooke*. This vessel, and her sister, *Prince Leopold*, were fitted with compound oscillating engines and carried their boilers aft of the paddle boxes. *Carisbrooke* is recorded as performing an excursion to Weymouth on 22 July 1876, and twenty years later as performing tender duties on 15 August 1896. The ship was reboiled in 1889, redecked in 1895, and in 1905 when she required another new boiler it was decided to sell the ship. A distinguishing feature between *Carisbrooke* and her sister was the position of the galley and stove pipe. Situated on the port paddle box of *Carisbooke*, they were on the starboard box of *Prince Leopold*.

Sold in 1906 to the Colwyn Bay & Liverpool Steamship Company Ltd she served for one season only, being transferred to the Mersey Trading Company in 1907 and renamed *Rhos Trevor*. At the close of the 1908 season, the Mersey Trading Company went out of business, and in November of that year the vessel was bought by Mr W Hawthorn of Rhyl. In May 1909, the vessel changed hands once again, the new owners being the well-established Liverpool & North Wales Steamship Co Ltd by whom *Rhos Trevor* was renamed *St. Trillo*. During the Great War *St. Trillo* served as a minesweeper (No. 837), but she ran as usual in 1915 and 1916, prior to being requisitioned as a minesweeper from October 1916 to June 1919. *St. Trillo* was released and refitted in time for the 1919 season. In September 1919 a rail strike caused *St. Trillo* to operate a special Menai Bridge-Llandudno-Liverpool service and return, and apart from passengers and parcels, she also carried mails, being the first and only steamer of the Liverpool & North Wales Steamship Co Ltd to fly the Royal Mail pennant. On 14 July 1921 *St. Trillo* grounded in the Menai Strait while returning from Caernarvon. The 290 passengers were quickly reassured by the Master and crew, and were

transferred by motor boats to the shore, and to the Liverpool steamer *Snowdon* and the Blackpool steamer *Greyhound*. On the rising tide, *St. Trillo* refloated and made for Port Dinorwic, some passengers still being aboard.

Old age and the condition of her boiler forced the company to part with her after the 1921 season. She was acquired by Marques de Olaso, Bilbao, Spain renamed *San Telmo*, and used on diverse rivers in connection with shooting parties, disappearing from the register during 1931/2. Later, *San Telmo* was reported as being in use as a floating hotel on the river Seville, Spain before being broken up in 1935.

Second of the Barclay, Curle & Co series of vessels, this photograph of CARISBROOKE clearly shows the wheel in front of the funnel on the deck below the bridge.
KEITH ABRAHAM COLLECTION

Between 1909 and 1921 CARISBROOKE operated in North Wales, she is shown here during that period named ST. TRILLO.
FRANK THORNLEY – RICHARD DANIELSON COLLECTION

PS PRINCE LEOPOLD

Built:	1876	*Tonnage:*	196 gross, 114 net.	
Withdrawn:	1905	*Dimensions: feet*	165' 6" x 20' 1"	
Wrecked:	1908	*metres*	50.44m x 6.12m	
		Builders:	Barclay, Curle & Co, Whiteinch, Glasgow. Yard No. 262.	
		Machinery:	Barclay, Curle & Co, Whiteinch , Glasgow. Paddle steamer, compound oscillating, 70 nhp.	

PRINCE LEOPOLD shown in her later life as RHOSNEIGR.
FRANK THORNLEY - RICHARD DANIELSON COLLECTION

Prince Leopold, which arrived at Southampton on 17 April 1876, was a sister ship of *Carisbrooke*, and the ship's career followed very closely that of her sister until *Prince Leopold* was wrecked in 1908.

The steamer was reboilered in 1889, redecked in 1895, and passed to the Colwyn Bay & Liverpool Steamship Company Ltd (1906), and the Mersey Trading Company (1907), becoming *Rhosneigr*.

On 20 July 1908 *Rhosneigr* was wrecked off Rhos Pier while on a trip from Llandudno to Blackpool. The wreck was dispersed with explosives in 1965.

PS PRINCESS BEATRICE

Built:	1880	*Tonnage:*	253 gross, 100 net.	
Withdrawn:	1930	*Dimensions: feet*	175' 7" x 20' 1"	
Scrapped:	1933	*metres*	53.5m x 6.13m	
		Builders:	Barclay, Curle & Co, Whiteinch, Glasgow. Yard No. 294.	
		Machinery:	Barclay, Curle & Co, Whiteinch, Glasgow. Paddle steamer, compound diagonal, 90 nhp.	

Princess Beatrice reverted to compound diagonal engines with the boiler forward of the paddle boxes, being an improved *Southampton*. The paddler made her maiden voyage to Alum Bay on 9 June 1880, and was the first steamer to call at Lee-on-the-Solent Pier on the day it was opened, 3 April 1888.

On 28 October 1897, she was cut through in the way of the foredeck by the Royal Mail Steam Packet Company's *Atrato* when berthed at Jersey Quay, Southampton Docks. *Princess Beatrice* was taken to Day, Summers & Company's yard at Northam, Southampton, and repaired, the costs being paid by the Royal Mail Steam Packet Company.

During 1908/9, she was fitted with electric light, and had been reboilered in 1893. The bridge was later removed from between the paddle boxes to forward of the funnel. During the Great War, *Princess Beatrice* served as a minesweeper (No. 555) from 23 April 1917 to 20 June 1919. *Princess Beatrice* made her last service runs on 19 December 1930. She was then laid-up at Northam, Southampton, until sold to Pollock, Brown & Company at Northam for scrap, in March 1933.

PRINCESS BEATRICE arriving at Cowes.
RED FUNNEL ARCHIVES

An angler relaxes in his deckchair as BALMORAL and PRINCESS ELIZABETH slumber at Southampton's Royal Pier. A late 1930s scene, both ships would soon be taking part in the war effort. Sadly, GRACIE FIELDS, from which this delightful photograph was taken, would not be coming home from her war.

RED FUNNEL ARCHIVES

PS PRINCESS HELENA

Built:	1883	*Tonnage:*	246 gross, 98 net.
Withdrawn:	1950	*Dimensions: feet*	175' 4" x 20' 2"
Scrapped:	1952	*metres*	53.44m x 6.15
		Builders:	Barclay, Curle & Co, Whiteinch, Glasgow. Yard No. 322.
		Machinery:	Barclay, Curle & Co, Whiteinch, Glasgow. Paddle steamer, compound diagonal, 118 nhp.

Launched on 22 June 1883, this steamer was proof of the longevity of the iron hull, and was a very similar ship to the *Princess Beatrice*. *Princess Helena* was reboilered in 1895 and during 1908/9 electric light was fitted, and also a captain's bridge (presumably forward of the funnel) and new steam steering gear. A new boiler, uptake and funnel were fitted in 1913, and during 1917 part of the main saloon aft were converted into a smoking room. *Princess Helena* replaced *Lord Elgin* on the summer Bournemouth to Swanage service in 1911, and remained on this duty until 1914. The Bournemouth station again saw the steamer when, in 1920, she returned to the Swanage service for one season only. Her funnel was painted red with a black top during her 1911-14 spell at Bournemouth, to emphasize the connection with the Bournemouth & South Coast Steam Packets Ltd which had been taken over by Red Funnel in 1908.

During World War I, *Princess Helena* was taken up for Admiralty service from August 1914 to January 1915, as a patrol vessel in the English Channel, but was returned to the company as unsuitable. During World War II, *Princess Helena* was left with the company, but joined the gallant band of ships which made the journey to Dunkirk in May 1940.

Princess Helena lost her mast around 1945 to allow better access for vehicles on the foredeck, her masthead light being placed on top of the wheelhouse; a wartime acquisition. With the arrival of the new *Balmoral*, in November 1949, the elderly vessel was withdrawn from passenger work and placed on the cargo service until 14 January 1950, relieving *Lord Elgin* for overhaul. She was retained as relief cargo steamer until 1952 and lay at Chapel Wharf. *Princess Helena* was sold for scrap and moved to Pollock, Brown's yard at Northam, Southampton, on 29 July 1952. On 9 August a high tide and gale caused her paddlebox sponson to override the quay wall, and when the tide ebbed she heeled over and sank. *Princess Helena* was pumped out, raised, and scrapped as planned.

PRINCESS HELENA wears the early 1930s livery of a white funnel with a black top.
H A ALLEN COLLECTION

PRINCESS HELENA embarks passengers and cars for Cowes in 1932. The canvas dodgers on the open bridge give little protection for the captain and helmsman.
RICHARD DANIELSON COLLECTION

On excursion duty, PRINCESS HELENA arrives at Ryde.
H A ALLEN COLLECTION

PRINCESS HELENA on the Cowes service with her foredeck well loaded with cars.
RED FUNNEL ARCHIVES

PS HER MAJESTY

Built:	1885	Tonnage:	325 gross, 131 net.
Withdrawn:	1940	Dimensions: feet	185' 2" x 20' 1"
Scrapped:	1941	metres	56.44m x 6.12m
		Builders:	Barclay, Curle & Co Ltd, Whiteinch, Glasgow. Yard No. 335.
		Machinery:	Barclay, Curle & Co Ltd, Whiteinch, Glasgow. Paddle steamer, compound diagonal, 135 nhp.

Opposite page.

Top:
In original condition HER MAJESTY arrives at Cowes with a fine motor vehicle prominent on the foredeck. The destination fan boards can be seen on the paddle box beside the galley stovepipe.
H A ALLEN
COLLECTION

Middle left:
With her mast moved to just forward of the bridge in 1927/8, HER MAJESTY is shown in her new role as car ferry.
H A ALLEN
COLLECTION

Middle right:
Shown in her last configuration, HER MAJESTY has no mast at all. It was removed in 1938 to facilitate tendering the liner NIEUW AMSTERDAM.
H A ALLEN
COLLECTION

This was the third similar ship and, until *Her Majesty* was altered, it was difficult to separate the trio for recognition purposes, as there was a tendency to alter the height of the funnels at various reboilerings, etc.

Her Majesty was sunk in a collision with the American Line's *Paris* in the Empress Dock, Southampton, on 13 February 1896. *Her Majesty* was at Transport Quay ready to act as tender to a North German Lloyd ship, and the *Paris* collided with the paddler, making a large hole in her side. She filled rapidly and sank, her mast and only 4 or 5 feet of her funnel being above water. The steamer was raised on 12 March 1896 by contractors for the London & South Western Railway Company (the dock authorities). The owners abandoned the vessel and action was taken against the American Line. The affair was satisfactorily settled, the vessel returned to Red Funnel and was repaired by J G Fay & Company, Northam, Southampton, the repairs being completed by January 1897. The American Line paid all the costs for raising the vessel and also a substantial sum to repair and reinstate her.

Her Majesty received a new boiler in 1901, was fitted with electric light in 1908, and received new steam steering gear during 1908/9. During the Great War, *Her Majesty*, served as a minesweeper (No. 554), from 23 April 1917 to 24 June 1919, partnering her fleet sister, *Princess Beatrice*, sweeping in the English Channel and Irish Sea.

After reconditioning, *Her Majesty* continued on passage service until 10 September 1927, when she began the second phase of her career with Red Funnel. Carriages and vehicles had been carried on the open foredecks of the passenger steamers, the pontoons at the terminals making for convenient loading and disembarking. An increase in this type of traffic caused the steamer to be converted into a car carrier, rather than a passenger ship with space for cars. The mast was set back immediately before the bridge, the companionway from foredeck to promenade deck being removed. The aft saloon was removed

completely, except for a deck house at the stern which housed the companionway to the dining saloon on the lower deck aft, and also provided support for the two lifeboats.

In this condition, *Her Majesty* could carry approximately 18 cars, and was used on holiday weekends and peak season Saturdays on unscheduled sailings for cars and their passengers, the steamer still possessing a passenger certificate. To enable vehicles to be put in the required positions on the steamers, skids were placed under the wheels and the cars manhandled, as necessary. The largest number of cars witnessed was 22, and this was achieved by manhandling a 'baby' Austin into the after engine room alley way. In this condition, *Her Majesty* was occasionally used on scheduled services, mainly for a few days towards the end of September, to enable *Medina* to receive pre-winter service attention. *Her Majesty* also took the cargo service in the 1930s during *Lord Elgin's* overhaul period.

When the giant French liner *Normandie* entered service in 1935, the ship was regularly employed as a car and mail tender to the liner, her mast being repositioned aft of the machinery area to enable her to tie up under the flared bows of the liner. Outgoing mail and luggage was loaded into Southern Railway containers stored on the deck of *Her Majesty*. The containers were lifted aboard *Normandie* by crane, unloaded and then lifted back onto the tender for return, empty, to Southampton. When *Normandie* was inbound the procedure for unloading was much simpler, mail and luggage being sent down a chute onto the deck of the tender by gravity.

In 1938 *Her Majesty's* mast was removed altogether, to enable similar tendering services to be performed to the new Dutch liner *Nieuw Amsterdam*. *Her Majesty* occasionally tendered the German ships *Bremen* and *Europa*.

While lying at Platform Wharf, the company's repair jetty, *Her Majesty* was sunk during an air raid on 1 December 1940, being later raised and broken up at Southampton.

Bottom:
Well loaded with cars on fore and after decks HER MAJESTY has her mast set abaft the funnel. The mast was moved to this position between 1935 and 1938 to enable her to tender the French liner NORMANDIE.
RED FUNNEL ARCHIVES

PS PRINCESS OF WALES

Built:	1888	Tonnage:		320 gross.
Lost in trials:		Dimensions: feet		215' 6" x 21' 1"
1888		metres		65.68m x 6.43m
		Builders:		Barclay, Curle & Co Ltd, Whiteinch, Glasgow. Yard No. 353.
		Machinery:		Barclay, Curle & Co Ltd, Whiteinch, Glasgow. Paddle steamer, compound diagonal.

This vessel never joined the Red Funnel fleet. She was run down, cut in two and sunk in a collision with the steamer *Balmoral Castle*, when on trials over the Skelmorlie measured mile on the Firth of Clyde. A Southampton party attending the trials escaped, but three painters working below were trapped and killed. *Balmoral Castle* (2,948 gross tons, 1877) was a former Castle Line mail steamer which had been sold to Spanish owners in 1882, and was on the Clyde for reconditioning after fire damage. The collision occurred at about 13:00 on Saturday 16 June 1888.

A report of the disaster stated that the new steamer was a two-funnelled vessel, with steam steering gear, and certified to carry 600 passengers. *Balmoral Castle* struck the *Princess of Wales* about two feet behind the paddle box, cutting her completely in two.

As the subsequent Board of Trade enquiry referred to the ship as 'virtually a total loss', it would appear salvage attempts were abandoned. The enquiry found both pilots guilty of negligence.

Later it was reported that *Princess of Wales* had not been worked up to her maximum speed, but it was felt unlikely that she would have attained the contract speed. Her replacement, *Solent Queen* (I), incorporated several improvements including more powerful engines and taller funnels.

PS BANGOR CASTLE

Built:	1864	Tonnage:		250 gross.
Chartered:	1888	Dimensions: feet		191ft x 22ft
Scrapped:	1899	metres		58.22m x 6.71m
		Builders:		Thomas Wingate & Co, Glasgow. Yard No. 84.
		Machinery:		Thomas Wingate & Co, Glasgow. Paddle steamer, simple diagonal, 2 cylinder 74 nhp.

This vessel was chartered for three months during the summer of 1888 to take the place of *Princess of Wales*, sunk on trials. She was originally named *Palmerston* and served on the Thames until transferred to the Belfast to Bangor service in 1873, on charter.

She took the name *Bangor Castle* when her registration was transferred to Belfast in 1877. Her owners became the Belfast, Bangor & Larne Steamboat Company in 1877, and *Bangor Castle* was sold in 1894 to the Plymouth Excursion Steamboat Co Ltd. She was a two funnel ship with the bridge between the funnels, and enormous paddle wheels, but, like the Red Funnel ships, had an open foredeck and narrow saloon aft. Her first sailing from Southampton to Southsea was on 26 June 1888.

An historic photograph taken in August 1888, the chartered BANGOR CASTLE carefully threads her way amongst sailing vessels at Cowes, much as happens with Red Funnel's vessels to this day.
TOM LEE COLLECTION.

In a view taken before 1910, LORD ELGIN lies at Boscombe Pier with Cosens' EMPRESS in the background. One hundred years later no steamers call at Boscombe and the present pier lacks the style of the 1889 structure.
PADDLE STEAMER PRESERVATION SOCIETY ARCHIVES

PS SOLENT QUEEN (1)

Built:	1889	Tonnage:	324 gross, 184 net.
Withdrawn:	1948	Dimensions: feet	215' 6" x 21' 1"
Scrapped:	1948	metres	65.68m x 6.43m
		Builders:	Barclay, Curle & Co Ltd, Whiteinch, Glasgow. Yard No. 354
		Machinery:	Barclay, Curle & Co Ltd, Whiteinch, Glasgow. Paddle steamer, compound diagonal, 217 nhp.

Opposite bottom: Although mostly used on excursions, this photograph shows SOLENT QUEEN on passage duties with vehicles on the foredeck.
KEITH ABRAHAM COLLECTION

In this early photograph of SOLENT QUEEN, the small work boat retrieved from PRINCESS OF WALES can be seen just forward of the port paddle box.
H A ALLEN COLLECTION

Solent Queen was built to replace the ill-fated *Princess of Wales* and arrived at Southampton on 18 May 1889. She had been launched on 3 April, and ran an official trip in the Gareloch on 29 April 1889, obtaining a mean speed of 14.5 knots. Throughout her life, *Solent Queen* carried a small work boat on the port side, abreast of the funnels, this boat being a relic of the *Princess of Wales*. *Solent Queen* was Red Funnel's first two-funnelled steamer and carried her bridge aft of her funnels. Unlike her fleet sisters, the bridge remained in this position until her end. The Board of Trade took an interest in its position, the minutes recording that in November 1915 the BoT requested it to be moved. However, this was not practicable and it was agreed that a man would always be placed as a lookout forward.

Except for the extra funnel, she was generally similar to the other vessels produced by these builders, but was 30ft. longer than *Her Majesty*. In her early days, *Solent Queen* performed a great deal of excursion work. She remained on Red Funnel service during the Great War and, from 1921 to 1931, spent each summer on the Bournemouth station, serving Swanage.

On 27 April 1893, *Solent Queen* was severely damaged by fire while lying at the Royal Pier, Southampton. Day, Summers & Co, Northam, Southampton was awarded the contract to renovate and repair the ship, the anticipated date of return to service being 1 July 1893. In the event, a strike of joiners caused *Solent Queen* to be sent to Cowes for completion. She returned to Southampton for docking and cleaning on 15 July, and was due to re-enter service on the 20th of that month. A new boiler was fitted in 1902, and electric light in 1907.

Solent Queen's load line certificate expired early in 1936 and the directors resolved that only a steam IV passenger certificate should be applied for from then. Her place in the longer distance excursion fleet was taken by *Gracie Fields*.

Solent Queen, with Captain A G Gattrell in command, went to Dunkirk and had the same bad luck as *Princess Helena*, returning without troops. Never a good-looking ship, because of her two thin funnels and large paddle wheels, her appearance was further marred, during World War II, by the loss of her mast, this being substituted by a stump mast with cross trees placed on the promenade deck immediately forward of the funnels. She was fitted with a wheelhouse during the War.

In August 1948, *Solent Queen* suffered boiler failure and was withdrawn, being sold for scrap to T W Ward Ltd of Grays, Essex, where she arrived on 31 October 1948, towed by *Topmast No. 14*. Her binnacle is now in the National Maritime Museum archives at Greenwich. *Solent Queen* was the last iron-hulled steamer built for Red Funnel.

The master can be seen on the bridge wing, ringing full astern on the telegraph, as SOLENT QUEEN slows for the photographer. Her bridge remained behind the funnels all her life, and a seaman was detailed to be looking forward, perhaps the figure on the starboard paddle box.
PADDLE STEAMER PRESERVATION SOCIETY ARCHIVES

PS PRINCE OF WALES

Built:	1891	*Tonnage:*	280 gross, 117 net.
Withdrawn:	1937	*Dimensions: feet*	185' 5" x 22' 2"
Scrapped:	1938	*metres*	56.5m x 6.77m
		Builders:	Southampton Naval Works Ltd, Woolston. Yard No. 271.
		Machinery:	Southampton Naval Works Ltd, Woolston. Paddle steamer, compound diagonal, 119 nhp.

The building of this steamer marked a departure from the Clyde firm of Barclay, Curle & Co Ltd. After using the Scottish yard for 19 years, this order went to the Southampton Naval Works Ltd, a short-lived firm that operated from the yard that was eventually to become that of John I Thornycroft from 1904. The firm's manager was John H Biles, who had been a successful shipbuilder on the river Clyde and later became the chair of naval architecture at the University of Glasgow.

Prince of Wales followed the same general design as her predecessors, with an open foredeck, narrow deck saloon aft with an alleyway around the sides. However, a tall single funnel and small paddle boxes distinguished the ship from other members of the fleet. She was unusual in being designed by Biles with a hogged keel, intended to counterbalance the tendency for paddle steamers to sag amidships with the weight and vibration of machinery and paddle wheels. However, *Prince of Wales* did not sag and carried her hogged keel throughout her life.

The first steel-hulled ship built for the company was launched at Woolston by Miss Beatrice Peglar on 7 July 1891. It was reported that the ship lacked speed, taking 90 minutes between Southampton and Cowes. After various alterations were made she could eventually sail at 15 knots.

During the winter of 1893/4 *Prince of Wales* was fitted with new paddle wheels with wooden floats instead of her original steel floats. Runs over the measured mile were satisfactory and much of the excessive vibration associated with the vessel was cured. Electric lights were fitted to the ship in 1908 and a smoking room, within the main lounge, was constructed in 1917. She was not requisitioned during World War I, continuing to work the packet service during the hostilities.

Red Funnel placed the order for their new motor ship, *Vecta* (I), with Thornycroft's in May 1937. At their meeting on 27 September 1937 the directors offered *Prince of Wales* for sale through the agent, Kellocks. By February 1938 they agreed to sell her to the highest bidder, subject to her not sailing on the South Coast. Eventually, she was sold in March to ship breakers S G Rees & Co of Llanelli for £600 with an undertaking that she would not be used for further trading.

This early view of PRINCE OF WALES shows the bridge abaft the funnel. The paddle boxes were noticeably smaller than those fitted to other ships in the fleet at that time.
H A ALLEN
COLLECTION

In the early 1930s, PRINCE OF WALES lies at the pontoon at Southampton's Royal Pier.   KEITH ABRAHAM COLLECTION

Near the end of her working life, PRINCE OF WALES heads up Southampton Water. Her successor in the fleet, VECTA, would have a very different profile.
RED FUNNEL ARCHIVES

PS DUCHESS OF YORK/ DUCHESS OF CORNWALL

Built:	1896	Tonnage:	302 gross, 127, net.
Sold:	1916	Dimensions: feet	185' 5" x 22' 1"
Re acquired:	1921	metres	56.5m x 6.73m
Withdrawn:	1949	Builders:	Barclay, Curle & Co Ltd, Whiteinch, Glasgow.
Scrapped:	1949		Yard No. 406.
		Machinery:	Barclay, Curle & Co Ltd, Whiteinch Glasgow.
			Paddle steamer, compound diagonal, 135 nhp.

Bottom Right:
The scene aboard
DUCHESS OF
CORNWALL on 9 July
1939. The open
alleyways, around the
saloon aft of the
paddle boxes, were a
feature of the early
steamers before full
width saloons came
into favour.
H A ALLEN
COLLECTION

For this ship a return was made to Clydeside and the yard of Barclay, Curle & Co. *Duchess of York* was ordered as a replacement for *Her Majesty* which had been abandoned by Red Funnel on being sunk (although in fact *Her Majesty* later returned to service). Launched on 28 May 1896, she averaged 14.86 knots on 4 runs over a Clyde measured mile, the fastest single run being 16.14 knots. She ran local trials in Stokes Bay on 4 July 1896. She was similar to *Prince of Wales*, but with slightly bigger paddle boxes and a fatter funnel. Electric light was fitted in 1908. Her bridge was abaft the funnel, on top of a large deckhouse over the main companionway.

In May 1916, *Duchess of York* was sold to the Admiralty, becoming minesweeper No. 0102, and with *Stirling Castle*, *Queen* (II) and *Princess Mary*, was one of four local steamers which sailed for service in the Mediterranean and Aegean Sea until May 1918. Red Funnel repurchased the ship in 1921 and she was refitted and returned to service. She presented a much neater appearance, her bridge had been moved forward of the funnel during Admiralty service and the companionway deckhouse disappeared after the War.

In 1928, Canadian Pacific Steamships were building four 'Duchess' class liners, and requested that Red Funnel relinquish the name of their steamer so that they could use it on one of their new ships. So our *Duchess of York* took the name of *Duchess of Cornwall* in 1928.

Duchess of Cornwall was again called up for war service in September 1939, but she was returned the following month as being unsuitable. She headed east along the coast during the Dunkirk period in 1940, but did not cross from Dover owing to fuel problems. Later in 1940 she was sunk at the Royal Pier during an air raid, but was raised and returned to service. In July 1945, she performed the first post-war excursion to Ryde, the last such sailing having taken place at Whitsun 1940.

The ship was withdrawn from passenger service at the end of the 1946 season. Her last sailing was on 16 October when, with *Princess Elizabeth* and *Solent Queen* (1), she accompanied the Cunard liner *Queen Elizabeth* at the start of her first commercial voyage to New York. She was retained, minus her mast, as reserve cargo steamer until going to Pollock, Brown's yard at Northam, Southampton for scrapping on 19 December 1949. Her last spell on the cargo service was at the end of March 1949.

The crew of DUCHESS OF YORK have already opened the hull doors in preparation for their arrival at Cowes. Her bridge was moved forward of the funnel by 1921 and her name changed to DUCHESS OF CORNWALL in 1928.
H A ALLEN COLLECTION

In a photograph taken in the last pre-war summer on 28 July 1939, DUCHESS OF CORNWALL arrives at Southampton.
KEITH ABRAHAM COLLECTION

The master leans out over the bridge wing as he brings DUCHESS OF CORNWALL alongside at Cowes.
RED FUNNEL ARCHIVES

PS LORNA DOONE (1)

Built:	1891	Tonnage:	427 gross, 83 net. (later 410 gross, 112 net)
Acquired:	1898	Dimensions: feet	220' 5" x 26'
Withdrawn:	1947	metres	67.19m x 7.92m
Scrapped:	1948	Builders:	Napier Shanks & Bell, Yoker, Glasgow. Yard No. 54.
		Machinery:	D Rowan & Son, Glasgow Paddle steamer, compound diagonal, 248 nhp.

During the 1897 season Red Funnel faced serious competition from P & A Campbell Ltd's magnificent steamer *Cambria*. Red Funnel needed to charter a vessel to compete and the choice fell on *Lorna Doone*. Her owner, John Gunn of Cardiff, was only interested in selling the ship. Consequently, Red Funnel purchased the vessel that was to serve them for almost fifty years and become one of their most popular ships. *Lorna Doone* was a pleasure steamer built for Edwards, Robertson & Co of Cardiff, who competed with P & A Campbell in the Bristol Channel trade. At the end of the 1895 season Edwards, Robertson gave up the struggle and their ships were purchased by John Gunn. He continued the fight against the Campbell's White Funnel fleet, until he too succumbed to the competition and sold out in 1898, his best ship coming to Southampton. While under Gunn's ownership, *Lorna Doone* had been chartered for several weeks in 1896 by the Brighton, Worthing and South Coast Steamship Company, to compete against the *Plymouth Belle*, a newcomer to the Sussex coast resorts.

Lorna Doone had an open foredeck with a short fore saloon having side alleyways (although the promenade deck above was of full width) and a full length, full width, saloon aft. She carried one mast, an open bridge forward of a rather short

insufficiently raked funnel, and her paddle boxes had seven groups of horizontal slats, divided vertically.

The new vessel arrived at Southampton on 1 April 1898. On trials she averaged 16.3 knots over two runs and was granted a Steam III passenger certificate for 706 persons and 818 on a Steam IV certificate. *Lorna Doone* performed her first excursion on Easter Monday, 11 April, to Bournemouth and Swanage, sailing via Southsea, Ryde and Cowes with 300 passengers. A newspaper report suggested that her superior accommodation (compared to the other ships in the fleet) met with approval, as the day was stormy with heavy rain showers.

In the winter of 1898/9 she was reboiled by J Samuel White & Co Ltd of Cowes with improved water tube boilers from the Haythorn Tubulous Boiler Syndicate. The boilers vented into two funnels, both forward of the paddle box. Her machinery also needed a thorough overhaul, the engine was removed from the ship and rebuilt with a new high pressure cylinder before being refitted.

After the re-boiling it was stated that the ship would have increased speed and complaints about soot and grit falling on the deck would be eliminated. The initial enthusiasm for the new installation soon evaporated and in 1901 she was

LORNA DOONE looks grand carrying two funnels during the 1899 and 1900 seasons.
KEITH ABRAHAM COLLECTION

again re-boilered, this time with a locomotive type boiler, reverting to one funnel.

During the 1906 season *Lorna Doone* was badly damaged in rough weather and her forward saloon was flooded. She emerged for the 1907 season with promenade and topside plating carried forward to the bows. The dining saloon was placed on the main deck aft and the lower saloon made into a lounge bar called the 'Retreat'. This layout later became common to many other ships of her type. At the entrance to the dining saloon, on the starboard side, was a bar named 'Half Way Doone'. Forward on the main deck was austere passenger accommodation with spar seating around the sides, while on the lower deck were the officers quarters and a small basic saloon.

In the Great War, *Lorna Doone* was taken over by the Royal Navy in August 1914 and used as a patrol vessel in the Solent area. From December 1915 to February 1919 she became a minesweeper (No 575) in the English Channel and with Dover Patrol, being released on 30 December 1919.

When Red Funnel made a determined attempt to enter the Bournemouth excursion trade, competing against Cosens & Co Ltd, *Lorna Doone* was stationed at Bournemouth in 1907/8. In the 1920s she often carried out day trips from Southampton to Brighton and Weymouth at Whitsun before *Balmoral* (I) entered service for the summer season.

Generally *Lorna Doone* operated the day excursions from Southampton, the timings of

which were most convenient to holiday makers, thus increasing her popularity.

Lorna Doone also saw service in World War II, being requisitioned in December 1939 serving as a minesweeper (No. J.135) and later as an anti-aircraft ship (No. 4.402) until September 1943. After these duties she became an accommodation ship on the Clyde until being released in January 1947.

When *Lorna Doone* returned from War service, she was laid-up at Northam, Southampton. It was decided that her condition was so poor that reconditioning was uneconomic. Eventually, on 14 October 1948 she was moved to Pollock, Browns yard at Northam for breaking up. *Lorna Doone*, known locally with great affection as 'Lorna', had been one of Red Funnel's most successful ships and her scrapping caused much regret.

LORNA DOONE is seen alongside Ventnor Pier in the 1920s.
TIM COOPER COLLECTION

LORNA DOONE in the early 1930s, with a black top to her white funnel, approaching Ryde.
H A ALLEN COLLECTION

PS BALMORAL (1)

Built:	1900	*Tonnage:*	473 gross. 97 net.
Withdrawn:	1947	*Dimensions: feet*	236' x 27' 1"
Scrapped:	1949	*metres*	71.93m x 8.25m
		Builders:	S McKnight & Co, Ayr. Yard No. 60.
		Machinery:	Hutson & Son, Glasgow.
			Paddle steamer, compound diagonal, 300 nhp.

Opposite page.

Top left:
Pictured in the early 1930s BALMORAL arrives at Ryde.
H A ALLEN COLLECTION

Top right:
BALMORAL on the slip having some hull plates replaced.
RED FUNNEL ARCHIVES

Middle left:
BALMORAL pictured in her final years, but not 1939 when a small wheel house was fitted. She was always flagship of the Red Funnel fleet.
H A ALLEN COLLECTION

Middle right:
Proudly wearing her new red painted funnel, BALMORAL is pictured on 16 July 1936. Her chime whistle, presented by P & A Campbell, is highly polished.
IAIN QUINN COLLECTION

The order for *Balmoral* (I) was placed in 1899 with Hutson & Son, Glasgow, who sub contracted the hull to McKnight of Ayr. Hutson had promised delivery of *Balmoral* for the 1900 season. She ran trials on the Clyde on 10 July, achieving a maximum speed over the measured mile of 19.51 knots, with a mean average over four runs of 19.25 knots. Her Steam II certificate was for 1,033 passengers and she was the first Red Funnel vessel to have a full length promenade deck.

Balmoral arrived at Southampton on 14 July 1900. Her first trip on 17 July was for directors, shareholders and invited guests. On the return sailing from Bournemouth she encountered *Cambria*, *Balmoral* winning the first tussle with the ship she was specifically built to compete with. This does not prove she was the faster ship, they were evenly matched. *Balmoral* immediately became flagship of the fleet and held this position until the outbreak of war in 1939. An expensive ship to operate, her season was always the shortest of any in the fleet. However her work was arduous as she undertook the long day excursions and cross Channel trips. Eastbourne (from 1930), Brighton, Weymouth, Torquay (until 1929 and again in 1939) and Cherbourg were her main destinations.

Balmoral received new boilers in 1907/8 and again in 1920 after war service. Her accommodation was refurbished as necessary and her lower lounge bar was renamed the 'Bal Drop Inn' during the 1930s. Some time after the Great War a stump main mast and wireless installation was fitted, and a thick rim fitted to the funnel top. In 1939 she appeared with a wheelhouse fitted on the bridge. In the mid-1930s Campbell's fitted chime whistles to their fleet. An extra one was cast and presented to Red Funnel who immediately fitted it to *Balmoral* as a tribute to a worthy competitor, *Cambria*.

Balmoral was requisitioned in February 1915, her first trip providing troop transport to Le Havre. For about three months she was employed on cross Channel trooping trips, before being converted into a minesweeper (No. 583). Off Ostend, she was apparently shelled by shore batteries. Near the end of the war she was based at Portland, and was returned to her owners in February 1919. After refit she re entered service in 1921. During World War II, *Balmoral* was requisitioned on 29 April 1940 and fitted out as an auxiliary anti-aircraft ship (No. 4.241). In September 1943 she was transferred to the Clyde as an accommodation ship for men working on a floating dock; some reports say she also provided some lighting and power to the dock.

At the end of the war, *Balmoral* was towed back to Southampton in a very poor condition, arriving on the mud berth at Northam in January 1947. It was not until 31 December 1948 that she was moved to Pollock, Brown's yard for breaking up. The competition for which *Balmoral* was built ceased after the 1902 season when Campbell's moved their South Coast operation to the Sussex coast. The short excursion seasons and high operating costs caused constant concern to the directors and shareholders. In the 1905 annual report the chairman summed up the situation -

'*Balmoral* worked eleven weeks in 1905 and was laid-up on the mud for forty one weeks, wasting money all the time; yet people run away with the idea that because she was fully loaded for a few days or weeks she is a gold mine for the company. The company did not think so, she was an unavoidable evil, yet the company could not do without her.'

According to the general manager's weekly working sheets *Balmoral's* final excursion sailing took place on Sunday 3 September 1939 at 14:15 from Southampton to Ryde, Southsea, Sandown, Shanklin and Ventnor. The same working sheets record her final cross Channel sailing to Cherbourg, via Bournemouth, from Southampton at 07:00 on Thursday 31 August. However Ron Adams understood this sailing to have been cancelled, in which case her last Cherbourg visit would have been on 30 August, via Southsea, Sandown and Shanklin. The outbreak of war brought all long distance excursion sailings to an end. Things would never be the same again; it was the end of an era.

Bottom:
After wartime service, BALMORAL lay on the mud berth at Northam during 1947 and 1948, never to sail again for Red Funnel. Next to her is UPTON, which served the company between 1946 and 1950. In the background, far right, the landing craft moored in the river may be the vessel destined to become Red Funnel's NORRIS CASTLE (II).
KEITH ABRAHAM COLLECTION

PS QUEEN (II) /MAURETANIA / CORFE CASTLE

Built:	1902	Tonnage:
Withdrawn:	1938	Dimensions: feet
Scrapped:	1939	metres
		Builders:
		Machinery:

345 gross, 106 net.
200' 3" x 24' 1"
61.04m x 7.34m
J Reid & Co Ltd, Whiteinch, Glasgow.
Yard No. 325.
Barclay, Curle & Co Ltd, Glasgow.
Paddle steamer, compound diagonal, 185 nhp.

The second two funnelled ship in the fleet was launched on 10 May 1902 by Mrs F J Burnett, wife of the company secretary. She arrived at Southampton on 8 June, running trials on 18 June when she achieved a mean average over four runs of the measured mile of just over 15 knots.

Queen was a further development of the 'packet' class of ships for the Cowes service, although she was mainly used on excursion services throughout her life. She carried the buff funnel colours of the 'packet' ships until 1931 when they became white with black tops. They changed again in 1935, when the fleet adopted the unified colour scheme of a red funnel with black top.

The promenade deck extended the full width of the hull, although the alleyways still persisted around the after saloon. *Queen* was fitted with a small fore saloon, having a short open foredeck, one mast, with the bridge forward of the funnels. Paddle box platforms were fitted in 1907/08. Unusually the promenade deck covered the mooring deck aft, but this was cut back in 1911/12 to make her similar to *Princess Mary*. At this time her paddle boxes were painted black, the normal colour of the passage boats, but they became white after the Great War. Originally she had a large deckhouse over the saloon companionway, but this was removed sometime after the Great War, and definitely before she took up the Swanage service in 1933.

In the Great War *Queen* was requisitioned, named *Queen IV* (No. 0104) and in May 1916 made ready for service in the Mediterranean. She sailed in convoy, with her fleet mates *Princess Mary*, *Stirling Castle* and *Duchess of York*, reaching Malta in July 1916 where they were used on patrol and minesweeping duties. At the end of the War *Queen* remained on Government duties, partly reconditioned at Gibraltar and did not return to passenger service until 1920.

During the winter 1927/8 *Queen* was fitted with new paddle wheels and steel floats. This improved her speed and she became equal to the then new *Princess Elizabeth*, making the two ships interchangeable on the excursion duty roster.

She was transferred to Bournemouth for the Swanage service in 1933, remaining on that duty until withdrawn at the end of the 1938 season with terminal boiler problems. She was broken up in Holland during 1939.

This ship was unusual as she was renamed twice without a change of ownership. In 1936, Cunard White Star Line asked Red Funnel if she could be renamed *Mauretania* to preserve the name for their new liner. Cunard asked for the return of the name in November 1937. The Red Funnel directors met on 22 November 1937 and discussed a new name for the ship. They agreed that she should be *Corfe Castle*, *Purbeck* or *Branksome* in that order of preference. Thus it was that she was renamed *Corfe Castle* for her final season in 1938.

Pictured in 1935 with a red funnel, QUEEN moves astern from Bournemouth Pier on a ferry trip to Swanage.
H A ALLEN
COLLECTION

As built, QUEEN's promenade deck extended right to the stern and covered the mooring deck. It was cut back in the winter of 1911/12.
PADDLE STEAMER PRESERVATION SOCIETY ARCHIVES

Taken in 1909, this photograph shows QUEEN arriving at Victoria Pier Cowes after being fitted with paddle box landing platforms.
PADDLE STEAMER PRESERVATION SOCIETY ARCHIVES

This image shows QUEEN as MAURETANIA heading back to Bournemouth from Swanage, passing the Old Harry Rocks in 1936.
RED FUNNEL ARCHIVES

PS PRINCESS ROYAL

Built:	1906	*Tonnage:*	428 gross as built. (later 487 gross,
Not accepted –			later 533 gross)
Lengthened:	1907	*Dimensions: feet*	195' 6" (later 217' 2") x 25' 1"
Scrapped:	1957	*metres*	59.59m (later 66.2m) x 7.64m
		Builders:	John I Thornycroft & Co Ltd,
			Woolston, Southampton.
			Yard No. 430.
		Machinery:	John I Thornycroft & Co Ltd,
			Woolston, Southampton.
			Paddle steamer, compound diagonal, 138nhp.

Most references to this steamer say she was not accepted by Red Funnel, owing to her speed not coming up to contract requirements. However, press reports at the time, indicate that the vessel was accepted and ran for two or three weeks.

A press report of 2 June 1906 stated that 'the vessel will be on service at Whitsun, with Captain Goldsmith in command'.

Princess Royal was launched on 10 April 1906 and trials took place on 28 May. Six runs over the measured mile achieved an average of 14.75 knots which, under all circumstances, were considered by the directors at a meeting held on board before returning to the Royal Pier, to be sufficiently satisfactory to justify taking over the vessel. Mr Calloway, technical director of John I Thornycroft & Co Ltd stated that he might say they had not had the time to tune up the machinery as they would wish, and he hoped the speed would work out alright.

The Red Funnel minute books and other records provide the following information. *Princess Royal* entered public service on Thursday 8 June on the 09:20 sailing to Ryde, Southsea, Sandown and Ventnor. It was clear all was not well as special tests were carried the following Saturday 'in consequence of serious discrepancies in her draught which her working had disclosed'. The vessel's draught was measured with three different weights of coal aboard.

Mr Calloway, the Thornycroft technical director, was summoned to a meeting of the board the following Tuesday. The chairman explained the unsatisfactory nature of the vessel and declined to accept the vessel or pay the last instalment. It was agreed that the matter be left for one week to enable the builders to consider their position. Mr Calloway asked that instead of immediately laying up the vessel, Red Funnel continued to use her until Monday next.

Red Funnel did continue to operate the vessel and her last sailing was to Alum Bay at 13:00 on Sunday 24 June; on the Monday morning she was taken to moorings on the river Itchen, never to sail in public service for the company again.

Various meetings and discussions took place through the summer and in October a supplementary agreement was agreed for the ship to be lengthened. The work was carried out and *Princess Royal* was floated out of the dock on 28 January 1907. The engine must have then been moved forward and further trials took place on 13 March. She still did not meet the required speed and Thornycroft's wrote to Red Funnel on 8 April suggesting that the failure was due to abnormal circumstances and requesting another trial. Presumably the Red Funnel directors lost patience at this stage, because Thornycroft's solicitors then wrote saying their client did not intend to contest the action entered by Red Funnel and suggested repayment terms. The Red Funnel board agreed.

Matters then rested until a letter from Thornycroft's was received on 13 January 1908. They were keen to bring things to a conclusion on 15 January and the company seal was fixed to the bill of sale.

In the event, *Princess Royal* was purchased by Cosens of Weymouth in 1908, sailing mainly from Weymouth until World War I. After that her station was Bournemouth, until her final season in 1956. Cosens renamed the ship *Emperor of India*.

To increase her buoyancy, the builders had added a 21ft. 8in. section inserted 4ft. aft of the original centre line, and moved the engine 6ft. 6in. forward. This appears to have helped matters, but she still did not reach the Red Funnel contract speed hence their rejection of her. However, Cosens were clearly delighted with their new acquisition and they sent the steamer to Day, Summers & Co to be fully plated with a full length promenade deck to the bows. Boiler, funnel and bridge were moved 7ft. aft. Unfortunately this upset her trim again, and she sat very low in the water. With her powerful engines, she should have been capable of much greater speed than that usually attained, and in consequence *Emperor of India* could not be described as a successful vessel.

As well as the usual local trips, she cruised to Cherbourg and Alderney prior to 1914. She saw service during the Great War in the Eastern Mediterranean as a troop transport, hospital carrier and mine-sweeper (No. 0106) under the name *Mahratta*, returning to Weymouth in 1920. The year 1922 saw her chartered by the Cinque Ports S N Company to operate from Sussex Coast piers in the absence of P & A Campbell's steamers. At the end of the season she returned to her owners and resumed her normal Bournemouth sailings in 1923.

Service in World War II was as a minesweeper (J.I06) and latterly as an anti-aircraft ship (No. 4.237) in the Thames estuary. She was flagship of the anti-aircraft flotilla, but the weight of her armament reduced her speed to six knots.

After refitting, *Emperor of India* returned to service in 1948, presenting a new appearance. Converted to oil burning, she had a much larger funnel with a fan casing at its front, a large bridge with wheelhouse, and for a few years carried a stump mainmast. There was also a large deckhouse over the main companionway, although this was later removed. This additional top hamper further affected her performance, and it was so poor in 1955, that from mid-season she was often relegated to the Swanage service. However, it must be stated that at this period she was the most luxurious steamer on the South Coast. The ship's panelling and furnishing was of the finest quality timber, including teak from the houseboat *Florinda*, originally owned by Lillie Langtry, and cedarwood panelling which had been stored at a country estate.

She was on charter, under Red Funnel arrangements, at the Coronation Naval Review in 1953, and hoisted her original house-flag for the day. *Emperor of India* was broken up at Bruges, Belgium, having left Weymouth in tow of the tug *Bulldog II*, on 24 January 1957.

PRINCESS ROYAL is seen here during trials. She has the black painted paddle boxes usually associated with the passage service.
RED FUNNEL ARCHIVES

As EMPEROR OF INDIA, Cosens had her open foredeck plated-up and the promenade deck extended to the bows.
H A ALLEN COLLECTION

PS STIRLING CASTLE

Built:	1899	Tonnage:	271 gross, 47 net.
Acquired:	1907	Dimensions: feet	170' x 24' 2"
War loss:	1916	metres	51.82m x 7.36m
		Builders:	J Scott & Co, Kinghorn, Fife. Yard No. 108.
		Machinery:	J Scott & Co, Kinghorn, Fife.
			Paddle steamer, compound diagonal, 141 nhp.

During 1907, her first season at Southampton, STIRLING CASTLE ran with the short telescopic funnel of her previous owners. In this condition she approaches Southsea's Clarence Pier.
PADDLE STEAMER PRESERVATION SOCIETY ARCHIVES

The failure of *Princess Royal* interrupted Red Funnel's push to gain more traffic from Bournemouth, as they had stationed the *Solent Queen* there for a Bournemouth to Swanage service in the summer of 1905.

Red Funnel purchased *Stirling Castle* from the Galloway Steam Packet Company Ltd of Leith and she entered service on 20 May 1907. She had a short open foredeck leading to a small foredeck saloon and a full width promenade deck aft. The bridge was abaft the funnel, which was telescopic enabling the ship to pass under bridges on the Firth of Forth. After one season at Southampton, during which *Lorna Doone* and *Solent Queen* were Bournemouth-based, she received an extensive overhaul during the 1907/8 winter, emerging with a normal funnel of pleasing dimensions, but her bridge was still aft of the stack, and she was fitted with new steam steering gear.

On 6 April 1908 she was placed on the Bournemouth station for the Swanage service, later being joined by *Lorna Doone*, which operated the day excursions. When the new *Bournemouth Queen* entered service in July 1908, *Stirling Castle* returned to Southampton. The following year, however, a return to the Bournemouth station was made, and the steamer subsequently spent each season there up to 1914, operating the Swanage service and local trips.

On 5 July 1911 *Stirling Castle* was involved in a tragic collision with a small sailing craft off the Old Harry rocks at Swanage. The occupants of the boat, a mother and her two children, and the boatman were all drowned. The case went to court and Red Funnel finally settled by paying out £2,552 in November 1911. The Board of Trade took an interest in the position of the ship's bridge and wrote in August 1912 enquiring why it had not been moved as desired. After they wrote again it was then moved forward of the funnel in time for the 1913 season.

Stirling Castle was one of a quartet of the company's ships (No. 0105) that sailed in convoy for war service in the Mediterranean in July 1916. The vessel was sunk by an explosion of unknown cause off the west coast of Malta on 26 September 1916, and became the company's first war loss.

During her short career with Red Funnel, this ship is reported to have changed her funnel colours several times during the first three years of service; 1907 - deep buff; 1908 - white until July, then buff again; 1909 — red with black top.

STIRLING CASTLE approaches Swanage. She has a conventional funnel, fitted for the 1908 season, which is painted red and black indicating the photograph was taken after 1909.
RED FUNNEL ARCHIVES

PS BOURNEMOUTH QUEEN

Built:	1908	*Tonnage:*
Withdrawn:	1957	*Dimensions: feet*
Scrapped:	1958	*metres*
		Builders:
		Machinery:

353 gross, 139 net. post WW2 428 gross 155 net
200' 1" x 24' 1"
60.98m x 7.34m
Ailsa Shipbuilding Co Ltd, Troon. Yard No. 209.
Hutson & Sons, Glasgow
Paddle steamer, compound diagonal, 94 nhp.

This steamer was the second and last vessel built for Red Funnel as a purely excursion class ship and, as her name suggests, was destined to spend the greater part of her service at her namesake port. She was similar to *Balmoral* in appearance and layout, but with less powerful engines. Her speed was about 15 knots and she was much more economical to operate.

The trial trips were run on 7 July 1908, and she started operating the Swanage service on 20 July 1908. At first her funnel was white, but on the acquisition of Bournemouth & South Coast Steamers Ltd for the 1909 season, a red, black-topped, funnel appeared, but in her case for one season only, she reverted to the white funnel in 1910 to emphasize her association with *Balmoral* and *Lorna Doone*.

In 1909 and during the remainder of her service, until the outbreak of World War II, she was the full day excursion boat from Bournemouth and, when new, was tried on the long trips to Brighton, Torquay and Dartmouth. However, this did not last long as she had insufficient speed for such long distances, especially when sailing against the tide. These excursions then became the preserve of *Balmoral* which made an early morning departure from Southampton.

Bournemouth Queen saw naval service as HMS *Bourne* during World War I, and served from March 1915 to April 1919. As a patrol and minesweeping vessel (No.188) she worked in the English Channel, North Sea, West Coast of Scotland and Northern Ireland, and during this service circumnavigated the British Isles.

Returning to her normal station and work, she took up her old runs from Bournemouth to Yarmouth or Totland Bay, thence to Cowes and Southampton; or to Cowes, Ryde, Southsea and Portsmouth Harbour cruise or 'Round the Island'. *Bournemouth Queen* usually, at least during the 1930s, commenced work at Easter, and was joined by the Swanage boat at Whitsun. The funnel stay ring on this vessel was rather low and, consequently, when in 1931 black tops were added, *Bournemouth Queen's* was very deep. Subsequently, this was altered to about half the depth and in some opinions, did not suit her so well.

Early in the 1939 season, *Bournemouth Queen* experienced boiler trouble and was withdrawn and spent the months of July, August and September laid-up on a mud berth at Northam. Requisitioned on 7 February 1942, *Bournemouth Queen* served in her second war as an anti-aircraft

This photograph typifies the end of an era. It shows an immaculate BOURNEMOUTH QUEEN at Swanage in 1939, just before the start of World War II. The position of the black top to the funnel in relation to the stay ring, referred to in the text, can be clearly seen.
LAURENCE PRITCHARD – PETER LAMB COLLECTION

ship (No. 4.270) on the Firth of Forth or on the Tyne, and later, from October 1943, became an accommodation ship at Fort William. The ship was returned to Red Funnel in December 1945.

It was July 1947 before the vessel returned to service, after substantial rebuilding had taken place. However, she was not converted to burn oil fuel, remaining coal-fired to the end. Her passenger accommodation had been modernised. A new larger funnel, pear-shaped and fitted with a cowl top, improved her appearance. A larger bridge sported a wheelhouse, solid bulwarks forward replaced the canvas laced rails and, when in 1954 she appeared with a main mast in compliance with new navigation light arrangements, she looked very well indeed. However, after her post-war alterations, *Bournemouth Queen* had become very 'tender', and listed at the first opportunity.

Her duty as a day excursion ship ended in 1949, when the newly arrived larger *Lorna Doone* (II) relegated her to the Swanage service. Her last season at Bournemouth was 1950, and this finished in mid-September because of lack of traffic caused by a polio scare in the Isle of Wight. *Bournemouth Queen* remained at Southampton in 1951 and operated the local excursion services until 1957, mainly on the Southampton, Ryde, Southsea triangle. During 1951, she introduced a service from the above three places to Totland Bay, with a short cruise from the pier. This proved unsuccessful and was not repeated in subsequent seasons. Also, at the beginning of the 1951 season, *Bournemouth Queen* ran to Shanklin and made a cruise to the Nab Tower. Later in the season, she was restricted within Steam IV passenger certificate limits. With other members of the fleet she attended the Coronation Fleet Review on 18 June 1953.

An unusual duty came her way on 28 July 1956 when, in place of the rostered *Princess Elizabeth*, *Bournemouth Queen* tendered the French liner *Liberte*. Her last sailing was on 29 August 1957 and she then lay at Berth 7 at the Royal Pier. Under tow of the tug *Bulldog II* she departed on 18 December 1957 to be scrapped by Van Heyghen Bros, at Ghent.

BOURNEMOUTH QUEEN returns to her builder's yard at Troon after trials on 7 July 1908. The beautiful finish to the gloss black paint on the stern is very noticeable. Eventually withdrawn in 1957, she was to serve Red Funnel for fifty years.

RED FUNNEL
ARCHIVES

BOURNEMOUTH QUEEN in the early 1930s, sporting a white funnel with a black top.

H A ALLEN COLLECTION

BOURNEMOUTH QUEEN in her immediate post World War II condition. Her propensity to list is clear from this photograph.

H A ALLEN COLLECTION

A well loaded BOURNEMOUTH QUEEN heads away from Ryde towards Southampton in the early 1950s.

RED FUNNEL ARCHIVES

BOURNEMOUTH QUEEN on Thornycroft's slip at Northam in spring 1957, being prepared for her final season.

CAPTAIN P D JONES - DON JONES COLLECTION

BOURNEMOUTH QUEEN laid-up at the Royal Pier awaiting disposal in autumn 1957. Alongside is PRINCESS ELIZABETH which had one more season to serve before steam propulsion finally gave way to diesel. In the background is one of Union Castle's mail boats and a troop ship is underway with assistance from tugs.

CAPTAIN P D JONES - DON JONES COLLECTION

PS LORD ELGIN

Built:	1876	*Tonnage:*	203 gross, 119 net.
Acquired:	1908	*Dimensions: feet*	160' x 20'
Withdrawn:	1955	*metres*	48.77m x 6.1m
Scrapped:	1955	*Builders:*	Richardson Duck & Co, Stockton-on-Tees. Yard No. 216.
		Machinery:	T Richardson & Sons, Hartlepool. Paddle steamer, compound diagonal, 75 nhp.

LORD ELGIN in service as passenger steamer before her conversion to a cargo boat in 1911.
H A ALLEN COLLECTION

During the latter part of 1908, Bournemouth & South Coast Steam Packets Ltd sold their business, with its goodwill and their steamer *Lord Elgin*, to Red Funnel. *Lord Elgin* had been built in 1876 for service by John Kidd, predecessor of the Galloway Steam Packet Co. Ltd. of Leith, for excursion services on the Firth of Forth. The ship was purchased by the Bournemouth company in 1881, and during her last years at Bournemouth, ran in conjunction with Cosens' steamers under a common programme.

At the annual general meeting for the year ending 30 September 1908, in reply to a question the secretary replied that *Lord Elgin* was in a good condition and, after serving as a passenger ship, she would make a perfect cargo steamer. This did, indeed, prove to be the case, because after continuing to serve Bournemouth for her new owners until the end of the 1910 season, *Lord Elgin* was converted into a cargo steamer to replace the old *Vectis*, and sailed in this capacity until her final sailing in 1955.

Lord Elgin, as a cargo vessel, had clear fore and aft decks with a derrick to serve the hold. Her funnel was upright, and wheel and telegraphs were on deck level. She maintained the run to Cowes on six days each week until World War II, this later being reduced to five days upon the introduction of the five day working week. In the

1930s and again after the war, the ship was used on summer Saturdays as a relief car ferry.

In September 1952, her place on the cargo service was taken by the car ferry *Norris Castle* (II), which introduced Red Funnel's policy of all freight being carried on the roll-on roll-off principle. However, *Lord Elgin* was kept on to maintain the service during *Norris Castle's* overhaul periods. Her last sailing eventually came on 11 May 1955 when the old steamer made the Solent crossing for the last time. Two days later, under her own steam, she sailed round to the Itchen berth of Pollock, Brown & Company Ltd for scrapping. She carried the distinction of being the last cargo paddle steamer in the British Register.

Synonymous with the name of *Lord Elgin* was that of Captain Joseph Sewley, who had commanded the old ship from 1923 until he took her to the scrap yard. It is estimated that this partnership made 8,607 sailings to Cowes, travelling 223,790 miles. In the company's pre-war handbook, Captain Sewley is described as 'a versatile, razor-blade-keen individual, who is as unmoved by the presence of 75 head of goggle-eyed cattle on her foredeck on a market day as he is of 600 ewes aft'. Captain Sewley later worked in the Pier office and eventually retired in December 1965.

LORD ELGIN at the Southampton Royal Pier Pontoon. A few interested bystanders wait to see the cattle unloaded from her foredeck.
RICHARD DANIELSON COLLECTION

LORD ELGIN lies at the Town Quay with some heavy machinery on her after deck. IAIN QUINN COLLECTION

A flock of pensive sheep await disembarkation from LORD ELGIN. RED FUNNEL ARCHIVES

The end of the steam cargo paddle boat era. Bedecked with flags, LORD ELGIN is about to sail from Berth 1 at the Royal Pier to the breaker's yard on the river Itchen. 13 May 1955.
IVAN BOVEY

PS PRINCESS MARY

Built:	1911	*Tonnage:*	326 gross, 130 net.
War loss:	1919	*Dimensions: feet*	195' 2" x 24' 1"
		metres	59.49m x 7.34m
		Builders:	Day, Summers & Co Ltd, Northam Southampton. Yard No. 148.
		Machinery:	Day, Summers & Co Ltd, Northam Southampton. Paddle steamer, compound diagonal, 137 nhp.

The first public sailing of this steamer was on 17 June 1911, after completing trials on 14th June. These trials had not been entirely satisfactory because a special meeting of the board was held on 15 June to discuss their non-compliance with the building contract. The next trials took place on 4 July when the highest speed recorded was 14.42 knots. It was agreed to accept the ship, on condition of a reduction of £400 from the contract price.

Princess Mary followed the usual company practice of building general-purpose ships, that is a vessel for the passage service, but capable of taking her place in the excursion programme and performing tender work when necessary. The usual open foredeck appeared, but the promenade deck was the full width over a narrow saloon with side alleyways which were enclosed by large windows, able to be opened in fine weather. Her bridge was placed before the funnel, which was fatter and shorter than those of her predecessors. Unfortunately, *Princess Mary* had a short life as she became the company's second war loss. She was the last unit of the four ships taken over in May 1916 that sailed in convoy to the Mediterranean, reaching Malta in July. She served as an auxiliary patrol vessel (No. 0103) under the name of *Princess Mary II* until April 1919, and was then used as a minesweeper. On 2 August 1919, she had the misfortune to run over the wreck of HMS *Majestic*, which had been mined during the Dardanelles operation; her bottom was ripped open and *Princess Mary* became a total loss.

PRINCESS MARY on the slip for final fitting out at Day, Summers yard.   LAURENCE PRITCHARD - IAIN QUINN COLLECTION

PRINCESS MARY not long before launching.
LAURENCE PRITCHARD – PSPS ARCHIVES

PRINCESS MARY, just launched into the waters of the river Itchen, being assisted by tug AJAX. The famous sheerlegs of the Day, Summers yard are seen on the left of the photograph.
LAURENCE PRITCHARD – PSPS ARCHIVES

PRINCESS MARY setting off down the river Itchen for trials on 14 June 1911. The wooded area on the riverbank behind the steamer is now the suburb of Southampton known as Chessel.
LAURENCE PRITCHARD – PSPS ARCHIVES

PRINCESS MARY awaiting trials.
DON JONES COLLECTION

PRINCESS MARY in service.
RED FUNNEL ARCHIVES

PS PRINCESS ELIZABETH

Built:	1927	*Tonnage:*	338 gross, (later 371 gross, later 388 gross)
Withdrawn:	1959		151 net.
Remains in		*Dimensions: feet*	195' x 24' 2" this is registered length
static use.		*metres*	59.44m x 7.36m
		Builders:	Day, Summers & Co Ltd, Northam Southampton. Yard No. 190.
		Machinery:	Day, Summers & Co Ltd, Northam Southampton. Paddle steamer, compound diagonal, 94 nhp.

Close to the end of her service with Red Funnel, PRINCESS ELIZABETH, nears Dockhead on her return excursion from Ryde on 29 August 1958. The photograph was taken from the Cowes service boat, VECTA, which had met the paddler off Calshot and then raced with her up Southampton Water. The steamer was about to let VECTA pass and berth at the pontoon, while PRINCESS ELIZABETH would follow to berth at the Royal Pier.
DON JONES
COLLECTION

Launched on 2 June 1927 by Mrs Cyril Sharp, daughter-in-law of the Red Funnel chairman, *Princess Elizabeth* appeared as a repeat of the ill-fated *Princess Mary*, but with refinements in accommodation and engineering departments. Stokes Bay was the venue for trials on 25 August 1927, and the speed of 14.5 knots was considered satisfactory, and in excess of contract requirements. At first, she was generally employed as a passage steamer, but when *Solent Queen* returned to the Southampton station in 1932, *Princess Elizabeth* spent much of this season at Bournemouth. However, 1933 saw *Queen* on the Bournemouth sailings and *Princess Elizabeth* became useful as the 'local' excursion steamer from her home port until the arrival of *Gracie Fields*. The withdrawal of *Queen* at the end of 1938 (by then she carried the name *Corfe Castle*) caused a return to the Bournemouth sailings until the outbreak of war.

In 1936 her funnel was lengthened and was fitted with a cowl top, which improved the appearance of the ship. A small wheelhouse was fitted in 1938.

The ship was taken over by the Admiralty in September 1939 and converted to a minesweeper (No. J.111). Four trips were made from the Dunkirk beaches with troops in May 1940. Reports say that she rescued 1,673 men. In 1942 HMS *Princess Elizabeth* became an anti-aircraft vessel (No. 4.403), being returned to her owners in 1944.

Refitted and converted to oil burning, she returned to service in 1946 on the Ryde excursion service. On 19 August she ran a special excursion to Yarmouth, Bournemouth and Swanage, reopening the latter two piers; this being the first pleasure steamer call since 1939. This excursion was repeated, usually twice weekly, for the remainder of the season. During her refit, the accommodation was improved, the dining saloon aft on the main deck becoming full width.

The year 1947 saw *Princess Elizabeth* again stationed at Bournemouth, replacing the screw steamer *Upton*, which had proved unsuitable for open pier work, and the following year she was Southampton-based, reintroducing sailings to Southsea, South Parade Pier and Shanklin, the piers there having been repaired. With larger second-hand vessels joining the fleet in 1949, *Princess Elizabeth* lost her place as a day excursion ship and was employed on passage work and excursions as required. At Easter 1952, she spent a week stationed at Bournemouth, turning out to be the last Red Funnel ship to operate from there.

From 1953 onwards, the description 'stand-by' steamer would be appropriate until 1958, when the season was occupied by local excursions, sometimes in lieu of *Bournemouth Queen*. During the 1954/55 period she had a short charter to British Railways and operated on their Clarence Pier, Southsea to Ryde service. With the building of the new car ferry *Carisbrooke Castle*, she performed her last scheduled passage sailing on 12 September 1958 on the first run up from Cowes, having made her last departure from Southampton the previous evening. Her final Solent cruise was on 14 September and from then on she was 'stand-by' vessel until the arrival of the new ship in May 1959. She made a service run, taking the 16:30 departure on 23 February that year, while the regular vessel was carrying out tender duties. She moved from Berth 8 at the Royal Pier to the mud berth at Northam on 17 July 1959.

Before leaving her Red Funnel career, it should be noted that she was regularly used during the summer as a passenger tender to the French liner *Normandie*, until 1938. She also relieved *Norris Castle* (II) on the cargo run during that ship's first overhaul after *Lord Elgin's* retirement. To comply with new navigation light regulations, *Princess Elizabeth* appeared in 1954 with a main mast which completely spoilt her appearance, being shorter than the foremast and placed in front of the companionway deckhouse. In November 1954, during survey, she needed to be fitted with new shafts and did not return to service until Whitsun 1955. The ship was always renowned for the splendid cleanliness and polish of her engine room metalwork.

In 1959 the vessel was sold to Torbay Steamers Ltd and was refitted by Thornycroft's at Northam. Trials were held on 26 April 1960 and she left Southampton for Torbay on 5 May 1960. The owners operated the ship from Torquay in 1960 and 1961. However, a dispute with the Torquay Harbour Authorities caused reconstitution as Coastal Steamers and Marine Services Ltd and preparations to operate from Brighton in 1962. Surprisingly, however, she turned up at Bournemouth and ran a short season of sailings from that resort.

At Weymouth, Cosens had withdrawn their steamer *Consul* at the end of the 1962 season. With the expectation of no steamer at the resort in 1963 *Princess Elizabeth's* owners moved her to Weymouth under the name of Coastal Steamers (Weymouth) Ltd. She completed three summers at Weymouth and was withdrawn at the end of the 1965 season.

This photograph taken aboard PRINCESS ELIZABETH encapsulates the pleasure of sailing on the open foredeck of a paddle steamer.
KEITH ABRAHAM

PRINCESS ELIZABETH waits to sail from the Royal Pier pontoon on 3 September 1951.
CYRIL PERRIER – PADDLE STEAMER PICTURE GALLERY

After 38 years service it was a reasonable expectation that *Princess Elizabeth* would be heading for the scrap yard. However, most remarkably, she was destined to become a great survivor and enjoy a greatly extended life in static use. The ship's subsequent movements can be summarized as follows:

1966 – Sold to A W Render to be used as a casino. The plan did not materialise.

1967 – Sold for scrap to Metrix Ltd, Newhaven and resold to Ferry Services and Supplies Ltd, Itchen, Southampton. She arrived on 24 October 1967, engine room and other equipment were removed and it was assumed that the ship would be scrapped.

1968 – Sold to Butler Holdings (Havant) Ltd and towed to Northney Yacht Marina, Hayling Island for use as a clubhouse. The plan did not materialise.

1969 – Sold to Don Hickman.

1970 – Received maintenance at Husbands Shipyard, Marchwood, Southampton and was then towed to London for use as a floating pub/restaurant. Underwent several changes of ownership, but continued in use moored bow up river at St Katherine's Dock just downstream of Tower Bridge.

1975 – Moved up river and moored at Old Swan Pier, immediately above London Bridge.

1987 – Moved to become headquarters of a yacht club near Gravesend, but not developed.

1987 – In December purchased by Association de Defence des Arts Typographics (ADAT) and towed to Rouen for refit, sheltering in Dover Harbour during the tow.

1991 - Moved to the river Seine in Paris and opened by ADAT as an art gallery.

1999 – Moved to Dunkirk and opened as a conference centre.

PRINCESS ELIZABETH fitting out under the sheerlegs at the yard of Day, Summers & Co Ltd.
LAURENCE PRITCHARD - IAIN QUINN COLLECTION

PRINCESS ELIZABETH approaches Sandown in her original condition, still with her short funnel.
H A ALLEN COLLECTION

PRINCESS ELIZABETH arrives at the Southampton pontoon with a well filled car deck, one owner has taken special precautions against sea spray reaching his car.
RED FUNNEL ARCHIVES

Now fitted with a taller funnel and cowl top, PRINCESS ELIZABETH arrives at Southampton on 23 August 1937.
IAIN QUINN COLLECTION

Showing her with a varnished finish to the front of her bridge, PRINCESS ELIZABETH transports another load of cars.
KEITH ABRAHAM

Taken from BALMORAL this view shows PRINCESS ELIZABETH on the inside berth at Ryde. Beyond, at the railway berth, one of the Denny-built motor vessels waits to return to Portsmouth.
ALAN BROWN – KEITH ADAMS COLLECTION

PRINCESS ELIZABETH waits for her next sailing 19 August 1956. BOURNEMOUTH QUEEN is in the background.
IVAN BOVEY

The small steam tug BANTAM lies alongside PRINCESS ELIZABETH at Southampton Royal Pier on 9 November 1957. In the background is the already withdrawn BOURNEMOUTH QUEEN.
IVAN BOVEY

TS MV MEDINA (III)

Built:	1931	*Tonnage:*	347 gross, 157 net. 339.47 gross as built	
Withdrawn:	1962	*Dimensions: feet*	143' x 28' 1"	
Scrapped:	1998	*metres*	43.59m x 8.56m	
		Builders:	John I Thornycroft & Co Ltd, Woolston, Southampton. Yard No. 1105.	
		Machinery:	Originally Twin screw, diesel total 456 bhp. by Gardner & Sons, Manchester. New engines 1953 by Crossley Bros Ltd, Manchester, total 640 bhp.	

The subject of this paragraph broke with tradition; gone were the paddle wheels and steam reciprocating engine, and present was a rather stubby vessel propelled by diesel engines. *Medina* (III) was the first motor passenger vessel on any of the three Solent passages, although the Southern Railway had introduced diesel motor car ferries on their Portsmouth to Fishbourne route in 1927.

Inspection of the ship, however, showed that she had the usual accommodation of the passage steamer, but the 'other way round'. Her first class accommodation was forward, and an open deck aft carried the cars. With the dining saloon below the main deck, the lounge had the usual walkway round the sides, enclosed by plate glass windows. A small bar was fitted right forward, with a small cabin below, forward of the dining saloon.

With short funnel and mast with little rake, a bridge fitted with a wheelhouse, and a cruiser stern, she was shorter than her consorts and, with open deck aft, gave the impression of stumpiness and excessive freeboard forward.

Launched on 6 January 1931, by Mrs J D R Atkey, wife of a director, she made her first run to Cowes on 12 February, having arrived at Southampton Royal Pier from her builders the day before. On Monday 16 February, she made an official cruise with a trial run, and luncheon on-board.

From press reports it would seem that she made 'show the flag' visits to some of the local piers, including Bournemouth. However, she proved unsuitable for pier and tender work, although designed as a general-purpose vessel, owing to her large flare at the bows, and was consequently restricted to the Southampton to Cowes passage where pontoons were in use. Nonetheless she did make a few visits to Ryde as a relief ship immediately after the war, when wind and tidal conditions were suitable. She also called at Ryde on 5 July 1959 when rostered as standby boat, a number of parties had booked for Ryde instead of Cowes, and conditions being suitable, *Medina* made her last call there.

Apparently *Medina* was designed primarily with winter service in mind, and Thornycroft's, building their second passenger ship for the company, did not give sufficient consideration to her possible use for tender and excursion work - in point of fact neither did the owners!

During the 1932 season, *Medina* made a series of Friday evening dance cruises from Southampton, and she took part in the non-landing cruises in the post-war years around the docks, and to meet the 'Queens' and other large liners. On 20 July 1935, the French liner *Normandie* was opened to the public when anchored off Castle Point, and trips were run from Southampton, and *Medina* took part in these. The Royal Fleet reviews of 1935, 1937 and 1953 also saw the vessel diverted from her usual roster to take passengers to these events. *Medina* helped maintain the passage service throughout the war years, but in the post-war period she found it difficult to maintain schedule. In the spring of 1953, *Medina* was re-engined with Crossley diesels, giving her a speed of 13 knots, an improvement over the 11 knots of which she had previously been capable. The Crossley machinery evidently found favour with the engineering department as that maker's engines were subsequently used in twelve more of the company's fleet. A new pear-shaped raked funnel was also fitted to *Medina* at this time.

In the late 1950s, *Medina* went to Cosens' at Weymouth for overhaul, receiving underwater attention at Southampton. On 5 March 1962, *Medina* made her last sailings on the advent of the new car ferry *Osborne Castle*, and was sold to M H Bland & Co Ltd Gibraltar. She was towed away from the Royal Pier on 8 March by the steam tug *Hamtun*. After slipping at Husband's Shipyard, Marchwood, she left Southampton on 28 April 1962, and was renamed *Mons Abyla* for use as a passenger tender to liners calling at Gibraltar. Alterations were made to her promenade deck to enable her to go alongside the liners. At the same time the deck was extended to cover the former car deck. Her subsequent movements are as listed below:

May 1968 - Sold to the Gibraltar Government (Port Department) — name unchanged.

May 1971 - Sold to W J Havens and later to Esme Lucas, Gibraltar.

Dec 1971 – Sold to R Mills of London.

May 1972 - Sold to Marilu Intermediterranean Transport Shipping S.A., Panama, and renamed *Marilu* – in use at a yacht marina in the Old Albert Dock, London. (Some reports also refer to her renamed as *Moroccan Belle* under the ownership of Moroccan Enterprises (Ships) Ltd)

Oct 1973 - Used as a floating office at Lymington Yacht Haven (Hampshire) reverting to the name of *Medina*.

Feb 1976 - Moved to Ramsgate, Kent, for use as a floating restaurant.

1977 - Moved to Brighton Marina as a floating club house.

Oct 1982 - Towed to Newhaven scrap yard.

One would have thought the last move would have been the end of *Medina*, but in October 1983 she was reported at Rotherhithe on the Thames, and in July 1984 had opened as a floating restaurant at Canary Wharf in the West India Docks, London.

Later she appeared on the Tyne as *Island Pride* in May 1992, after sale by owners on the Medway. Work commenced to convert her into a Chinese restaurant, but was never completed and from early 1996 she was moored in a derelict condition up river from South Shields. No further work was carried out and she was sold in September 1997 to G O'Brien & Sons and broken up.

Towards the end of her life at Southampton MEDINA heads towards the Royal Pier. The removal of the cream bands leaves her hull looking rather austere. In the background are the remains of the flying boat berths at Berth 50 and Cunard's 1939 built MAURETANIA lies in the Ocean Dock.
IVAN BOVEY

PS GRACIE FIELDS

Built:	1936	*Tonnage:*	396 gross, 180 net.
War loss:	1940	*Dimensions: feet*	195' 11" x 24' 11" Loa 202' 2"
		metres	59.72m x 7.6m
		Builders:	John I Thornycroft & Co Ltd, Woolston, Southampton. Yard No. 1149.
		Machinery:	John I Thornycroft & Co Ltd, Woolston, Southampton. Paddle steamer, compound diagonal, 137 nhp.

Surprisingly, Red Funnel reverted to steam paddle propulsion for their next new ship, and introduced a change of naming policy. Miss Gracie Fields, the film and stage star, launched her ship on 8 April 1936 with the song 'Sing as we go', which became the steamer's signature tune. *Gracie Fields* ran trials on 29 May, and on 9 June guests were entertained to lunch and a six hour cruise on the new ship to the Nab Tower and St. Catherines Point. Her first revenue-earning cruise took place on the following day to witness a unique event - *Normandie* and *Queen Mary* in the Solent within a few hours of each other.

Gracie Fields was an improved *Princess Elizabeth*. A bow rudder was fitted, enabling her to manoeuvre out of Cowes quickly. A raised forecastle kept some of the spray from the cars on the fore-deck in rough weather, and a deck strake across her paddle boxes, although unsightly, gave protection when going alongside piers. She was coal-fired, and had a cowl on her large oval funnel. Her promenade deck was square at the forward end instead of curved. The dining saloon was full width on the main deck aft, with the lounge below, while below the car deck was a lounge bar. In 1938 a wheelhouse was fitted to her otherwise open bridge.

On 26 July 1936, *Gracie Fields* sailed to Brighton and embarked her sponsor, with children from an orphanage run by Miss Fields, for a cruise. Also in 1936, the steamer was at Bournemouth during the period when Miss Fields was appearing at the Bournemouth Pavilion.

Gracie Fields was a general purpose ship and during her short life performed excursion, tender and passage services admirably, and became a very popular steamer.

Gracie Fields was requisitioned at the outbreak of war in 1939, and was converted for minesweeping duties (pennant No. J.100). She became a unit of the 10th Division stationed at Dover. When the Dunkirk evacuation began, the flotilla was in the thick of it. After being employed on preliminary sweeping operations, they began lifting troops on Tuesday, 28 May, when HMS *Gracie Fields* made a successful run. The next day, however, saw the steamer meet her end. A bomb hit her, causing damage to the engine room and jamming the rudder. HMS *Pangbourne* spotted her out of control, came alongside, and took off the troops and some of the crew, leaving a skeleton crew on-board to attend the tow lines. HMS *Pangbourne* then commenced to tow the casualty, but she made a bad tow with her jammed rudder, and was taking water, so *Pangbourne* closed and took off the remaining crew, as it became clear there was no hope of saving her. She sank in the early hours of 30 May. So Red Funnel lost one of its finest ships. Her peacetime Master, Captain N R Larkin, went to war with his ship and happily survived the sinking, returning to the company to serve until his retirement on 2 January 1962.

GRACIE FIELDS at speed, taken from one of the towage fleet. RED FUNNEL ARCHIVES

The seaman hauls in the stern rope as GRACIE FIELDS leaves on an excursion. Note the extra deck strake near the top of her paddle box – unsightly but giving effective protection. IAIN QUINN COLLECTION

On 24 July 1939 GRACIE FIELDS passes QUEEN MARY at Southampton's Ocean Terminal. Both new ships at the time, only QUEEN MARY returned from war service to her country.
KEITH ABRAHAM COLLECTION

GRACIE FIELDS heads down Southampton Water on excursion duty. RED FUNNEL ARCHIVES

With coal smoke drifting from her funnel, GRACIE FIELDS heads up the Solent. H A ALLEN COLLECTION

TS MV VECTA (I)

NOTES:

Vecta and Balmoral had the same midship section, 27ft on the waterline, sponsoned-out to 30ft at main deck level plus 12" fender port and starboard to give 32ft beam overall.

1946, *Vecta* retained original diesel engines but converted to conventional rudder and twin screw via d.c. electric drive.

Built:	1938	*Tonnage:*	622 gross 362 net later 630 gross, 390 net.
Withdrawn:	1965	*Dimensions: feet*	199' 6" x 32'
Scrapped:	1996	*metres*	60.81m x 9.76m
		Builders:	John I Thornycroft & Co Ltd, Woolston, Southampton. Yard No. 1180.
		Machinery:	Originally Voith-Schneider (twin units aft) powered by twin English Electric diesels totalling 1,300 bhp.

Gracie Fields proved to be the last paddle-steamer built for Red Funnel, as their next new building was, for the late 1930s, an unusual vessel. *Vecta* was a motor ship, propelled by two Voith-Schneider units and at the time of her launching was only the second British passenger ship of any size to have this method of propulsion; the first being the Southern Railway's *Lymington* of 1938. This method of propulsion gave the ship exceptional maneuverability making her capable of turning to port or starboard without the need of a rudder, rotating in her own length, going ahead or astern without gears and of sideways movement also.

Ordered in April 1937, *Vecta* was launched on 14 July 1938. Delays in delivering machinery prevented the new ship entering service in 1938,

and it was in March 1939 when she made her maiden voyage. The speed attained on trials was 15.6 knots. Much thought and research had gone into her planning and the result was an attractive looking motor ship, with her two Voith-Schneider propellers both placed at the stern. She was designed mainly for the regular Cowes service, but was also able to take her place in the excursion fleet and to undertake tender duties. *Vecta* was far superior in size, appointment and speed to the older ships on the service. A forecastle and high bulwarks, with side openings, protected the largest car deck in the fleet, whilst below the car deck was a large lounge bar for second class passengers. The small engine room casing allowed double rows of seats in each alleyway, which led from the car deck aft to the

On 18 September 1965, her last day with Red Funnel, VECTA arrives at Southampton. Two days later she left for Cardiff and service with the White Funnel Fleet of P & A Campbell.

IVAN BOVEY

spacious full width dining saloon. The lower deck aft was given over to officers' quarters and the crew lived forward. The promenade deck was raised over and covered part of the car deck, giving added protection to vehicles from inclement weather. The first class observation saloon and bar was forward on the promenade deck, and above it was the bridge, wheelhouse, wireless room and a small bridge deck used when on tender work, or going alongside a pier at low water. Aft on the promenade deck was, for the first time, a section allocated to second class passengers with its own comfortable observation saloon. A full length foremast, with cross trees, and a stump main mast were fitted, and a particularly well-shaped funnel completed the pleasing design.

The bridge, of course, was interesting. The wheelhouse contained an engine room telegraph, for starting purposes only; two levers for operating the speed of the propulsion units ahead and astern, and a motor car type steering wheel for side thrust of the propellers. All of these being under the control of the Chief Officer, when coming alongside or leaving piers. There were docking telegraphs on the bridge wings.

Vecta had only one season before the outbreak of war in September 1939, and she proved to be a versatile ship. One unusual sailing occurred, when she operated a special visitors' day excursion to a Territorial Army Unit encamped for annual training at one of the old forts between

In June 1963 VECTA is ready to load passengers and cars for the next passage sailing to Cowes. The wooden planks used for loading vehicles from the pontoon can be clearly seen.
TONY HORN

Yarmouth and Colwell Bay, Isle of Wight. *Vecta* sailed direct to the fort's own jetty.

At Whitsun 1940, a programme of excursions was advertised to Ryde and Southsea, and *Vecta* performed these on 11, 12 and 13 May. A similar programme was issued to run from 1 June to 31 August 1940, but a sailing bill in the author's collection carries a note that these did not operate after the fall of France. *Vecta* made her way to Dover during the Dunkirk evacuation, and when crossing to Dunkirk she broke down and had to limp back to port.

The ship ran on the Cowes service with her upperworks painted grey and a concrete 'umbrella' protecting her wheelhouse. *Vecta* seems to have been cursed with engine trouble during the war years, and was laid-up at Northam for a considerable period, being described as a 'navigator's dream and an engineer's nightmare'.

The impossibility of obtaining spares from Germany caused Red Funnel to convert the ship to a diesel-electric twin screw arrangement. The stern of the ship had to be redesigned to take twin shafts, conventional propellers, rudders and steering gear, and the bridge was fitted with normal equipment. The propulsion motors were bridge controlled. Originally the Voith-Schneider units were powered directly from the diesel engines. Now the engines drove two electric generators which fed electrical power to new electric drive motors, one on each propeller shaft. In order to accommodate the electric propulsion equipment, further space was required in the engine room and this was provided by moving the forward bulkhead by two frame spaces for the generators. A recess was also made in the aft bulkhead to house the propulsion motors.

Owing to wartime priorities, it was not until February 1946 that *Vecta* eventually returned to service. Soon after the war, second class accommodation was abolished on all Red Funnel ships, and *Vecta* became a single class vessel. In 1954, a full length main mast was fitted in accordance with new regulations.

While heading for Cowes in the Thorn Channel during rough weather on 29 July 1956, *Vecta* shipped green seas onto her car deck. She returned to Southampton and later the two forward openings were plated-in on both sides. Her dining saloon was converted to a cafeteria in 1960.

Vecta tendered many liners and was frequently used for French Line ships, especially the *Liberte*. After the disposal of *Princess Elizabeth*, she became the second excursion ship until her withdrawal in September 1965. *Vecta* went to Cosens' at Weymouth for overhaul from the late 1950s, receiving underwater attention at Southampton.

Vecta made her last Red Funnel sailing to Cowes on 18 September 1965, and on 20 September sailed to Cardiff, having been bought by Townsend Car Ferries Ltd for use by their subsidiary company P & A Campbell Ltd on their Bristol Channel excursion routes. Still carrying her Red Funnel livery she entered Bristol Channel service immediately. During the ensuing winter she returned to Cosens' at Weymouth, where her car space was enclosed and decked over, rubbing band fitted and a cowl added to the funnel. She returned to Mount Stuart dry dock at Cardiff where windows for the new saloon were cut in the steelwork, paintwork completed in Campbell's livery, and she was renamed *Westward Ho*.

Between 1966 and 1971 *Westward Ho* tendered the Swedish America Line's cruise ships when they called off Clevedon in May each year on their 'Round Britain' cruise. At 17:00 on 29 April 1969, she left Cardiff for Cobh, Eire, arriving some 15 hours later. At Cobh she tendered *Orsova*, and then proceeded to Bantry Bay where she undertook similar duties during celebrations at the oil terminal. She was back in Cardiff on 8th May at 09:30 after a crossing of $16^1/_2$ hours.

Westward Ho was joined by her former fleet mate *Balmoral* in 1969, and the two ships operated together on the Campbell's so-named White Funnel services until 14 September 1971, when *Westward Ho* was withdrawn. She was laid-up at Barry and later at Hayle, Cornwall, having experienced increasing engine trouble, and was offered for sale. In October 1972 she was bought for use as a floating restaurant at Pomona Docks, Manchester, by Compass Caterers Ltd, and was renamed *North Westward Ho*.

After being at Pomona Docks, Manchester for over twelve years, she was sold and towed to Bromborough Dock on 19 March 1985. It was reported she was to be refitted for static use on the Thames and at the end of the year she was in Millwall Docks, London. Thus there were three ex-Red Funnel ships in the London area at that time, *Vecta*, *Medina* and *Princess Elizabeth*, the same numerical strength as the present operational vehicle ferry fleet between Southampton and East Cowes.

By 1991 *North Westward Ho* had been moved from the Thames to the historic Ballast Pond, Torpoint, Cornwall, her interior gutted and everything apart from the funnel and forward observation lounge removed. It was intended to convert her into a yacht clubhouse, but her rather exposed mooring proved not to be suitable and in March 1997 she was reported as having been scrapped.

In early post-war years VECTA chases UPTON down Southampton Water. RED FUNNEL ARCHIVES

In September 1952 Chief Officer P D Jones oversees the backing of a car onto VECTA, Captain Diaper looks on from the bridge wing. DON JONES

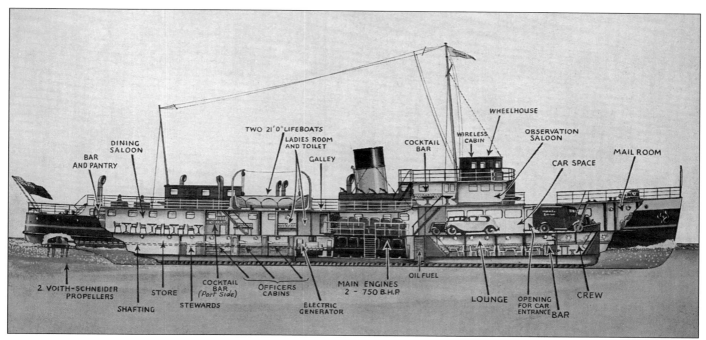

This exploded drawing was used by Red Funnel to publicise their new VECTA – note the twin Voith-Schneider propellers.
RED FUNNEL ARCHIVES

VECTA as built showing the nine openings in her car deck plating. Later the front two on both sides were filled in and replaced with portholes. H A ALLEN COLLECTION

This photograph was taken at the end of September 1965 and shows VECTA still in Red Funnel livery, sailing in the Bristol Channel for P & A Campbell. In 1966 she was altered and renamed WESTWARD HO. KEITH ABRAHAM COLLECTION

VECTA, about to depart from Fountain Pier at Cowes in the mid 1950s.
KEITH ABRAHAM

In August 1967, VECTA, now a Bristol Channel passenger vessel, has been renamed WESTWARD HO and had her car deck converted to passenger accommodation.
R D CHARNOCK

VECTA at her final resting place, photographed in August 1991. Having, spent the early 1990s here at the Ballast Pond, Torpoint waiting for conversion to a clubhouse, by early 1997 she had been scrapped.
RICHARD DANIELSON

TSS UPTON

Built:	1925	*Tonnage:*	374 gross, 127 net.
Acquired:	1946	*Dimensions: feet*	145' 1" x 32'
Withdrawn:	1950	*metres*	44.2m x 9.75m
Scrapped:	1953	*Builders:*	Cammell Laird & Co Ltd, Birkenhead. Yard No. 914
		Machinery:	Cammell Laird & Co Ltd, Birkenhead. Twin screw, triple expansion steam reciprocating. 1,300 ihp.

Immediately after the ending of World War II, Red Funnel went into the second-hand market, and purchased *Upton*. She was one of five ships built for Birkenhead Corporation between 1925 and 1933 for their ferry service to Liverpool. *Upton* was slightly smaller than her sisters, being intended for the Rock Ferry service, and took the last sailings on this route when it was abandoned on 30 June 1939. *Upton* was requisitioned by the Ministry of War Transport and used as a tender in Liverpool Bay. She was almost sold to the Galway Harbour Commissioners in 1945. However her release from war service was

delayed and she was then sold to Red Funnel, arriving at Southampton in May 1946. She was immediately overhauled and refitted, entering service in September of that year for a fortnight on the Southampton to Ryde excursion service.

The main visual alterations were the construction of a navigating bridge, the Birkenhead ferries having side cabs and a wheelhouse on the promenade deck, and the addition of a lifeboat and davits on each side of the ship. *Upton* had no space for cars and no accommodation below the main deck, but on this deck there was a lounge bar forward and a refreshment lounge aft and toilets, all surrounded by alleyways. The promenade deck was full width and extended nearly to the bows. Her speed was about 10 knots and, with her stout build, great beam, and massive belting round the hull giving her bulwarks a distinct 'tumble-home', she had difficulty in

keeping her scheduled timings.

In May 1947, *Upton* was sent to be Poole-based to operate the Bournemouth to Swanage service, but proved very unpopular with the pier authorities due to ranging alongside the stages. She was returned to Southampton at the end of June, where the ship concentrated on the Southampton to Ryde service for the remainder of her career. This service consisted of three return trips a day, but, in 1950, it was amended to two, the evening sailing being cancelled and a later return sailing given on the afternoon trip.

The summer of 1950 saw a serious outbreak of polio on the Isle of Wight, and this naturally had an adverse effect on the number of passengers carried. Being unsuitable to call at Southsea, because of her draught, *Upton* was withdrawn on 2 September 1950 when the Southampton to Ryde service was extended to Southsea. *Upton* retired to a mud berth at Northam on 14 September 1950. She was then laid-up and not used in 1951. However, she did return to steam between 21 April and 7 May 1951, when trials were carried out to test her capability for use as a tug tender. These proved unsuccessful, and *Upton* returned to Northam and moved from her mud berth to the adjacent Pollock, Brown's yard for breaking up on 3 March 1953.

Left:
UPTON approaches Ryde on 28 May 1950, her last year of operation.
IVAN BOVEY

Below:
This photograph gives UPTON the appearance of sailing at great speed, but her maximum was about 10 knots.
KEITH ABRAHAM

TSS ROBINA

Built:	1914	*Tonnage:*	306 gross, 121 net.	
Acquired:	1948	*Dimensions: feet*	159' 6" x 26' 1"	
Withdrawn:	1949	*metres*	48.62m x 7.96m	
Scrapped:	1953	*Builders:*	Ardrossan Dry Dock & Shipbuilding Co Ltd. Yard No. 259.	
		Machinery:	McKie & Baxter, Glasgow. Twin screw, triple expansion steam reciprocating.	

This steamer was purchased on 11 August 1948 and, as *Solent Queen* (I) had been withdrawn with terminal boiler trouble in the same month, it is understood that *Robina* was taken up as a temporary replacement.

We have seen that *Queen* (II) was noteworthy in bearing three names under the same ownership; *Robina* was also noteworthy as she retained her name under several owners and led a rather nomadic existence, details of which follow.

Built in 1914 for the New Morecambe Central Pier Company Ltd she operated excursions from Morecambe. During World War I, she became an auxiliary patrol vessel of Portsmouth extended defences from late 1914 until November 1918. The 1919 season saw her on charter to Blackpool Passenger Steamboat Co. Ltd for excursions from the Lancashire resort. Her owners then chartered her to W. H. Tucker & Co. Ltd for a winter service from Cardiff to Bristol, from 1 November 1919. Early in 1920, the service was abandoned due to lack of traffic, but *Robina* was retained by Tucker's, and from 13 March 1920 until after Easter, when withdrawn for overhaul, she operated a Cardiff to Weston service. She returned to service on 13 May, and remained on the Weston ferry until 25 September, after which she made one unadvertised sailing to Ilfracombe; her only call at that resort, and her last Bristol Channel passenger sailing.

She was not used in 1921, but in July 1922 her owners became Messrs W & P Cordingley and, from 14 August until 24 September, she operated a service for the Furness Railway Company from Barrow to Fleetwood, with excursions from Barrow on Sundays. The following two years were spent at Blackpool under charter in 1923 to the Blackpool Steam Shipping Co. Ltd and in 1924 to Mr H D Bickerstaffe. From 1925 to 1939 she enjoyed her most stable and successful period as a tender and excursion vessel at Belfast, her owners being William McCalla, until August 1927, then William Trevor McCalla, who traded as the Ulster Steam Tender Co. In 1937 a company with this title was incorporated, and in March 1941 the ownership of *Robina* was transferred to this concern, following the death of Mr W T McCalla. *Robina* was a Naval examination service vessel in Belfast Lough from June 1940 to May 1941 and, in 1942, was sent to the Clyde to spend the rest of the war serving as a troop tender under the management of the Caledonian Steam Packet Company.

In January 1946, she was bought by Coast Lines Ltd for excursion service from Falmouth, but it was later realised she had too deep a draught for the projected programme of cruises. Coast Lines made use of the vessel by chartering her to two of their associated companies. She served David MacBrayne Ltd from 12 May 1946, and remained

On 9 January 1949, four vessels slumber at the Royal Pier. ROBINA, at Berth 6, joined the fleet in 1948. To the left at Berth 8, QUEEN OF KENT has just arrived from the Medway to become LORNA DOONE (II). Behind her at Berth 7 is PRINCESS HELENA and to the right of ROBINA at Berth 5 is PRINCESS ELIZABETH. RICHARD DANIELSON COLLECTION

under their control until the spring of 1948, serving as secondary Oban excursion steamer in 1946, then in the autumn relieving on the West Loch Tarbert to Islay route, and in the 1947 season operated a revived but poorly patronised Gourock to Lochgoilhead service. In 1948 she was chartered by the Island Shipping Co. Ltd to run between Guernsey and Sark, commencing on 1 June 1948, but on 5 June she collided with the same company's *Herm Coast* off Sark, both vessels receiving damage, and after repairs she moved to London. She appeared at Southampton Town Quay, still in her Channel Island livery, in July, and was eventually purchased by Red Funnel. A twin screw steamer, she had finer lines than *Upton*, and was a faster ship. Again, accommodation was on the main deck only, with a lounge forward and dining saloon aft. Her promenade deck did not extend to the side forward of the bridge, and her two lifeboats restricted the space on the deck aft. Aft of the funnel there was a platform deck, probably a legacy of her tender work. *Robina* carried two masts, both rather short and, like the funnel, insufficiently raked, and with a straight stem and elliptical stern she did not present a pleasing appearance. She was a comfortable ship to travel on but, when carrying a fair number of passengers, movement around the ship was somewhat restricted.

Immediately after purchase, she was drydocked at Southampton on 17 August 1948, and undocked ten days later. It was intended to get her into traffic before the end of the season, as the last excursion bill of 1948 was headed, *Princess Elizabeth*, *Robina*, etc. She ran a trial trip on 1 September when boiler trouble developed, and nothing more was heard of her until it was announced that she would operate on the Cowes winter service from 27 September 1948, vehicle facilities being withdrawn from the 10:45 and 15:45 sailings from Southampton and the corresponding return sailings from Cowes. This was a retrograde step, and a storm of protest ensued. However, it was not until 9 November that *Robina* finally took up service, having experienced further boiler trouble. From the beginning of December she was withdrawn on Fridays, the number of car sailings being increased to five on that day, a small measure of success for the protesters.

She was withdrawn from the Cowes service at the beginning of April 1949, but returned to service at the end of the month to replace *Princess Elizabeth*, which had gone to Bournemouth, relieving *Bournemouth Queen* for about a week. During the 1949 summer her name appeared at the head of the Bournemouth sailing bills, but her name was the only appearance, as the volume of traffic did not warrant a third Southampton steamer at Bournemouth. She remained at Southampton, relieving *Upton* on Tuesdays and Fridays, and also appearing at Cowes on relief sailings. Her last sailing for Red Funnel was on 13 September 1949 when, returning from Cowes, she broke down with boiler trouble off Calshot, and was subsequently withdrawn.

In February 1950, she was slipped at Northam for inspection by prospective buyers, but nothing came of this. Before the 1951 season, preparations were made to return her to service as reserve steamer, but this plan was abandoned when the ship was already half-painted. In July of the following year she was reported to have been sold to Italian buyers from Rome to run from Genoa, but it was not until 5 August 1953 that *Robina* was moved from Northam to Southampton Docks, and was then to depart for Rotterdam under tow of the Smit's tug *Noord Holland* for scrapping.

ROBINA during her short period of about twelve months operating for Red Funnel.
RED FUNNEL ARCHIVES

TS MV NORRIS CASTLE (II)

Built:	1942	*Tonnage:*	473 gross, 302 net.
Acquired:	1947	*Dimensions: feet*	180' x 38' 1"
Withdrawn:	1962	*metres*	54.86m x 11.61m
		Builders:	Alexander Findlay & Co Ltd, Old Kilpatrick, Glasgow. Some of her parts were constructed at Motherwell before being assembled and fitted at Old Kilpatrick.
		Machinery:	Twin screw, diesel by Davey Paxman & Co Ltd, Colchester (part of Ruston & Hornsby).

This landing craft vessel was assembled and completed during World War II by A Findlay of Old Kilpatrick with frames prefabricated by Joseph Park, Northwick, as *LCT 828* (LCT Mk.4), later becoming NSCL1. Service between Poole and the Normandy beaches occupied the ship at the time of 'D' day and the subsequent period, and later she carried out experimental work in Poole Harbour.

Deciding that an ex-LCT would prove suitable to cope with the increasing vehicle traffic to the Island and possible competition, Red Funnel purchased this vessel in March 1947. The ship had to be remodelled and partly reconstructed, and this work was undertaken by Thornycroft's at their Northam yard. She emerged virtually a new ship with small, but well-appointed, passenger accommodation, carrying the name *Norris Castle*. She ran trials on 7 July 1948 and entered service on 23 July.

Her service was supplementary to the main timetable and her voyage time was often as long as an hour and a half. She could side-load vehicles at the pontoons at Southampton and Cowes, but later used her bow ramp when a buffer pontoon was provided at Southampton and a slipway at East Cowes. Her complement was 250 passengers and 30 cars. A gantry mast was fitted foreward and she carried a tripod type main mast on top of the wheelhouse. To comply with new navigation light regulations in 1954 she was fitted with a tall pole main mast, and a year or so later the tripod mast was removed.

Her main advertised service was summer only, until she took over the cargo service from *Lord Elgin* on 29 September 1952, after which she was in service all year around until her withdrawal. She began running to East Cowes in 1950 when arrangements had been made to use her ramp on the concrete slipway.

Norris Castle was occasionally used as a cargo tender in her first two years and as a cargo ship in 1948 when *Duchess of Cornwall* broke down in August while relieving *Lord Elgin*. She occasionally took on the cargo service while *Lord Elgin* was being overhauled, until taking it over

NORRIS CASTLE passes Netley Military Hospital. The photograph must have been taken in the late 1950s as the original tripod mast has been removed from the top of the wheelhouse and replaced with a pole main mast.
BERT MOODY COLLLECTION

full time in September 1952. The traditional time of departure had been 11:00, but this was brought forward to 09:00 to enable *Norris Castle* to make two return trips each day.

Until the arrival of *Carisbrooke Castle* in 1959, the cargo service had to be suspended during *Norris Castle's* overhaul. It was expected that she would be withdrawn as soon as the new ship arrived, but she survived until *Osborne Castle* was delivered in 1962. This was remarkable performance for a landing craft built solely for the wartime 'D' day operations.

During her time at Southampton she served as a car ferry on summer Saturdays, and on occasions as a passenger vessel. In 1953 a new pontoon was being installed at Cowes and *Norris Castle* remained at East Cowes acting as a floating landing stage, passengers and vehicles being unloaded over her decks to the service ship.

On Coronation fleet review day, 16 June 1953, she was the only ship sailing from Southampton to Cowes, as all other members of the fleet were engaged in excursion work. After completing three round trips, *Norris Castle* was herself advertised for an excursion from Cowes to view the evening illuminations, perhaps the only excursion sailing she ever made.

Her final sailing from East Cowes was on 16 March 1962. *Norris Castle* was then sold to Compania Maritima Santa Kynaki S.A., Panama for service around the Greek islands. She left Southampton on 27 May 1962 named *Nereis*. Later in the year she was sold to D Filipopoulos

and renamed *Aghios Dionisios*.

In 2000 she was renamed *Galina S*, owned by the National Shipping Co and registered at San Lorenzo, Honduras. The 2000/1 supplement to Lloyds Register showed the deletion of her owners and port of registry. The ship's name continued to appear in the 2008/9 register, but with no details of owner or flag. Therefore, however unlikely for such a vessel built in 1942 for the immediate and short term needs of War, it would seem just possible that she may still be in existence, somewhere.

The pierman hauls in the second bow rope as NORRIS CASTLE arrives at the Royal Pier pontoon. She is well loaded with cars which will disembark using the side doors.
RED FUNNEL
ARCHIVES

Taken early in 1955, this photograph shows NORRIS CASTLE with both pole and tripod masts. She approaches the buffer pontoon with a full load of cargo whilst her predecessor, LORD ELGIN, lies at Berth 1.
KEITH ABRAHAM

PS LORNA DOONE (II)

Built:	1916	Tonnage:	798 gross, 379 net.
Acquired:	1948	Dimensions: feet	235' 2" x 29' 1"
Withdrawn:	1952	metres	71.67m x 8.86m
Scrapped:	1952	Builders:	Ailsa Shipbuilding Co Ltd, Troon. Yard No. 298.
		Machinery:	Ailsa Shipbuilding Co Ltd, Troon.
			Paddle steamer, compound diagonal, 1,600 ihp.

LORNA DOONE shown as QUEEN OF KENT in New Medway Steam Packet Co livery. She almost joined the Red Funnel fleet in 1939, but eventually arrived at Southampton in 1949.
H A ALLEN COLLECTION

In January 1949 Red Funnel purchased two paddle steamers from the New Medway Steam Packet Co Ltd. *Queen of Kent* was first to arrive. The ship had been built during World War 1 as HMS *Atherstone*, one of a large class of minesweepers based on the design of a Bristol Channel paddle steamer. Laid up after her war service, she was purchased from the Admiralty early in 1928 and converted into a pleasure steamer by the New Medway Steam Packet Co Ltd, entering service for the summer season. She was used on cross Channel excursions to Calais, Boulogne and Dunkirk from Gravesend, Margate, Clacton and also to and from Yarmouth, Southend, Dover and Sheerness. She was withdrawn in September 1938, replaced by new motor vessels and not used in 1939.

At the outbreak of World War II *Queen of Kent* was requisitioned and again took up minesweeping duties, under pennant number J74. During the war the New Medway Steam Packet Co suffered losses to their fleet and *Queen of Kent* returned to excursion services for the 1947 and 1948 seasons.

During spring 1949 she was refitted at Thornycroft's Northam yard and renamed *Lorna Doone* (II). She was a very distinctive vessel, having widely spaced, raked funnels, one forward and one aft of the paddle boxes. The bridge was forward of the funnels, but the wheelhouse was not fully enclosed, the back being open to the

elements. Unusually, her dining saloon was on the main deck forward and her saloon aft, there being general accommodation on the lower deck both forward and aft.

Lorna Doone entered South Coast service on 10 May 1949 as the company's Bournemouth-based steamer. Captain Clarke, Red Funnel's general manager, had noted that the ship, and her sister *Solent Queen* (II), were capable of sailing cross Channel and expressed the desire to resume these excursions when the landing restrictions were lifted. Because of these plans *Lorna Doone* retained her six lifeboats and carried a radio officer during her first season. The two stern boats were removed before the 1950 season.

Lorna Doone returned to Bournemouth for the 1950 season and also commenced the 1951 sailings until recalled to Southampton in July to take the place of her sister *Solent Queen* (II) which had been seriously damaged by fire. *Lorna Doone* was the last Red Funnel steamer to be permanently based at Bournemouth.

On 28 November 1951 she was slipped at Whites' shipyard for survey and preparation work to replace a number of hull plates. The defective plates were removed, but in January 1952 the work was stopped, the old plates replaced, and the ship returned to the mud berth and was advertised for sale. She was towed away for scrapping at Dover by the tug *Brahman* on 15 March 1952.

LORNA DOONE (II) looks most impressive as she steams away from the photographer.
ALAN BROWN – KEITH ADAMS COLLECTION

LORNA DOONE's bow has a flare, ideal for the cross Channel excursions she undertook before joining Red Funnel.
GEOFFREY GRIMSHAW - H A ALLEN COLLECTION

After only three seasons at Southampton LORNA DOONE is pictured at the Dover Industries Ltd scrapyard in the Eastern Docks at Dover in 1952 where her fire-damaged sister ship SOLENT QUEEN had also been scrapped the previous year.
ALAN BROWN – KEITH ADAMS COLLECTION

LORNA DOONE under tow from Southampton to the Dover scrap yard, March 1952.   RED FUNNEL ARCHIVES

PS SOLENT QUEEN (II)

Built:	1916	*Tonnage:*	792 gross, 382 net.
Acquired:	1948	*Dimensions: feet*	234' 9" x 29' 1"
Withdrawn:	1951	*metres*	71.55m x 8.86m
Scrapped:	1951	*Builders:*	W Hamilton & Co, Port Glasgow. Yard No. 317.
		Machinery:	W Hamilton & Co, Port Glasgow.
			Paddle steamer, compound diagonal, 1,600 ihp.

The career of this steamer closely followed that of her sister, *Lorna Doone* (II), with the exception of being purchased by the New Medway Steam Packet Co Ltd in 1929 from Hughes Bolckow Shipbreaking Co Ltd, to whom she had been sold by the Admiralty in 1927. Built as HMS *Melton*, she was renamed *Queen of Thanet*.

In September 1939 she again served her country as a minesweeper, taking pennant number J30. She was very active in the Dunkirk evacuation, bringing back about 4,000 men from the beaches. Later she served as the control ship *Selsey* at the 'D' day landings in Normandy, becoming the base for directing operations at the Mulberry artificial harbour.

Queen of Thanet arrived at Southampton a week after her sister and, following refit, entered service on Whit Sunday, 5 June 1949, as *Solent Queen* (II). Her stern lifeboats had been removed and this provided an easy means of distinguishing her from *Lorna Doone* (II) in her first season. From 1950 the main difference between them was her varnished wood cladding on the bridge, compared to her sister's cream painted canvas.

Solent Queen offered day excursions from Southampton sailing to Ryde, Southsea, Shanklin and either Bournemouth, Swanage or 'Round the Island'. When the Cunard 'Queen' liners were around she would often retrace her calls from Shanklin, providing a cruise to see the liners in port at Southampton or witness their arrival or departure.

Having sailed satisfactorily during 1949, boiler trouble caused her withdrawal in July 1950. Repairs were unsatisfactory and her timekeeping was poor, resulting in her excursion programme being undertaken by the new motor vessel *Balmoral*. *Solent Queen*, a large and expensive ship to operate, spent the rest of the season relieving *Upton* on the service to Ryde or on local cruises to witness the arrival or departure of the liners at Southampton.

On 28 March 1951 she followed her sister, *Lorna Doone*, onto the slipway at Whites Shipyard for survey and repair. Significant work was required by the surveyor and repairs were progressing until a serious fire aboard on 22 June. The fire started in the aft saloon and gutted the ship aft of the engine room, while smoke, heat and water damaged the fore part. So much water was pumped into the vessel that there was a danger the slipway cradle might collapse under the extra weight. Workmen placed extra baulks of timber under the ship to support her and a hole was cut in her stern to release some of the water.

Solent Queen left the slipway on 15 July and was declared a total constructive loss. She lay at Whites' yard until leaving Southampton on 2 October 1951 under tow for Dover Industries Ltd's shipbreaking yard in the Eastern Docks at Dover.

QUEEN OF THANET in New Medway Steam Packet Co livery. Her stern lifeboats were removed before entering Red Funnel service.
H A ALLEN
COLLECTION

SOLENT QUEEN lies at Southampton. A couple of crewmen eye the photographer with unease. She only operated as a main excursion vessel in 1949 and until July 1950 when boiler trouble caused BALMORAL (II) to undertake her all-day cruises for the rest of that season.
ALAN BROWN – KEITH ADAMS COLLECTION

SOLENT QUEEN approaches Ryde. During the last part of the 1950 season she shared the Ryde service with UPTON, not an economic use of a large paddle steamer.
KEITH ABRAHAM

MV BALMORAL (II)

NOTE:
Originally Newbury
Sirron total 1,200
bhp.
New engines fitted
at Bristol, May 2003,
Grenaa Motorfabrik
(Danish) 1,600 bhp.

Built:	1949	*Tonnage:*	688 (later 735) gross, 298 net.
Withdrawn:	1969	*Dimensions: feet*	203' 6" x 32'
Remains in		*metres*	62.03m x 9.75m
service with		*Builders:*	John I Thornycroft & Co Ltd, Woolston,
Waverley			Southampton. Yard No. 4120.
Excursions Ltd.		*Machinery:*	Twin screw, diesel.

THE LAST RED FUNNEL EXCURSION SHIP.

Balmoral is now one of the great survivors of coastal passenger shipping, having reached her diamond jubilee in June 2009. She celebrated the event by sailing round the Isle of Wight from Southampton, sponsored by Red Funnel, on the exact anniversary of her launch in 1949.

However, back in 1949, with the war years still in recent memory, and Red Funnel's finances in a poor state, there had been talk of her being sold even before entering service. Thankfully, it was decided to keep her at Southampton and her luck has held ever since that time.

Balmoral was launched by Mrs C D Pinnock, wife of Red Funnel's chairman, on 27 June 1949. She was given the name of the famous paddle steamer *Balmoral*. Her predecessor was built in 1900 and, as related elsewhere, was a fast excursion steamer performing long day excursions from Southampton, including cross channel trips to Cherbourg via Bournemouth or the Isle of Wight piers. The first *Balmoral* was broken up in 1949 on the river Itchen, very close to where her successor was being built at Thornycroft's yard at Woolston.

The new ship may have carried the same name, but she was a very different vessel in every respect. She was primarily designed as a passage service ship, but able to take part in tendering duties and operating excursions as required. She was quite similar to *Vecta*, but her partly enclosed car deck was aft, instead of forward and surprisingly there was space for fewer cars. Consequently her lower deck lounge bar was aft, under the car deck. Her dining saloon was forward on the main deck, with the purser's office just outside it on the starboard side, a mail room taking the similar position on the port side. There was a small bar/cash desk at the entrance to the dining saloon, which has survived the alterations to that room over the years, although it is now used as a store.

Two observation saloons were built on the promenade deck. The forward one, under the bridge deck, contained a small bar. *Balmoral's* fitting out was to a generally high standard, in keeping with Red Funnel's normal practice. Two life boats were carried. Her original stump main mast was replaced in 1954 by a full length mast to

This photograph shows BALMORAL (II) as a brand new ship in December 1949, probably on a press trip. She looks exceptionally fine in full Red Funnel livery, including the cream stripe around the hull, sadly dispensed with in 1959, and a tiny sliver of cream paint separating the windows on the main deck from the black hull below. Her name is shown in small gold letters, later to be bolder plain black and set higher up on the hull topsides. For a few seasons at the end of the 1950s the front and sides of her bridge were scumbled (painted to look like wood grain) to resemble the varnished wood of VECTA.
RED FUNNEL
ARCHIVES

Top left:
In August 1962 BALMORAL disembarks her passengers at South Parade Pier, Southsea, after an excursion sailing round the Isle of Wight.
TONY HORN

Top right:
BALMORAL leaves South Parade Pier, returning to Sandown, Shanklin and Ventnor to pick up the passengers she left there earlier in the day. This trip could be taken as a late afternoon cruise from Southsea.
TONY HORN

Departing from Sandown Pier on 14 August 1966, BALMORAL's car deck is in use as a sundeck. In strong headwinds it provided a sheltered spot.
CYRIL PERRIER - PADDLE STEAMER PICTURE GALLERY

comply with changing navigation light regulations then coming into force. This improved her looks. Her funnel was distinctive in having a horizontal top which was similar in style to the one fitted by Thornycroft's to the luxury ocean going motor yacht *Shemara* in 1938. This style has been used in Red Funnel's marketing and was also instrumental in the *Waverley* organisation sometimes referring to *Balmoral* as a motor yacht and painting her hull white in the early years of their ownership.

As a ship intended for year-round passage service she was well designed, however for excursion work she lacked the spaciousness of her paddle predecessors. The deck saloons restricted space on the promenade deck, but the car deck provided a delightful sun trap and shelter from head winds. The small deck abaft the bridge was a good viewpoint, but some Red Funnel masters felt

passengers interrupted their view when berthing and had it closed. After *Carisbrooke Castle* entered service in 1959, a decline in restaurant service standards throughout the fleet took place when cafeterias were fitted. *Balmoral* did not escape and her silver service dining saloon became self service.

During her career *Balmoral* has had her share of berthing heavily at piers and pontoons. However on two occasions incidents were more serious. On 21 November 1961 she was in collision with the Sitmar liner *Fairsky* in Cowes Roads. *Balmoral* had moved out of Cowes to let *Medina* take the 15:45 sailing to Southampton, before going back into the pontoon to take her own 16:35 sailing. The collision occurred whilst she was waiting, her starboard lifeboat was smashed and there was a gash in the hull from the deck almost to the waterline. Fortunately there were no passengers

In her final season at Southampton the Coastal Cruising Association chartered BALMORAL on 16 June 1968. She left Southampton, called at Southsea's Clarence Pier then picked up by tender off-Littlehampton, called at Worthing, then operated an afternoon cruise to off-Peacehaven. This view shows her sailing past the derelict landing stages at Brighton's Palace Pier.
JUNE BUSHELL

aboard and she went to the repair yard the same day. The second incident took place in the same area late in the afternoon of 21 January 1964. In thick fog she ran aground off Princes Green at Cowes. Local launches took the passengers off and tug *Thorness* towed *Balmoral* back to Southampton 12 hours later. There was no hull damage, but the propellers and rudders were badly twisted. Radar was fitted a few months later in July 1964. With the modern aids available to mariners in the 21st century, it is sobering to reflect on the skills of the ships' masters when they navigated in all weathers and conditions using only their local knowledge and instinct to guide their ships and passengers safely to and fro. *Balmoral* became the main excursion ship from 1952. With the rest of the fleet, excepting *Norris Castle*, she attended the Coronation fleet review

on 15 June 1953. An unusual duty was a visit to Shoreham, on charter to the Shoreham Harbour Board, where H R H The Duke of Edinburgh boarded to open the new locks to the Aldrington basin on 20 May 1958. She returned to Sussex, chartered by the Coastal Cruising Association, on 16 June 1968, sailing to Littlehampton (embarking by tender) and Worthing with the cruise then continuing to beyond Brighton.

Concern over the deteriorating state of the local piers and Red Funnel's concentration on the car ferry and commercial traffic meant the ship's days at Southampton were numbered. There were occasional rumours about her conversion to take a greater rôle in carrying of vehicles, but nothing actually happened. The latest vehicle ferry, *Norris Castle*, was due to enter service in December 1968. *Balmoral's* last excursion was programmed for 16 September 1968. It was a day of torrential rain, there were few people about, and the sailing was cancelled. It was the end of an era, both for the ship and the local enthusiasts for whom *Balmoral* provided the only remaining opportunity to sail around 'the back of the Wight'. She was quietly withdrawn and made available for sale. No one could have foreseen how she was to survive and give pleasure sailings far away from her original home territory, roaming all around the coasts of the United Kingdom. *Balmoral* tendered the liner *Bremen* on 26 September and left the Royal Pier on 3 December 1968 for the short trip up the river Itchen to lay up at Thornycroft's Northam yard.

BALMORAL leaves the pontoon at Southampton. Behind her stern can be seen PRINCESS ELIZABETH and in the left background MEDINA and VECTA. Beyond MEDINA'S funnel, another cowl-topped Red Funnel ship is just visible.
KEITH ABRAHAM

Shown with a full length main mast at the end of the 1950s BALMORAL arrives at the Southampton pontoon. The funnel of the Royal Mail liner ANDES can be seen above the Town Quay warehouses.
BERT MOODY
COLLECTION

Once a regular scene, BALMORAL escorts QUEEN MARY up Southampton Water in 1959. The cream band on the hull looks to be broader in that season.
JUNE BUSHELL

Taken in the 1960s, after the cream band had been removed from the hull and radar fitted.
BERT MOODY
COLLECTION

THE CAMPBELL YEARS.

During the winter of 1968/69 several potential buyers came and looked at the laid-up vessel. P & A Campbell Limited was amongst them, but agreement was not reached in 1968. Campbell's returned with a charter proposal in March 1969 as a result of which *Balmoral* was slipped at Northam early in April, sailing to Cosens' at Weymouth on 16 April for survey. All was well and she arrived at Barry in the Bristol Channel on 16 May to take up duties with her old fleetmate *Vecta*, now renamed *Westward Ho*. Campbell's had operated a fleet of fine paddle steamers in the Bristol Channel for many years. The last of this fleet, *Bristol Queen*, had been withdrawn in 1967. *Balmoral* was effectively her replacement. At the time some Bristol Channel sailing enthusiasts were far from pleased with these developments. Gone were their magnificent paddlers, replaced with two second-hand Isle of Wight diesel ferries. Some have never got over the change, but for those who love the Bristol Channel as a place to sail there is still a thrill in going down the Channel to Ilfracombe and Lundy Island - without *Balmoral* it would just not be possible. The ship has built up her own band of enthusiastic followers over the years.

For her first season on the Bristol Channel a bareboat charter was agreed from 19 May to 22 September 1969 at £10,000. At the end of this period a demise charter was agreed, with Campbell's having the option to buy the ship after 10 years. In October 1979 Campbell's asked to extend the charter for 1 or 2 years. This was offered at £10,000 per year or £1,000 per month, however Campbell's then decided to take up their option to buy *Balmoral*.

In 1969 *Westward Ho* was struggling mechanically and often completed her sailings with only one engine and its generator supplying reduced power for her electric propulsion motors. *Balmoral* was reliable and, in comparison, fast. She entered service on 23 May, operating the Cardiff – Weston ferry and then made her first visit to Ilfracombe the following day from Penarth. During her first season she effectively took *Westward Ho's* sailings and the 'Ho' was relegated to dealing with those programmed for *St. Trillo*, which returned to North Wales for what turned out to be her final sailings from Llandudno and Menai Bridge. At the end of the season *Balmoral* returned to Weymouth for maintenance by Cosens. She broadly retained Red Funnel's hull and upperworks livery, but with a white funnel to which a Campbell-style cowl was fitted. Before her second Campbell season, the Paddle Steamer Preservation Society (PSPS) chartered her from Weymouth and she returned to her old haunts on 2 May 1970 calling at Swanage, Yarmouth and Shanklin cruising round the Isle of Wight.

Back on the Bristol Channel greater use was made of *Balmoral's* reliability and speed and she quickly took up the longer distance excursions and ranged all over the Bristol Channel reviving sailings to Tenby, Padstow and Clovelly. There was annual charter work in the 1970s tendering the Swedish America Line's *Kungsholm*. Most years, *Balmoral* would act as tender in the Bristol Channel and then set off overnight, following the liner, to be ready to perform again the following morning at Llandudno or Douglas in the Isle of Man.

Later she gained full P & A Campbell livery, the livery she now sails in for the *Waverley* organisation.

Among the many interesting sailings for Campbell's were the annual trips to the Isles of Scilly. *Bristol Queen* had started these as a three

Now with a white funnel, BALMORAL rolls lazily in the swell off Weston-Super-Mare. The ship acquired a quite different character while operating in the Bristol Channel. She would take campers and essential supplies from Ilfracombe to Lundy Island, where everything was unloaded into launches and transferred to the beach. Bristol Channel timetables varied each day, having to fit in with Bristol Channel tidal patterns, all quite different from the regular schedules in the Solent.
KEITH ADAMS

day excursion in springtime and *Balmoral* continued this pattern in 1971, but from 1972 they took place in October and were four day arrangements near the end of the season. These marathon excursions were advertised by the company as Mini-Cruises. The majority of participants were hardened steamer enthusiasts, but some 'ordinary' members of the public also joined for these most exhilarating of end of season finales. All who took part in those trips to the Scillies will retain very special memories of the occasions.

By the end of the 1971 season *Westward Ho's* engines were in terminal decline and she was withdrawn and sold. *Balmoral* was now the sole bearer of the Campbell flag, apart from seasons 1977 and 1978 when she was joined briefly by *Devonia*. *Devonia* was another product of Thornycroft's Woolston yard, being built as *Scillonian* (II) in 1956 for the all year service from Penzance to St Mary's.

Campbell's had become a small subsidiary of the European Ferries Group. By the end of the 1970s the parent company wished to concentrate on their cross Channel operations. It was only the charismatic and shrewd Campbell's managing director, Mr S C (Clifton) Smith-Cox, who kept his company going within the larger outfit. He ran the operation on a shoestring and unfortunately it showed. Catering on board was sometimes an embarrassment and *Balmoral* became very scruffy as only essential maintenance was being carried out. When financial deficits brought the end of Campbells sailing on their own account, Mr Smith-Cox negotiated a deal with the Landmark Trust (lessees of Lundy Island).

Balmoral would be operated by a jointly funded company, White Funnel Steamers, with Campbell's managing the ship. The arrangement was not a financial success for the Landmark Trust and that year's annual trip to the Scillies turned out to be her last sailing under traditional ownership. When her passengers left *Balmoral* on Monday 13 October 1980 at Portishead, most were unaware that it was the end of another chapter in the ship's life.

THE FLOATING PUBLIC HOUSE.

Balmoral sailed to Bristol for winter lay up as usual. The Landmark Trust had ideas of operating their own vessel to Lundy and consequently P & A Campbell put their ships *Devonia* and *Balmoral* on the sales list. *Devonia* went first in 1981, for further service with Torbay Seaways running from Torquay to the Channel Islands. *Balmoral* continued to lay idle until March 1982 when she was sold for static use as a floating pub and restaurant in Dundee. Her new owners were Craig Inns Limited. She sailed there under her own power, along the South Coast, past all her old haunts, and up the North Sea to the river Tay. She opened as 'The Inn on the Quay' but the venture was not a success and it failed after a few months. Another period of disuse followed, this time boarded up in a run down area of Dundee. There she was to remain, deteriorating, until just before Christmas 1984.

BALMORAL lies at Anderston Quay, Glasgow in January 1986. She had sailed there from Dundee, through the Pentland Firth, and would shortly be refitted to commence her new life with Waverley Excursions.
JOE McKENDRICK

THE PRESERVATION YEARS.

The *Waverley* organisation was looking for a supporting vessel to run with *Waverley*, replacing the short-lived *Prince Ivanhoe*, previously the Portsmouth based ferry *Shanklin*.

Waverley's Captain, David Neill, travelled to Dundee with Ken Blacklock, *Waverley's* Chief Engineer and enthusiast Ken Angell, who had previously worked in *Balmoral's* engine room. They examined the ship and, amazingly, after two years complete disuse started the generators and main engines. The *Waverley* threesome came away impressed and on 21 December 1984, Captain Neill reported to his fellow directors, recommending an offer be made to purchase *Balmoral*. At 35 years of age the ship's next, most exciting, era was about to begin.

The sale was agreed and *Balmoral* sailed from Dundee around the north of Scotland to Clydedock Engineering at Greenock to be significantly rebuilt. A new dining saloon and galley were built on the car deck, the previous dining saloon becoming a passenger lounge with a small bar forward on the port side. At the same time a new, larger wheel house was fitted. Her hull was painted white and with a yellow funnel she ran trials and set off for Bristol, her new home port, where she arrived on 12 April 1986. In the early hours of 11 April 1986, passing the Isle of Man en route for Bristol, she completed her first circumnavigation of the British Isles - a feat never

contemplated when she began working the Cowes passage service in 1949.

Balmoral then entered public service with a trip to Ilfracombe the following day and an unusual sailing from Gloucester down the ship canal the next weekend. At this time most of the money had been spent on the refurbishment of the ship's public areas, in the engine room a blue haze of diesel fumes still drifted above the reactivated Sirron diesels. The ship's engineers set about putting right years of accumulated neglect and gradually the polished metalwork returned and the blue haze disappeared.

This is not the place to list all the various ports *Balmoral* has visited while sailing in preservation. These details are well covered in specialist works published by the *Waverley* organisation where she is marketed as 'Britain's Classic Coastal Cruise ship'. It is sufficient here to confirm that in a normal season she will now visit the Clyde, Irish Sea, Bristol Channel, South Coast, Thames and the East Coast, providing opportunities for coastal cruising where the traditional operators gave up long ago. Mention should be made of *Balmoral* standing in at short notice for *Scillonian III* on the Penzance to St Mary's service in May 1991 and her only passenger sailing across the English Channel when she sailed from Eastbourne to Boulogne on 29 June 1996 to commemorate 40 years since P & A Campbell left the south coast. She also returned to Red Funnel territory, visiting the river Medina,

BALMORAL flies the Waverley Steam Navigation house flag from her mainmast as she revisits the Cornish port of Padstow in June 1988. This early preservation livery of a plain white hull and buff funnel was reportedly based on the colour scheme of the 1930s motor yachts built by BALMORAL's builders, the yard of John I Thornycroft & Co Ltd at Woolston, Southampton.
AGNES AND BUNTY HOSKIN

cruising to see paddle steamer *Ryde* at Island Harbour Marina on 7 June 1991 and actually visiting Newport on 6 June 1992.

Different colour schemes were experimented with in the early years, but in 1995 she returned to P & A Campbell livery. There has been a steady stream of projects to keep the vessel operating. Funding is always an issue and help has been received from the Heritage Lottery Fund. Major expenditure occurred in the winter of 2002/03 when the original, much respected, Sirron diesels were replaced. The old machinery had become difficult to maintain and *Balmoral's* future reliability rested on new machinery in the form of Danish built Grenaa engines.

Legally, *Balmoral* is now owned by Waverley Steam Navigation (WSN) who charter the ship to their operating company Waverley Excursions Limited. When first in preservation she was owned by Helseam Limited, which became Balmoral Excursions Limited in 1988. The transfer to WSN, a registered charity, was made in 1992 to help safeguard her future. In December 2002, *Balmoral* joined *Waverley*, by being listed in the National Register of Historic Ships.

Calshot – Hitching a ride.

For many years the RAF had a fairly large camp at Calshot and operated both flying boats and Air Sea Rescue launches from the Spit.

It was a regular practice for the Red Funnel Cowes to Southampton ferries to pick up and drop off RAF men off the end of Calshot Spit just up Southampton Water from the lightship.

The launch would come out from the RAF camp as the ferry approached, the ferry would momentarily stop and the airman would either climb up onto the ferry if he was going home to Cowes or alternatively clamber down onto the RAF launch if he was going back to camp.

In those days especially during the war years the passage service was very limited and the Calshot Spit light vessel was continuously manned – I remember the crew on the light vessel always came out and gave the Red Funnel boat a cheery wave.

The rescue launches at Calshot were locally named the 'Hants and Dorset' class boats. This was because they were tall ungainly looking craft and were said to resemble a double decker bus! Hence Hants and Dorset after the local bus operator.

Carrying cars on VECTA and MEDINA.

After the Second World War, I worked at High Wycombe for a few years and travelled via Cowes - Southampton. The passage service was maintained mainly by VECTA and MEDINA and from the floating pontoon at Cowes cars were loaded onto the ship through side gates in the ships' bulwarks. Once the vehicles were aboard, it was quite a performance with each car being skilfully manoeuvred into position to maximise the load. Jacks and skids were carried on the steamers to enable cars to be squeezed into tight spaces.

One of the regular users was the famous boat designer Uffa Fox. He had a great big old Humber car with a big angle iron frame bolted to it so he could carry boats up side down on the roof.

Now Uffa might have been a brilliant yacht designer but he knew his parking was not quite so good! The crew all rubbed their hands with glee when he arrived. The drill was he drove onto the pontoon, abandoned his car and strode off onto the boat, but he always gave one of the crew a pound note to load and unload the Humber for him. That was a pretty good tip in those days.

– by Ray Perkins

BALMORAL has regularly visited the Irish Sea and North Wales areas each spring. Returning from her cruise from Douglas, Isle of Man to the Calf of Man on 28 May 2007, BALMORAL is seen at Port St Mary, where she called to retrieve some of her mainland passengers who had gone ashore at Douglas for a steam train trip.
RICHARD DANIELSON

On 9 July 2006 in unseasonably boisterous weather, BALMORAL rounds Onchan Head, Isle of Man en route from Garlieston to Douglas, the Island's capital. RICHARD DANIELSON

BALMORAL runs alongside her fleetmate, paddle steamer WAVERLEY, on 26 May 2004 off Penarth. These two ships now provide the only opportunity for long day cruises around the coast of the United Kingdom. Both vessels are listed in the National Register of Historic Ships. They deserve every support in keeping alive a lengthy tradition of coastal cruising. CHRIS JONES

MV CARISBROOKE CASTLE

NOTE:
All 'Castle class' had a moulded breadth of 40 ft, i.e. 42 ft over the fenders. As built all had the same length and breadth however *Carisbrooke Castle* was 1ft less in depth to main deck and with a draft of 6 ft compared to 7 ft for the other three vessels. All four vessels had the same installed power of 2 x 900 bhp.

Opposite middle right:
CARISBROOKE
CASTLE *sailing in Italian waters as CITTA DI META, arriving at Capri from Sorrento, 24 September 1985.*
NORMAN BIRD

Opposite middle left:
Early in her career, before being fitted with radar, CARISBROOKE CASTLE calls at East Cowes. Passengers wait to board over the vehicle ramp. On the western bank of the river Medina can be seen one of the Princess flying boats, G ALUN, built by Saunders-Roe. At the time one of the largest aeroplanes in existence, two were also mothballed at Calshot Spit; all three were broken up without ever operating commercially. G ALUN, the only one to fly, was moved to East Cowes in May 1966 to clear the Cowes site for the Sea Speed hovercraft service.
KEITH ABRAHAM

Built:	1959	*Tonnage:*	672 gross, 246 net.
Withdrawn:	1974	*Dimensions: feet*	191' 2" x 42'
Scrapped:	2007	*metres*	58.26m x 12.85m
		Builders:	John I Thornycroft & Co Ltd, Woolston, Southampton. Yard No. 4183.
		Machinery:	Twin screw, diesel. Crossley Bros, Manchester, total 1,800 bhp.

The first of the 'Castle class' ships, named *Carisbrooke Castle,* took Red Funnel into a new era of profitability. Only a few years previously the last of the second-hand war replacement vessels had been disposed of. Now there was a purpose-built passenger/vehicle ferry on the Southampton - Cowes service. She was launched at Woolston on 27 November 1958 by Lady Hobart, wife of one of the directors. After sea trials, *Carisbrooke Castle* made her first revenue earning voyage to East Cowes on 23 May 1959.

Capable of carrying 45 cars (or less cars and a few lorries) the main deck, except for crew accommodation at the stern, was left free for vehicles. An articulated ramp was provided at the bow for loading and unloading. In order to help manoeuvring and stowage of vehicles on board, a 13 foot diameter turntable was installed on the car deck. For use alongside pontoons, the ship was fitted with sliding doors for access to the covered part of the car deck, with hinged bulwark doors forward for larger vehicles.

On the promenade deck were the public rooms, the buffet lounge being the full width of the ship, with large windows on three sides. Abaft this saloon there were enclosed alleyways both sides, passing the saloon bar, purser's office and toilets, eventually leading to a small open deck aft. In common with many vessels of that time there was no view ahead from the open passenger deck.

During her trials she reached a speed of 14.7 knots and there was pleasure at how the hull design produced very little water turbulence. The arrival of *Osborne Castle* brought an extending of *Carisbrooke Castle's* boat deck to the stern, so that both ships looked similar. The obvious distinguishing feature was the Thornycroft patented funnel top used on *Carisbrooke Castle,* but not repeated on her later sisters. Radar was fitted early in 1962.

There was a serious fire aboard in the early hours of 2 October 1971. Repairs began immediately, but it upset the overhaul programme for the whole fleet during that winter.

Plans to dispose of *Carisbrooke Castle* were wisely delayed until *Netley Castle* had been accepted and settled into service. She was effectively spare ship during summer 1974 and

sailed occasionally during *Netley Castle's* teething problems. Her last Red Funnel sailing took place on 27 August 1974.

She was sold in September and sailed on the 16th for Naples under her new name of *Citta di Meta.* Her new owners were Societa Partenopea di Navigazione (SPAN) and her sailings were from Naples to the Isle of Ischia. At the end of 1975 this operator was succeeded by Campania Regionale Marittima SpA (Caremar), a state/regional company which took over many of SPAN's ships. During this period *Citta di Meta* operated from Pozzuoli and Naples to Ischia but, by 1980 she sailed mainly from Pozzuoli to Ischia calling at the island of Procida. However, around 1982/3 she was transferred to Capri for the rest of her Caremar career, operating the service to Sorrento.

In the winter of 1986/87 she was sold to a private company, Maregiglio Societa di Navigazione, and renamed *Giglio Espresso 11*, and again by 1992 to become *Giglioespresso Secondo.* She was based at the island of Giglio and sailed to Porto S. Stefano on the mainland. Under the ownership of Maregiglio she underwent several alterations, including a narrow, open, viewing deck fitted immediately forward of the main saloon. During 1994 the ship was re-engined with Caterpiller diesels. In 2001 *Giglioespresso Secondo* was sold to state-owned Trasporti Regionali Marittimi (Tremar) to sail between Palau in the north of Sardinia to the island of La Maddalena. This was a short 20 minute crossing and her saloon accommodation was stripped to bare necessities. In 2004 she was reported to be in a scruffy condition and about this time Tremar was taken over by Enermar and *Carisbrooke Castle* entered service for her fifth and final Italian owner. It is not known when she was actually withdrawn from service, but she was reported sold to Turkish shipbreakers in 2007, arriving at Aliaga for demolition on 21 September 2007 after over 30 years service in Italy, following 15 years at Southampton.

CARISBROOKE CASTLE lies at Southampton pontoon on 24 February 1974 at the start of her last year in service with Red Funnel. The photograph clearly shows the design of her Thornycroft patent funnel.
KEITH ADAMS

Caption - see opposite

Caption - see opposite

CARISBROOKE CASTLE, before her boat deck was extended to the stern, passes the inward bound UNITED STATES. The American liner entered service in 1952 and was decommissioned in 1969. She was exceptionally fast, having been designed with a military rôle also in mind, and was the last Atlantic liner to hold the coveted Blue Riband. Red Funnel did a good trade in running excursions from the local resorts to see the liners on their way in and out of Southampton.
R D CHARNOCK

MV OSBORNE CASTLE

Built:	1962	*Tonnage:*	736 gross, 252 net.
Withdrawn:	1978	*Dimensions: feet*	191' 2" x 42'
Remains in		*metres*	58.26m x 12.83m
service in		*Builders:*	John I Thornycroft & Co Ltd, Woolston,
Canada			Southampton. Yard No. 4196.
		Machinery:	Twin screw, diesel. Crossley Bros, Manchester, total 1,800 bhp.

OSBORNE CASTLE pictured off the Town Quay, Southampton. During her time with Red Funnel she was the only member of the 'Castle' class not to have any significant structural alterations. However she ended up in Canada, the last of the class in operation and the one looking most different from the original design.
RED FUNNEL
ARCHIVES

The second of the new generation of ships was launched by Lady Ashburton on 23 November 1961. There were some detailed improvements over *Carisbrooke Castle*. The boat deck was extended right to the stern, thus giving greater open passenger space. This enabled the saloon accommodation to be improved, with toilets in a separate position further aft. After *Carisbrooke Castle* had her boat deck extended, the best way of recognising the two ships was by the funnel. The earlier vessel had a Thornycroft patented designed fluted top, but *Osborne Castle* was fitted with a slim oval funnel with a dome top.

Planned to enter service on 19 March 1962 she stood in for *Balmoral*, due to a breakdown, on the 14:15 service to Cowes on 16 March.

Osborne Castle's life at Southampton was generally unexciting, but she found herself pressed into excursion work on 31 October 1967 for the departure of the famous three-funnelled *Queen Mary*. She joined her fleetmates *Gatcombe* (I) and *Balmoral* for a public cruise escorting the famous liner down Southampton Water for the last time. She had also been out, with *Balmoral* and

Calshot (II), to meet *Queen Mary* on her final arrival.

In late May 1976 *Osborne Castle* was withdrawn from frontline service after her sisters *Cowes Castle* and *Norris Castle* returned from conversion to drive-through vessels. Together with *Netley Castle*, the newly converted ships were able to provide increased carrying capacity due to the quicker turn rounds. *Osborne Castle* remained at the Town Quay as reserve ship during the summer and moved to a mud berth at Northam for the winter. At this time consideration was given to converting her to drive-through operation, but the other three vessels were coping well enough with the traffic on offer.

However, while these decisions were being concluded, the Isle of Wight tourist authorities expressed concern over the capacity of routes to the Island. So she was reactivated in summer 1977 and operated unadvertised extra sailings on Fridays, Saturdays, Sundays and Mondays direct to East Cowes between June and early September. The Silver Jubilee Fleet Review took place on 28 June and *Osborne Castle* made some sailings to view the fleet prior to and on the evening of Review Day.

The decision was taken to sell her with availability from 3 September. Initially there was interest from Greece and British Rail considered her as a replacement for their former Lymington – Yarmouth ferry *Farringford*, then operating on the river Humber between Hull and New Holland. Eventually, *Osborne Castle* was sold in spring 1978 to a Canadian firm and renamed *Le Gobelet d'Argent* for service in the Gulf of St Lawrence. She was subsequently converted to drive-through operation. She was renamed *Le Maxim* in 1989 and *Cavalier Maxim* in 1993. In 1997 she was reported as still sailing under the Canadian flag operating between Quebec and Montreal as a mini cruise liner and sporting a swimming pool. Photographs show her bow now plated-up and operating as a passenger-only vessel.

OSBORNE CASTLE is launched into the river Itchen at Thornycroft's Woolston yard on 23 November 1961. RED FUNNEL ARCHIVES

OSBORNE CASTLE proudly flying the Red Funnel houseflag.
RED FUNNEL ARCHIVES

A builder's photograph of the bridge of OSBORNE CASTLE.
RED FUNNEL ARCHIVES

The former OSBORNE CASTLE at Montreal on 2 May 1998. The image shows how the vehicle ramp has been removed and replaced with a conventional bow. MARK JONES

MV COWES CASTLE

Built:	1965	*Tonnage:*	786 (later 912) gross, 287 (later 385) net.
Rebuilt:	1975	*Dimensions: feet*	191' 2" (later 221') x 42'
Withdrawn:	1994	*metres*	58.22m (later 67.36m) x 12.64m (later 12.82m)
Scrapped:	2008	*Builders:*	John I Thornycroft & Co Ltd, Woolston, Southampton. Yard No. 4209.
		Rebuilt:	Boele, Rotterdam.
		Machinery:	Twin screw, diesel. Crossley Bros, Manchester, total 1,800 bhp.

COWES CASTLE shows her manoeuvrability by swinging close to the ro-ro berth at Southampton.
RED FUNNEL ARCHIVES

Cowes Castle was launched by Lady Brabourne, daughter of Admiral of the Fleet, Earl Mountbatton of Burma, at that time Governor of the Isle of Wight. The ceremony took place at the Woolston yard on 11 October 1965. After running trials on 8 December she was accepted for service on 15 December. The bar on this ship was situated at the aft end of the main deck, thus allowing a full width, large saloon on the promenade deck. She was similar in looks to *Osborne Castle*, but had six large windows each side of the promenade deck, where her earlier sister only had three.

On occasions *Cowes Castle* performed charter sailings and, with her sisters, took the annual Cowes Fireworks cruise on the Friday of Cowes Regatta Week. She also provided cruises around the NATO fleet when they assembled at Spithead for review by HM The Queen on 16 May 1969. In her early years she also acted as venue for the Red Funnel annual general meetings. Taking over this duty from *Balmoral* she was moored at the Royal Pier for the formal meeting and afterwards a buffet was provided for the shareholders. *Cowes Castle* undertook an unusual duty on 28 November 1973 when she was chartered to attend the re opening of the Fibre Resin Co Ltd's factory at the Kingston power station site on the river Medina.

As related elsewhere it was decided to convert this ship, and her later sister *Norris Castle*, to drive-through operation.

Cowes Castle was the first to be dealt with and sailed to Bolnes, close to Rotterdam, in September 1975. Work proceeded to plan and she

COWES CASTLE leaves Southampton on 21 July 1973. Unusually, there is no sign of cars on the vehicle deck, but plenty of passengers watching the departure.
EDWIN WILMSHURST

was back in Southampton on 15 December. She re-entered service on 30 December 1975. Her bow thruster was not fitted until February 1976 and initially she sometimes berthed at Southampton with the aid of the small tug *Bonchurch*. When first fitted, the thruster unit, powered by a diesel engine, was retractable but later it was fixed in the down position. The bow ramp had been retained for East Cowes, with a new gate arrangement at the stern for loading onto the linkspan at Southampton. The side doors continued to be used at Cowes. Mezzanine decks, either side of the central engine room casing, were also fitted to enable her to carry an extra 25 to 30 cars.

The alterations provided an additional non-smoking saloon on the promenade deck. Additionally, with the removal of the funnel farther aft, the deck above the Master's cabin was opened up to passengers, giving an excellent view ahead. The ship's captains quickly mastered the new techniques of bow thrusters and berthing stern first at Southampton. The modifications enabled an efficient service to be operated by three ships and *Osborne Castle* was eventually sold in 1978.

Cowes Castle continued to serve the Isle of Wight until she was superseded by the new *Red Falcon* in 1994. She made a special farewell cruise to Cowes and back on 18 March, but actually finished with the 16:30 from East Cowes on Monday 21 March. She was then sold to Jadrolinija and sailed to Croatia on 26 March for further service around the Islands under her new name *Nehaj*. She remained in the same ownership, with the same name, until laid-up in 2008 and reported to be sold for scrap.

COWES CASTLE shows the improvement in looks a red line makes to hull. The addition was made in 1985, at the same time the topsides became magnolia.　　RED FUNNEL ARCHIVES

This rare view shows the extensive work to convert COWES CASTLE into a drive-through vessel at Bolnes in 1975. The new hull insert has been placed in position in the floating dock and her funnel lies on the quay.　　DON JONES COLLECTION

The bow thruster of COWES CASTLE can be seen in action as she turns off East Cowes to return to the mainland. The red hull appeared on the ferries in 1990, after the appointment of an advertising consultancy advised on signage and developing a new 'house style'.　　RED FUNNEL ARCHIVES

MV NORRIS CASTLE (III)

Built:	1968	Tonnage:	734 (later 922) gross, 250 (later 252) net.
Rebuilt:	1976	Dimensions: feet	191' 3" (later 221' 2") x 42'
Withdrawn:	1994	metres	58.29m (later 67.41m) x 12.83m
Scrapped:	2008	Builders:	Vosper Thornycroft , Woolston, Southampton. Yard No. 4226.
		Rebuilt:	Boele, Rotterdam.
		Machinery:	Twin screw, diesel. Crossley Bros, Manchester. Total power 1,800 bhp.

NORRIS CASTLE shortly after launching on 8 August 1968. She was the last Red Funnel vessel to be built at the Woolston yard.
RED FUNNEL ARCHIVES

NORRIS CASTLE passes the floating crane and heads for the Southampton terminal on 28 March 1980. She portrays the livery both she and her sister first carried after they became drive-through ships, until the changes shown on page 145.
EDWIN WILMSHURST

The fourth 'Castle class' ferry was ordered in October 1967. She was to be the last of her class and the last vessel built for Red Funnel at the former yard of John I Thornycroft at Woolston. Thornycroft's had merged with Vosper's in 1966 and the combined business was now known as Vosper Thornycroft. Third vessel to carry the name, *Norris Castle* had reduced passenger capacity in order to almost double the weight-carrying capacity for commercial vehicles.

Norris Castle was launched by Mrs R W B Lacon, owner of Norris Castle at East Cowes, on 8 August 1968. The ship was handed over and arrived at the Royal Pier on 6 December 1968. A demonstration trip was made on 10 December when Mrs Lacon presented, and unveiled, an oil painting of her home in the passenger lounge. Embarrassingly a steering fault developed during the cruise and tug *Dunnose* had to be summoned to assist the new ship back to Southampton.

However matters were soon righted and she entered service on 19 December, primarily on direct sailings to East Cowes with heavy vehicles although she did take her turn on the other rosters. On 3 January 1976 she followed her sister to Rotterdam for conversion to a drive-through ship. After surgery and modification she was back at Southampton on 16 March 1976, looking quite different. Her passenger certificate increased from 500 to 900 and she was now much closer to *Cowes Castle* in appearance than before the alterations. However, her mast was placed

forward of the funnel after her rebuilding, whereas *Cowes Castle's* remained abaft her funnel. *Norris Castle* re-entered service on 1 April.

Before the alterations, foot passengers were embarked through sliding doors onto the car deck aft and made their way up the companionway to the passenger accommodation. Afterwards, a raised covered way was constructed at all three terminals so that foot passengers could embark directly into the foyer on all three ships. This is similar to the system presently operating with the 'Raptor' ferries as this is written in summer 2010. On the arrival of *Red Osprey* in autumn 1994, *Norris Castle* was surplus to requirements. She made an official farewell cruise on 20 October 1994 with Mrs Lacon, who had launched her in 1968, as special guest of honour. A band was aboard, commemorative certificates issued, *Norris Castle* mugs were on sale and a special cake was cut. She made her final public crossings to Cowes at 08:00 from Southampton the following day, returning from Cowes at 09:30. The oil painting of *Norris Castle* donated by Mrs Lacon at the ship's launch was taken off the vessel and returned to her.

On 27 October *Norris Castle*, renamed *Lovrjenac*, set off on her delivery journey, following her sister to Croatia, under the new ownership of Jadrolinija. Like *Cowes Castle*, she remained in the same ownership and with the same name until laid-up in 2008. She is reported as having been sold for scrap, but definite confirmation of this is awaited.

NORRIS CASTLE as originally built. She was easy to distinguish from her earlier sisters as her accommodation was smaller leaving a larger vehicle deck for commercial traffic. This photograph was probably taken during Cowes Week as she has flags flying from the mainmast and a Trinity House vessel is at anchor in the background. RED FUNNEL ARCHIVES

NORRIS CASTLE in post-1983 condition, showing the extended bow ramp fitted to meet the new arrangements at East Cowes in that year. RED FUNNEL ARCHIVES

A Cowes Week scene from the Esplanade at Cowes. NORRIS CASTLE is about to pass HMY BRITANNIA, which has the Standard of Prince Philip Duke of Edinburgh flying from her main mast. HMY BRITANNIA entered service in 1954 and was decommissioned in December 1997, she is now berthed at Edinburgh's port of Leith and open to the public. RED FUNNEL ARCHIVES

MV NETLEY CASTLE

Built:	1974	Tonnage:	1,183 gross, 567 net.
Withdrawn:	1996	Dimensions: feet	242' 2" x 49' 9"
Still in		metres	73.81m x 15.16m
service with		Builders:	Ryton Marine, Wallsend-on-Tyne. Yard No. 531
Jadrolinija		Machinery:	Diesel Caterpillar Tractor Co Ltd. 4 x 500 bhp. Driving 4 in no. Aquamaster rudder propeller units

NOTE:
Breadth of *Netley Castle* was increased when the 'west' side was sponsoned-out to increase the car capacity in 1980.

From *Medina* (III) up to *Norris Castle* (III) all the passenger vessels built for Red Funnel came from Thornycroft's shipyard at Woolston, Southampton. However by the 1970s the Woolston yard was concentrating on warship construction and several other ship builders were asked to tender for the building of the new ship that was to become *Netley Castle*. Out of the 14 British and 13 foreign yards who were asked if they were interested in quoting, the final choice came down to Ryton Marine (Ryton's) at Wallsend on Tyne and Bolson's at Poole in Dorset. There was £250,000 difference in the tenders under consideration, but Ryton's had never built a vessel of this type before. The Red Funnel chairman visited the yard and was impressed with the facilities and the people he met. The price differential was too great to ignore and the order was placed with Ryton's in January 1972.

Although continuing the 'Castle' nomenclature, the new ship was a very different vessel from the previous four and cannot be regarded as a member of the 'Castle class'.

Netley Castle was to be a double-ended ship capable of carrying 1,000 passengers and 80 cars. A load of 200 tons was to be within her capability and individual lorries of up to 44 tons would be carried. On each side of the vehicle deck there were casings containing passenger entrances and accommodation. These casings supported a saloon deck over the full width of the vessel.

Portable car decks were fitted on the inboard side of the casings.

An unusual feature was the placing of a bridge at each end of the vessel. Both bridges had full access to propulsion and steerage consoles.

The launch was expected in May 1973, but this was soon put back to June. Subsequently, Ryton's proposed a launch of 31 July with handover on 15 August. Late in June it was clear there would be further delay and Ryton's admitted to cash flow problems and asked for a further payment on account. This was granted, the Red Funnel board being prepared to help, up to the value of the vessel at this stage. Unfortunately matters deteriorated and Mr W G Mackey of Whinney Murray was appointed receiver and manager of Ryton Marine on 3 October 1973.

Discussions with Mr Mackey took place immediately. It was agreed that the yard would complete the ferry and Red Funnel would pay instalments as the work progressed. A Red Funnel team, under the leadership of Captain Bowden, was assisting at Wallsend. It was hoped *Netley Castle* would be launched on 23 November, with completion within a month. Provisional arrangements were made for a tug to accompany her from the Tyne to Southampton.

This date was met and the chairman reported that his wife launched the vessel, followed by a modest reception in the works canteen. He had offered thanks for the high quality of the work carried out under very difficult circumstances at Ryton's. It was then hoped for completion at the end of January 1974. Trials were attempted on 4 February, but stopped by problems with the hydraulic steering system. Acceptance was delayed, *Calshot* (II) was sent for and she towed *Netley Castle* to Southampton arriving 22 February. Further work was carried out and after sea trials she was finally accepted on 17 May 1974. Berthing trials took place at East Cowes on 30 May.

Netley Castle entered passenger service on 24 June 1974. Until the arrival of Sealink's new 'Saint class' ferries on their Fishbourne service in 1983, she was the largest ship on any service to the Isle of Wight. Unusually, instead of a bow and stern she had a Cowes and Southampton 'end' with corresponding east and west sides.

NETLEY CASTLE waits to be launched from the yard of Ryton Marine at Wallsend-on-Tyne, 23 November 1973.
RED FUNNEL ARCHIVES

The saloon lights welcome night time passengers to NETLEY CASTLE.
RED FUNNEL ARCHIVES

Bottom left:
NETLEY CASTLE
leaves East Cowes,
about to be followed
by SHEARWATER 5.
The canting rope is
still attached to the
hydrofoil, the normal
practice was to berth
bow up the river
Medina on arrival
from Southampton and
then swing with the
aid of the rope before
returning to the
mainland. The RED
JETS now turn in the
river before berthing,
their twin waterjets
being more
maneuverable than the
single propeller of the
RHS70 hydrofoil.
RED FUNNEL
ARCHIVES

SIS, ex-NETLEY
CASTLE, at
Southampton on 23
January 1997 waiting
to sail for Croatia.
She sailed at 08:30
the following morning.
DON JONES

In 1976 the ship's Southampton end had its ramp removed by Cosens, and a replacement gateway fitted to work with the new linkspan at Southampton. This produced an odd look sailing to the mainland when she appeared to be sailing stern first. In 1980 additional space for 16/17 cars was created by removing the passenger accommodation on the west side, sponsoning-out the hull above main deck level and installing an additional mezzanine deck.

Netley Castle's appearance was improved when her funnel colours were changed in 1980 from the original cream with black top to red with black top. The ship experienced occasional problems with her control systems and a bout of troubles in May and June 1982 came to the board's attention. It was agreed that a fundamental review of the systems would be undertaken. This review was wide ranging and included the radical possibility of modifying the vessel to be single ended. Eventually technical changes were made to the steering system and subsequent trials were satisfactory.

When *Red Falcon* and *Red Osprey* entered service in 1994 it was intended that *Netley Castle* would have a major refit to run with them. The work was planned for winter 1994/95, but the subsequent ordering of *Red Eagle* caused its cancellation. *Netley Castle* began the 1996 summer three ship roster on 23 March 1996, until *Red Eagle* arrived and took her place.

Netley Castle gave a farewell cruise on 26 April 1996. Jadrolinija were keen to acquire her for use alongside *Cowes Castle* and *Norris Castle* in Croatia, but funding was an issue for them.

She had another spell in service on 31 July and 1 August replacing the failed *Red Osprey*. However, her passenger certificate had expired and she was limited to 12 passengers, cars being loaded on board and the drivers having to sail by *Red Jet* to pick up their vehicles at the destination. However, eventually agreement was reached with Jadrolinija and she sailed for the Adriatic in thick fog on 24 January 1997, calling at Gibraltar on 2 February, under her new name *Sis*. At the time of writing in Spring 2010, *Sis* is still in service and operating on local services from the City of Zadar.

MV BERGEN CASTLE

Built:	1976	*Tonnage:*	1,220 gross, 411 net.
Acquired:	2003	*Dimensions:*	66.02m x 12.55m
Withdrawn:	2005	*Builders:*	Loland Verft AS, Norway. Yard No. 42.
		Machinery:	2 variable pitch propellers (one fore and aft)
Still in			Single diesel engine by Bergeus, Bergen, Norway
service.			

The decision to send the 'Raptor class' ferries to Poland for rebuilding in 2003 left Red Funnel with a problem maintaining their established timetable. The solution was to purchase a temporary replacement that would stand in while each of the larger ships was absent.

Bergen Castle was built in 1976 as the *Nordhordland* of Norway's HSD (Hardanger Sunnhordlandske Dampskipsselskap). She arrived in Southampton on 11 September and was refitted in King George V dry dock. United Kingdom safety regulations required an additional watertight bulkhead to be fitted and unfortunately this divided the passenger saloon into two sections. Renamed, *Bergen Castle* was phased into service from 3 October taking her regular place in the roster from 10 October 2003. When *Red Falcon* re-entered service on 2 April 2004, *Bergen Castle* was laid-up on a stand-by basis. It was originally intended that she would stand in again when *Red Eagle* went for her rebuilding, however Red Funnel decided that the larger capacity of the two rebuilt ferries could cope on their own with a revised timetable.

Bergen Castle had two cargo decks and two passenger saloons accommodating about 250 passengers. Vehicle capacity was approximately 85 cars and 5 lorries. As is typical of Norwegian craft, the bridge was side mounted. Of greater draught than the existing ferries it was not possible to maintain the timetable at all states of the tide. The passenger accommodation was inferior to that of the 'Raptors' and her time with the company was problematical.

However, it was a sensible and brave commercial decision to provide a continuing service to customers. Withdrawn in spring 2004, *Bergen Castle* was laid-up at Berth 110, near to the container terminal, in Southampton's Western Docks until her sale was concluded on 27 October 2005. She left Southampton over the weekend of 19/20 November renamed *Stella*. Lloyds register shows her registered in North Korea, but no details of ownership are given.

Left:
BERGEN CASTLE undergoing survey and refit in the King George V dry dock at Southampton on 17 September 2003.
DON JONES

Right:
Work on the new double deck vehicle ramps at East Cowes continues as BERGEN CASTLE loads for the 12:30 departure on 14 December 2003.
DON JONES

Bottom:
BERGEN CASTLE in the river Medina, passes RED JET 3 which is preparing for the 17:30 departure from Cowes on 20 October 2003.
DON JONES

RED EAGLE arrives at dusk in Southampton after another crossing from East Cowes on 17 October 2008. RED JET 1 lies by; Red Funnel's first catamaran left the fleet in 2009 for further service in the Caspian Sea.
RICHARD DANIELSON

MV RED FALCON

Built:	1994	Tonnage:	2,881(later 3,953) gross, 864 (later 1,185) net.
Rebuilt:	2004	Dimensions:	83.54m (later 93.14m) x 17.5m.
Still in service		Builders:	Ferguson Shipbuilders Ltd, Port Glasgow. Yard No. 606.
		Rebuilt:	'Remontowa' Gdansk, Poland
		Machinery:	Stork – Wartsila 2 x 8 cylinder diesel 2,100kW 2,816bhp. Voith Schneider propulsion.

RED FALCON just prior to launching on 18 October 1993. DON JONES

Red Falcon was launched at Port Glasgow, on Monday 18 October 1993, by Mrs Kate Bradley, wife of Red Funnel's then chairman Stuart Bradley.

Trials took place at the end of January 1994 in unpleasant weather. On 26 January *Red Falcon* achieved 14.26 knots on the Skelmorlie measured mile, just over one knot greater than her design speed. The following day she was out on the Firth of Clyde in gale conditions that had forced most of the local Caledonian MacBrayne ferries to cease operating. The weather continued to be difficult and *Red Falcon* arrived at Southampton on 1 March 1994 after sheltering from poor weather and heavy seas on her journey from Port Glasgow. She had left the Clyde on 17 February, but spent two days in Belfast Lough and eight days at Milford Haven before arriving in the Solent.

In design she is similar to the earlier *Netley Castle* in that she does not turn around when sailing, however she does have a bow, the 'Southampton' end, and stern. The single funnel is on the port side just forward of the bridge wing.

Red Falcon carried out berthing trials at Cowes on 3 March 1994. A press preview trip took place on 23 March and she entered regular public service on Saturday 26 March. On her return sailing from Cowes she passed *Nahej*, ex-*Cowes Castle*, starting her delivery voyage to Croatia. The previous day she had operated an 'official'

maiden voyage at 11:15 from Southampton with a band on board and made a further relief sailing in the afternoon.

The vessel could carry 142 cars or a mix of vehicles, four separate mezzanine decks allowing for operational requirements. Foot passengers join the ship on the starboard side towards the bow. The vessel has two passenger lounges at each end of the ship, originally having smoking and non smoking areas. Due to public pressure the forward saloon, and cafeteria, were made completely non smoking in summer 1995. Facing the forward lounge is a small cafeteria. At the stern (Cowes) end on the same side is the bar area. On the opposite side is the information desk. Situated in the passageway on the starboard side is displayed the wheel of the *Cowes Castle*, and some pictures of the earlier ships in the fleet. One stairway from each lounge leads up to a spacious upper deck, where there are over 200 fixed plastic deck seats.

Red Falcon called at the Fountain Pontoon at Cowes for the first time on the evening of Friday 5 August to pick up returning passengers from the Cowes Week Firework display.

Red Falcon was the second of her class to sail for Gdansk for conversion to a double deck ferry. She left Southampton on 9 January 2004 and took *Red Osprey's* place at the Remontowa shipyard. She arrived back on 30 March and re-entered service on 2 April 2004.

RED FALCON, as built, passes Hythe Pier on her way to Southampton early on the morning of 29 March 1996. BARRY EAGLES

The arrival of the new era, RED FALCON nears the end of her lengthy delivery voyage on 1 March 1994. In Southampton Water she meets COWES CASTLE on the 10:30 service run from East Cowes. Both vessels are dressed overall to mark the occasion. DON JONES COLLECTION

Above left:
The dockyard cranes are lifting 327 tonnes of RED FALCON'S superstructure during her rebuilding at Gdansk on 22 January 2004. DON JONES COLLECTION

Above right:
Taken on 19 February 2004, RED FALCON has now been undocked. The hull insert can be seen and the new car decks are under construction. DON JONES

Left:
RED FALCON, with upper car deck well loaded, in Southampton Water, 18 October 2008. RICHARD DANIELSON

MV RED OSPREY

Built:	1994	Tonnage:	2,881(later 3,953) gross, 864(later 1,185) net.
Rebuilt:	2003	Dimensions:	83.54m (later 93.14m) x 17.5m.
Still in service		Builders:	Ferguson Shipbuilders Ltd, Port Glasgow. Yard No. 607.
		Rebuilt:	'Remontowa' Gdansk, Poland
		Machinery:	Stork – Wartsila 2 x 8 cylinder diesel 2,100 kW 2,816 bhp. Voith Schneider propulsion.

RED OSPREY on 28 April 1994, the day of her 'technical launch.'
DON JONES
COLLECTION

Red Osprey entered the waters of the Clyde at Port Glasgow on 28 April 1994. There was no ceremony, the event being known as a technical launch.

During the second day of trials on 1 September she passed the liner *Queen Elizabeth 2* which was visiting Greenock. Later that day everything was going well and in perfect weather conditions *Red Osprey* cruised round Bute, passing the village of Tighnabruaich before sailing through the famous narrows of the Kyles of Bute. Trials were completed in just two days and were regarded as very successful. Her delivery was five months ahead of schedule.

After the official handover on 22 September, *Red Osprey* left the Clyde the next day and arrived at Southampton at 08:00 on 27 September. She had sheltered in Penzance Bay for 36 hours after experiencing a heavy swell near Land's End. Familiarity trials took place over the next few days and on 7 October she crossed from Calshot to off-Cowes with *Red Falcon* so that publicity photographs could be taken.

She was pressed into service on 14 and 17 October to help clear traffic which *Norris Castle* was unable to carry. The official naming ceremony took place at Fountain Pontoon, Cowes on 19 October, when Mrs Judith Bland, wife of Red Funnel director Christopher Bland, officiated. Lunch was served to guests in a

marquee erected on the vehicle deck. A special party was brought from the mainland by *Red Jet 1*. *Red Osprey* undertook her official maiden voyage on 21 October, taking over from *Norris Castle* on the 11:00 departure from Southampton.

In 2002 the decision was taken to rebuild the three 'Raptor' ferries and *Red Osprey* was the first to set off for Poland, arriving at the Remontowa shipyard at Gdansk on 1 October 2003. She was made longer by 9.6m and higher by 2.8m, to allow the creation of a new car deck, taking approximately 70 vehicles.

Red Osprey arrived back at Southampton on 4 January 2004. After trial berthing at the modified linkspans that load the new upper deck of the ferries she re entered service on 8 January 2004. On 12 January *Bergen Castle* took a round trip on the service run, whilst *Red Osprey* operated an excursion to accompany the new Cunard liner *Queen Mary 2* at the start of her maiden voyage. Following completion of work on the upper deck linkspans, *Red Osprey* started carrying cars on her new top vehicle deck in early February 2004.

In January 2009 *Red Osprey* received a new colour scheme. In a commercial arrangement with the Swedish firm Ikea, the vessel's superstructure was painted yellow as part of the publicity for a new store opening in Southampton. She returned to Red Funnel livery early in 2010.

RED OSPREY is launched into the waters of the Clyde, 28 April 1994.
DON JONES

In glorious weather RED OSPREY passes through the Narrows of the Kyles of Bute during her trials on 1 September 1994.   DON JONES

Another heavy lifting operation takes place during the rebuilding of RED OSPREY, 12 October 2003.
DON JONES COLLECTION

A classic view of RED OSPREY taken on 3 September 2006. The marketing image on the side of the ship was inspired by the funnel of Red Funnel's BALMORAL, built in 1949.
TOM LEE

Taken from paddle steamer WAVERLEY on Sunday 20 September 2009, RED OSPREY displays a temporary livery advertising a new store in Southampton.
KEITH ADAMS

RED JET 3 sweeps behind RED OSPREY on 15 October 2008. In the background is Royal Caribbean Cruise Line's INDEPENDENCE OF THE SEAS, berthed at Southampton's City Cruise Terminal at Berth 101 in the Western Docks.
RICHARD DANIELSON

MV RED EAGLE

Built:	1996	*Tonnage:*	3,028(later 4,075) gross, 908 (later 1,222) net.
Rebuilt:	2005	*Dimensions:*	83.54m (later 93.14m) x 17.5m.
Still in		*Builders:*	Ferguson Shipbuilders Ltd, Port Glasgow.
service			Yard No. 611.
		Rebuilt:	'Remontowa' Gdansk, Poland.
		Machinery:	Stork – Wartsila 2 x 8 cylinder diesel 2,100 kW 2,816 bhp.
			Voith Schneider propulsion.

Opposite top:
The newest of the
three sister ships,
RED EAGLE was two
years old when this
photograph was taken
on 2 May 1998.
BARRY EAGLES

The contract for the third of the 'Raptor' class ferries was signed on 22 November 1994. The order was from Ferguson Shipbuilders at Port Glasgow for delivery in 1996. Similar to her earlier sisters, her superstructure was 3.6 metres longer to enable a retail facility to be added on the saloon deck. Additionally, she was to have an extra top deck executive lounge, and her bridge is about two metres higher than her sisters. The lounge has its own bar and a circular dance floor enabling private functions to be held.

Red Eagle was launched at Port Glasgow on 23 November 1995. Mrs Janice Whyte was her sponsor; wife of Red Funnel's then managing director Alistair Whyte. Later *Red Eagle* was dry docked in Yarrow's covered dock, returning to Port Glasgow in early March 1996. *Red Eagle's* engines were installed with a different number and varied stiffness of flexible mountings from those on her earlier sisters. Problems had been experienced with vibration on *Red Osprey* and *Red Falcon* and this was later corrected by modifications based on the experience with *Red Eagle*.

It was hoped that *Red Eagle* would be in service for Easter 1996, but there were delays, despite special efforts by all concerned and she did not arrive in Southampton until late on Good Friday,

5 April. She entered service on 16 April, her 'official' maiden voyage being the following day. There was a jazz band on board and a Caribbean cruise theme for the press and invited guests on 18 April.

The third ship to visit Poland for reconstruction, she left for Gdansk on 14 December 2004. A Red Funnel crew flew out on 12 March 2005 to carry out sea trials and sail her back through the Kiel Canal to Southampton. She arrived on 21 March, resuming service on the 23rd, in time for the Easter week-end.

Together with *Red Jet 4*, *Red Eagle* represented Red Funnel at the Trafalgar 200 Fleet Review by H M The Queen on 28 June 2005.

In a public relations exercise during autumn 2008, *Red Eagle* briefly became known as *Red Squirrel* for a few days to support the native species on the Isle of Wight. Press coverage was provided when mock protestors, dressed up as grey squirrels, demonstrated at the terminals.

Red Eagle, with her additional top deck accommodation, tends to be the first choice for any special sailings, such as the cruise to accompany *Queen Elizabeth 2* on her final departure from Southampton on 11 November 2008.

RED EAGLE about to
be launched at Port
Glasgow, 23
November 1995.
DON JONES (Both)

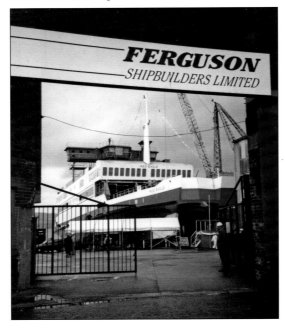

The cranes lift 380 tonnes of RED EAGLE'S superstructure during her rebuilding at Gdansk, 6 January 2005.

DON JONES *(Both)*

The unpainted hull insert can be seen and the new car decks are well advanced in this image taken on 5 February 2005. RED EAGLE returned to service at Southampton on 23 March 2005.

RED EAGLE is about to pass Cunard's transatlantic liner QUEEN MARY 2 on 12 July 2006.   RICHARD DANIELSON

TOWAGE

At the time Red Funnel was formed in 1861 the port of Southampton was undergoing tremendous expansion. The Outer and Inner docks had been constructed in the 1840s. One of the earliest vessels to enter the Inner dock in 1851 was the tug *Mary*, built for Andrew Lamb, Superintendent Engineer of P&O and later to be Red Funnel's first chairman. Regular towage in the port commenced with the formation of the Southampton Steam Towing Company in 1853, later renamed the Southampton New Steam Towing Company in 1870.

There was a depression in trade during the 1880s causing the Southampton Dock Co to enter into an arrangement with the London and South Western Railway to finance further expansion. The Red Funnel board could see that the future of trade in the port would be assured with railway support and looked for ways of involving the company more closely with the towage business. After negotiation during 1884, there was a formal purchase of the Southampton New Steam Towing Company on 1 January 1885, their vessels *Sovereign*, *Alexandra* and *Fawn* joining the fleet. Further investment was soon in evidence when the tug-tender *Albert Edward* was built in 1886 by Day, Summers & Co at Northam, followed by four twin screw tugs, *Hercules*, *Vulcan*, *Ajax* and *Neptune* (I) built by Barclay, Curle & Co at Glasgow between 1890 and 1896. For its next three tugs Red Funnel returned to Day, Summers with *Hector* arriving in 1903, *Neptune* (II) in 1910 and the larger and more powerful *Sir Bevois* (I) in 1916. After acquiring twin screw tugs since 1886, Red Funnel bought *Minas* in 1920, and then a pair of single screw vessels *Ascupart* and *Morglay* in 1922 from Bow, McLachlan & Co Paisley. The 1923 AGM referred to the sisters as having been purchased on 'very favourable terms' in view of anticipated rapid development at the port. However, the directors swiftly returned to twin screw operation and local builders, commencing their long association with John I Thornycroft & Co Ltd with the arrival of *Canute* in 1923. This was the first vessel built for Red Funnel by Thornycroft's since the unfortunate *Princess Royal* in 1906. Happily, *Canute* was a success and she was followed by a sister *Clausentum* (I) in 1926. In 1930 the tug-tender *Calshot* (I) entered service replacing *Albert Edward*. *Sir Bevois* (I) was lost during World War II and replacement came in 1946 with the acquisition of tug-tender *Paladin* (built 1913) from Clyde Shipping Co Ltd. These two vessels dealt with tendering, with help from the passage vessels when required.

After the Second World War, there had been increasing activity in the port. In 1946 Red Funnel acquired the small Dartmouth-built harbour tug *Bantam*. She was used to tow coal barges to the coal-fired passenger vessels moored at the Royal Pier and for other domestic company work. She replaced *Princess Louise*, which was very much a 'maid of all work' in the company, being able to carry a small number of passengers and to carry out light towing duties. Built in 1871, she had unfortunately been sunk near Southampton's Town Quay in 1944.

Also, development of the Esso oil refinery at Fawley continued with completion of the jetties in 1951. In the short term, the single screw tug *Beamish* was chartered with a view to purchase, but her owners were not agreeable to selling. Orders were placed with Thornycroft's for two new tugs. Delivered in 1953, *Hamtun* (I) and *Sir Bevois* (II) were the first to be oil fired and destined to be the last steam powered vessels built for the company.

Red Funnel always worked closely with Esso in providing towage and fire fighting services at the refinery jetties. Their agreement was extended in 1954 for a further ten years, with special fire fighting requirements. The latter resulted in the building of the first twin screw diesel tugs, *Atherfield* and *Culver* entering service in 1956. The end came for the little *Bantam* in 1958. She was sold after the company's last coal burning passenger ship *Bournemouth Queen* had gone for scrap at the end of the previous year.

Towards the end, *Paladin* was generally used for towage, but her 1960 replacement was *Gatcombe*, a fine purpose-built tug-tender. *Calshot* (I) was now incurring increasing costs of maintenance and the decision was made to replace her in 1964 with a ship similar to *Gatcombe* whilst retaining the old name to become *Calshot* (II). With hindsight, patterns of shipping were changing and the old order was disappearing quickly. *Gatcombe's* tug-tender design was surplus to requirements after just nine years and she was sold in 1969. *Calshot* (II) survived in the fleet until 1985 but latterly, little use was made of her extensive passenger accommodation. In 1969 *Culver* was fitted with a high tower to assist with fighting fires on large oil tankers.

For ordinary towage work *Dunnose* arrived in 1958, followed by her sisters *Thorness*, the centenary building in 1961, and *Chale* in 1965. Following the tug-tender *Calshot* (II), *Chale* was the first tug to have a fully enclosed bridge. She was also the last tug to be built for Red Funnel by Thornycroft's.

In 1966 the small tug *Bonchurch* joined the fleet. By then already 20 years old, her acquisition was specifically to compete against the increasing work being carried out in the port by the small tugs operated by Husbands Shipyard. She was sold in 1983.

The increasing size of tankers caused Red Funnel to replace the fire fighting tugs at Fawley in 1970. Richard Dunstan (Hessle) Ltd delivered *Gatcombe* (II) and *Vecta* (II). The sisters each had

CALSHOT (I)

CALSHOT (I)

CHALE

CLAUSENTUM (I)

HECTOR

SIR BEVOIS

PALADIN

VULCAN

This splendid publicity photograph shows DUNNOSE escorting QUEEN MARY in the Solent. DUNNOSE joined the fleet in 1958, followed by sisters THORNESS and CHALE, she was sold in 1980.
RED FUNNEL ARCHIVES

REDBRIDGE, delivered in 1995, became the last tug built for Red Funnel. She was part of the remaining towage fleet sold to Adsteam Marine Ltd in 2002.
RED FUNNEL ARCHIVES

Seen here in the Ocean Dock in April 1960, NEPTUNE joined the fleet in 1910. She was replaced by THORNESS in 1961 and then broken up.
PHIL FRICKER – RICHARD DANIELSON COLLECTION

a single screw with Kort nozzle and also had their superstructure and exhausts painted light green, in 1984 the exhausts were painted red with a black top. They were sold out of the fleet in 1997 and 1999 respectively.

Returning to conventional twin screw propulsion for towage work, *Clausentum* (II) was built by Richards (Shipbuilders) Ltd at Lowestoft in 1980 and remained in the fleet until sold to the port of Londonderry in 1993. In 1981 Red Funnel looked at four tugs for sale at Bantry Bay, but these were unsuitable and in 1982 a change to twin Voith propulsion units arrived in the form of second-hand acquisitions from Rotterdam. Formerly *Aziebank* and *Europabank*, they were renamed *Gurnard* and *Totland* respectively. These sisters, although not in the fleet for long, enabled valuable experience to be gained in operating 'tractor' tugs and subsequent acquisitions were to be of this type. New vessels *Hamtun* (II) that remained in the fleet until sold in 2006, and her sistership *Sir Bevois* (III) both arrived from McTay Marine Ltd in 1985 and were propelled by twin Schottel azimuthing propulsion units.

Changes within the shipping industry in the port of Southampton and increasing concern about environmental issues were of continual concern to the Red Funnel directors over many years. Traditional liner work declined in the 1960s. The port invested heavily in facilities for container ships, but this had not replaced the traditional work as quickly as hoped for. Additionally, the shipping industry had been beset by industrial unrest, the national seamen's strike in 1966 hastening the end of conventional towage work. Ironically, the strike provided some short term advantage to Red Funnel in the work of moving dead ships around the berths at Southampton.

As well as investing in *Hamtun* (II) and *Sir Bevois* (III), Red Funnel also chartered the new Swedish reverse tractor tug *John af Goteborg* from the Swedish Roda Bolaget AB. She was renamed *Portunus* and provided escort and ship handling services at Fawley. Unfortunately, the Esso contract, which Red Funnel tugs had enjoyed at Fawley for very many years, was not renewed in 1993, so the charter was terminated and *Portunus* returned to her owner.

Perhaps surprisingly, following the end of the Fawley contract, two years later in September 1995, Red Funnel took delivery of a new tug, named *Redbridge*, built for them by the Yorkshire Drydock Co Ltd, Hull. She had cost £3.5 million pounds, and was of 399 gross tons. Her main engines were by Stork-Wartsila and produced over 4,000 bhp, powering twin Voith Schneider propulsion units. *Redbridge* was often used for escorting tankers using the oil jetties at Hamble.

In March 2002, with Red Funnel now owned by international bankers J P Morgan Partners and with their tugs hived-off into a separate subsidiary, it was decided to sell the whole towage business. This enabled Red Funnel to concentrate on its main ferry, tourism and goods delivery business in the Isle of Wight. The successful purchaser, who paid AU$25million (about £10 million) for Red Funnel Towage Ltd was the Australian company, Adsteam Marine Ltd. They had developed a huge business by acquiring and consolidating many local towage operations. With world salvage and towage becoming ever more concentrated in the hands of a few big operators, Adsteam were themselves taken over by the global Danish giant Svitzerwijsmuller A/S in 2007. At the time of writing, *Redbridge* (now renamed *Svitzer Redbridge*) and *Sir Bevois* (III) were still in their vast international tug fleet.

The tug-tender CALSHOT, seen at Berth 42, Southampton docks on 22 May 2010. After being sold in 1964, CALSHOT was converted to diesel propulsion, equipped with a short funnel and operated from Galway, Eire, under the name GALWAY BAY, until bought by Southampton City Museums in 1986. Her original name was restored and recently a new taller funnel fitted; now cared for by the Tug Tender Calshot Trust Ltd it is hoped CALSHOT will be part of a new maritime museum complex planned for part of the old Trafalgar dock area at Berth 50 in the Eastern Docks.
RICHARD DANIELSON

BONCHURCH

CLAUSENTUM (II)

CULVER

HAMTUN (I)

HAMTUN (II)

CALSHOT (II)

PALADIN

VECTA (II)

COSENS & CO LTD

Cosens & Co Ltd (Cosens) was a long established operator of pleasure steamers based at Weymouth, having been incorporated in 1876 but with origins going back to 1848 and its founder Mr Joseph Cosens. As well as operating the fleet of paddle steamers, their business included major ship repair and marine engineering facilities in Weymouth Harbour and an adjacent, substantial cold storage and ice making plant. In their heyday they had also operated tugs, launches and speedboats offering trips around the bay. Their paddle steamers ranged far and wide along the South Coast often well into Red Funnel territory. For this latter reason, it came as no surprise to find that in 1946 Red Funnel were trying to acquire Cosens rather than see them sold to clients of London merchant bankers, the well known Charterhouse Finance Corporation Ltd. The fear was that if Charterhouse were successful, their clients might no longer be cooperative with Red Funnel at the various resorts both companies had previously served reasonably harmoniously.

Thus it was towards the end of 1946, that Red Funnel acquired a controlling interest in Cosens by purchasing all the shares held by the firm's directors. This amounted to over 70% of the capital of Cosens, which was more than enough to enable it to appoint its own directors and pass resolutions as required to suit the newly combined operations.

The benefits of the takeover included cutting out wasteful competition between the two companies, and made the Weymouth ship repair and marine engineering facilities available to Red Funnel. In good seasons, it was hoped that Cosens positive cash flow would help to swell their new parent company's coffers.

The 1946 season, so soon after the end of the Second World War, was a difficult one for pleasure steamer operators with their ships needing restoration if not complete rebuilding after war service, and with many piers and harbours still out of action.

The Cosens fleet was popular but their ships were universally old, even by the standards of that era which was renowned for the longevity of such vessels.

Under Red Funnel stewardship after the takeover, one by one the obsolete members of the Cosens fleet were withdrawn and scrapped. At the start of 1950, the first to go was Monarch dating from 1888. Early in her sixty-two years she had had her foc's'le enlarged and extra lifeboats fitted making her seaworthy enough to venture across the Channel to places such as Cherbourg carrying 300 passengers; quite a feat for a pleasure steamer of just 309 gross tons. Then it was the turn of

Victoria (built in 1884) followed by Empress (built in 1879) and Emperor of India (built in 1906 as Red Funnel's Princess Royal). They were withdrawn in 1953, 1955 and 1956 respectively. Meanwhile, the motorboats and launches had restarted operations after the end of the Second World War and were still providing trips around Weymouth Bay.

All was not gloom and the first Monarch's place in the fleet was filled by the acquisition of Shanklin (built in 1924) from the British Transport Commission's railway ferry fleet at Portsmouth. She entered Cosens' service in July 1951 renamed Monarch (II) and went on to give 10 years popular and reliable service. When she was withdrawn, there was talk that Red Funnel's motorship Medina, nearing the end of her days at Southampton, might be moved to Cosens at Weymouth but the idea came to nothing. Whether she could have ever been a popular excursion ship like Monarch and others before her is debatable. Medina was renowned for rolling mercilessly, even in the enclosed waters at Southampton, and there simply was not the will to see her redeployed for open sea work.

The launches and motorboats continued running until 1956 when they finally ceased due to declining business and the increasing cost of maintaining the old boats. In the end they all found new owners and varying degrees of continuing service. Cosens kept two workboats functional for use in and around the harbour where the ship repair and engineering business still continued.

After Monarch (II) had been scrapped, only two paddle steamers remained in the fleet. These were Consul (built in 1896) and Embassy (like Monarch (II), she was also a former Portsmouth railway ferry, but built in 1911 as Duchess of Norfolk). Embassy ran from Bournemouth, Poole and Swanage often to the Isle of Wight and Consul was based at Weymouth running local trips to Portland Harbour and Lulworth Cove. With what little business that remained available in the area being shared with Croson's, the Poole boat operator, the prognosis was not good. All that could be said was that at least Cosens and Red Funnel were no longer in competition with each other. Consul was withdrawn following the 1962 season but reappeared under new ownership for the following two seasons before ending her days as a floating club house bearing her original name Duke of Devonshire. She was scrapped in 1966.

Meanwhile, Embassy became the sole survivor to proudly fly the Cosens & Co Ltd house flag. Her end finally came following her 1966 season that had been marred by mechanical breakdowns and some indifferent weather. Despite efforts to try to find a way to maintain their paddle steamer service the directors of Cosens finally had to admit defeat. The 55-year old *Embassy* was placed in the hands of brokers, offices were closed and the staff dismissed. In May the following year *Embassy* was boarded up and towed away for scrap in Ghent.

Embassy's departure marked the end of 119 years of pleasure steamer operation by the company and its forebears.

Happily, the ship repair and marine engineering side of the business began to expand again including some general engineering work following redevelopment by Cosens of the old harbourside workshop buildings. New purpose-built facilities, completed in 1971, enabled them to compete with other engineering business in the area. In the end, the potential investment value of the Weymouth Harbour site began to be appreciated and the Cosens engineering business was moved to Portland. In 1990 Red Funnel, who were by then wholly owned by Associated British Ports and not that interested in their small Portland based subsidiary, disposed of Cosens & Co Ltd. Thus, a management buyout took a renamed Cosens Engineering Ltd business back to independence but sadly, not many years later, the venture ended in receivership.

This is the heading of the June 1951 Bournemouth sailing bill listing ships from Red Funnel and Cosens' fleets. In fact, apart from Easter 1952, no Red Funnel vessel was based at Bournemouth after May 1951.
KEITH ADAMS
COLLECTION

Cosens' EMBASSY was the last paddle steamer in the Red Funnel group fleet. She survived until the end of the 1966 season and was broken up in 1967.
KEITH ABRAHAM

VICTORIA departs from Swanage, leaving MONARCH (I) at the pier.
P S P S ARCHIVES

MONARCH (I) leaving Weymouth.
H A ALLEN COLLECTION

MONARCH (II) arriving at Bournemouth.
H A ALLEN COLLECTION

EMPEROR OF INDIA arrives at Totland Bay Pier.
H A ALLEN COLLECTION

EMPRESS at Lulworth Cove.
ALAN BROWN – KEITH ADAMS COLLECTION

CONSUL crossing Weymouth Bay.
RICHARD DANIELSON COLLECTION

MONARCH (II) heads across Bournemouth Bay.
H A ALLEN COLLECTION

MEDINA CROSSINGS

The main history section of this book mentions the purchase of the small paddle boat *Precursor* (I) in July 1866. This acquisition marked the start of Red Funnel's involvement in the river crossing between Cowes and East Cowes. The service appears to have been initially maintained all year round, but after World War I it became seasonal until again becoming all year round in the mid-1930s.

Precursor (I) was joined by *Princess Louise* in 1871. She ended up being used as a small general purpose tug at Southampton. One of her regular duties was hauling coal barges from the Town Quay to the Royal Pier for coaling the passenger steamers. *Princess Louise* had a very long life, surviving until being sunk by a landing craft off the Town Quay in 1944.

A more powerful version of *Princess Louise*, named *Medina* (II), was acquired in 1884 and *Precursor* (I) was disposed of. *Precursor* (II) arrived in 1898 and was converted to diesel power in 1935. *Medina* was disposed of in 1931.

Just before World War II a new motor launch, *Norris Castle* (I) was purchased. In January 1942 both *Precursor* and *Norris Castle* were requisitioned by the Admiralty. The minutes noted that the hire of *Norris Castle* was agreed at £22.50 per month, a sum considered very satisfactory by the board. Red Funnel were also prepared to sell the launches.

There was no further mention of the launches in the minutes, but it is known that both vessels went overseas. They did not return and the service did not resume after the War.

Red Funnel trialed a water taxi service from East Cowes marketed 'JetConnect' from November 2003. It was designed for commuters joining the *Red Jet* service at Cowes, but ceased in April 2005.

Red Funnel also took over the Cowes Floating Bridge Company in 1868. They ran it until an Act of Parliament enabled the East Cowes and Cowes Councils to operate the floating bridge on a 31 year lease from 1901. Eventually the ferry rights were purchased by the Councils in 1915.

MEDINA (II), the third of the launches built for the river crossing between East Cowes and Cowes. She entered service in 1884 and was eventually sold in 1931; being converted into a private yacht and surviving until after World War II.
DON JONES
COLLECTION

NORRIS CASTLE (I) was the last launch built for the Medina crossings. Shown here, just launched from Clare Lallows yard on 12 July 1938, her time with Red Funnel was short as she was taken over by the Admiralty on the outbreak of War in 1939 for service in the Mediterranean and did not return.
RED FUNNEL
ARCHIVES

VECTA heads down Southampton Water, keeping company with Cunard's transatlantic liner QUEEN ELIZABETH. At the time she was the world's largest passenger liner. Whether on a special excursion or a service run, passengers are always keen to see the liners at close quarters. The interest has returned to Southampton with the recent influx of cruise ships and QUEEN MARY 2 sailing regularly to New York. The smaller local operators and steamship SHIELDHALL often arrange pleasure trips to see the ships depart in the afternoon.
RED FUNNEL ARCHIVES.

RED FUNNEL DISTRIBUTION FORMERLY VECTIS TRANSPORT

At their board meeting on 3 October 1967 the Red Funnel directors considered a letter from the chairman of Vectis Shipping Ltd, Mr Vivian Leighthomas, suggesting an amalgamation of his business with Red Funnel. Several meetings took place and eventually an offer document to acquire Vectis Shipping was sent out by Barings Bank, Red Funnel's advisors, on 30 August 1968. The contract bringing Vectis Shipping and Vectis Roadways into the Red Funnel Group was signed in September. The three significant motor barges acquired were *Murius*, *Riverclose* and *Newclose*. Other barges in the fleet, and sold over the next few years, were *Oceanic*, *Match* and *Seaclose*. Also disposed of was *Vectis Isle*, a typical Dutch built coaster.

The barge service from Southampton to Newport was quickly discontinued and at their meeting on 23 January 1970 the board noted that the new trailer service, started on 6 October 1969 using the Red Funnel vehicle ferries, was working well. The barge service from Flathouse Hard at Portsmouth to Newport continued to provide for loads not suitable for the trailer service. The 1970 AGM noted that more traffic was being transferred to the trailer service and this was providing benefits to the parent company via its ferry operation. By 1972 the size of the road fleet had been reduced, but vehicles were newer and the financial results improved.

The shipping operation suffered a decline in turnover and profitability during 1974, but the acquisition of the Island Transport Company Ltd brought benefits. This company, wholly owned by J Samuel White & Co Ltd, was set up at the end of World War 1 to carry materials from Southampton to Cowes for its parent's shipbuilding activities. As the shipbuilding decreased they became competitors of Vectis, carrying general cargoes. Their fleet of barges included *Arreton*, *Calbourne* and *Shalfleet*.

On 21 February 1975 the directors noted that a meeting had taken place with British Road Services (BRS) to consider whether that company's services might be amalgamated with those of Vectis Shipping and Roadways. Nothing appeared to come from these possibilities but on 1 January 1976, the Vectis Roadways operation was merged with Vectis Shipping to form Vectis Transport Ltd, effecting economies in administration costs. The results were regarded as satisfactory by the Red Funnel board, but the activity was very vulnerable to disputes in the road haulage industry and the general recession at that time.

In 1978 the directors noted that the reduction in demand for the barge service continued, although they were receiving work from the new power station at Kingston, on the river Medina, and carrying grain supplies from the Rank Hovis Mills at Southampton. In 1980 there was more concern, with business from Elliot Turbomachinery, the successor to J Samuel White's, halving in two years and having to tender against very low rates from others.

Red Funnel allowed the Vectis board considerable autonomy and in October they were considering their own ro-ro service from either Portsmouth or Southampton to East Cowes. They also set up a special committee to report on the future of barge service. This service had contributed towards the company's overheads, but it really needed an increase of 10% in sales to become profitable. The board realised this was an unlikely possibility and resolved to carry on as previously, the ro-ro idea not being cost effective.

The final straw came in March 1981 when Portsmouth Council announced increases in charges of 15% from 1 April 1981. The council also had plans to enlarge Flathouse Quay to ease congestion and meet increased demand.

At the board meeting on 30 July it was resolved to cease the barge service on 31 October 1981. It would be replaced by a trailer service, using the Red Funnel ferry, provided by the local mainland haulage firm of Meachers Transport. The barge *Riverclose* made the final sailings. Subsequently barge *Marius* was sold to Williams Shipping for £15,000; *Riverclose* went to D W Hale for £12,000 and *Newclose* to J W C Gallop for £15,000.

On 26 August 1988 Mr Archdeacon retired from the Red Funnel board and as company secretary. He had been chairman of Vectis Transport and his place was taken by Island based director Mr Christopher Bland.

In November 1991 consultants recommended that the Andover Transport, formerly Grays Transport, operation be formally merged with the Vectis Transport business. In practice there had been close cooperation between the entities from 1 July 1989, the date that Grays Transport was taken over by Red Funnel.

In spring 1993 Red Funnel Distribution was set up to combine the two entities administratively, but the Vectis name was retained and used on the Island. The arrangement was short-lived as the Andover operation was sold out of the group on 30 June. The integration had been problematic and now efforts could be concentrated on the Island based operation.

Vectis Shipping had been incorporated on 7 December 1918 by Leightomas and Co Ltd, the Newport grain merchants and millers, so its 75th anniversary coincided with the new 'Raptor' ferries being introduced in 1993. The extra space on the ferries enabled a fresh marketing exercise to generate extra business. The cutting of a birthday cake was publicised in the Isle of Wight County Press.

Medina Borough Council made a formal offer to acquire the Newport Town Quay premises in May 1994. The company had one year to find a new operating base and they moved to the former BRS site at the Riverway Industrial Estate in Newport. Contract completion took place on 1 August 1995. Ironically, this warehousing and distribution facility had been set up by BRS in December 1975 when they ceased their own barge service between Cowes and Portsmouth, transferring their traffic to the Red Funnel ro-ro services.

The separate identity of the Vectis Transport board ended when it was merged into Red Funnel Ferries Limited, the last formal board meeting of Vectis Transport taking place on 25 August 2004. The Red Funnel Distribution activity continues to provide every service for the haulage industry. If a vehicle can drive under a motorway bridge then it can drive onto a 'Raptor' ferry. The division also offers a contract distribution and drop trailer service where the mainland haulier can leave their trailer at the Southampton Terminal; Red Funnel then taking responsibility for its onward journey and delivery to Island premises, before returning the trailer to Southampton. Smaller consignments can be grouped together for transport between Southampton and Newport and a home delivery service is also offered. The division is the Island agent for BOC gases, based at the Distribution Centre in Newport. Any abnormal, or dangerous, loads are also dealt with by Red Funnel Distribution.

Red Funnel Distribution handles Red Funnel's freight, goods distribution, hazardous cargo and abnormal loads business. Their articulated lorries and trailers are to be seen everywhere in and around the Southampton terminal and throughout the Island, collecting and delivering everything required for life in the Isle of Wight.
RICHARD DANIELSON

In this late 1940s view at Southampton, a few passengers are already aboard PRINCESS HELENA, with her foremast removed to facilitate better vehicle loading, necessitating her forward-facing white light to be wheelhouse-mounted. MEDINA is loading for her next passage service to Cowes and VECTA may be seen in the background.
TERRY CRESSWELL COLLECTION

Tug-tender VULCAN on the slipway at Northam displaying a build-up of marine growth needing to be removed as it will significantly impair the ship's performance. If a ship regularly berths with the same side in the sun, marine growth will be very much more pronounced on that side.
RED FUNNEL ARCHIVES

Coal-fired to the end, BOURNEMOUTH QUEEN in her final post-war guise presents the photographer with her lovely, period counter stern while the ropeman finishes stowing his rope. A poorly patronised excursion; a small crowd is gathered on her foredeck leaving the rest of the ship almost deserted.
DON JONES COLLECTION

With only four weeks left of her final season with Red Funnel at Southampton, BALMORAL arrives at Shanklin Pier on Sunday, 18 August 1968. Culver Cliff and the Yarborough Monument can be seen behind the vessel. The published timetables give the following details of BALMORAL'S excursion sailing that day:

Southampton (depart10:45); Ryde (12:05/18:10); Southsea (12:40/17:20); Shanklin (14:10/15:50) – from where a cruise along the Island coast was offered calling at Sandown (14:30/16:10). The fare for the full day cruise from Southampton was 17 shillings (85 pence), from Southsea 10 shillings (50 pence) and from Shanklin and Sandown 5 shillings (25 pence).

The master, without his uniform jacket, stands at the engine room telegraph. The purser, Mr Ted Angel, is standing on the bridge wing. He had been on BALMORAL for many years, finally retiring at the end of the 1968 season.

JUNE BUSHELL

SOURCES

COMPANY PUBLICATIONS

Official Guide (Second Edition) 1913
South Coast Guide – Years 1924, 1936
Red Funnel Stuff – Years 1937, 1938, 1939
Red Funnel Steamers – Years 1953 – 1962 (6 editions)
Red Funnel Steamers – Years 1970, 1971 (Captain F T O'Brien)
The First Hundred Years – Centenary book - 1961 (G W O'Connor)
Red Funnel- A Pictorial History - 1997 (Michael Archbold)

NEWSPAPERS AND PERIODICALS

Black Jack (Newsletter of the Southampton branch of the World Ship Society)
Clyde Steamers (Magazine of the Clyde River Steamer Club)
Cruising Monthly (Magazine of the Coastal Cruising Association)
Isle of Wight County Press, The
Ship Ahoy (Magazine of the South Wales branch of the World Ship Society)
Ships Monthly
Southern Evening Echo, The
Trip Out
Paddle Wheels (Magazine of the Paddle Steamer Preservation Society)

BOOKS

Adams, R B. *Red Funnel and Before*. Kingfisher Railway Productions, 1986

Arnott, Alastair and Wragg, Rachel. *Images of Southampton*. Breedon Books, 1994

Barnaby, K C. *100 Years of Specialised Shipbuilding and Engineering*. Hutchinson & Co, 1964

Box, Peter. *Belles of the East Coast*. Tyndale and Panda Publishing, 1989

Brown, Alan. *Lymington – The Sound of Success*. Allan T Condie Publications, 1988

Brown, Alan. *Shanklin – Ill Fated Prince*. Waverley Excursions Ltd, 1985

Burtt, Frank. *Cross-Channel and Coastal Paddle Steamers*. Richard Tilling, 1937

Chalk, David L. *Any more for the Skylark* – The Story of Bournemouth's Pleasure Boats. David L Chalk, 1980

Clammer, Richard. *Cosens of Weymouth 1848 – 1918*. Black Dwarf Publications, 2005

Clammer, Richard. *Cosens of Weymouth 1918 – 1996*. Twelveheads Press, 2001

Danielson, Richard. *The Honourable Balmoral – Her Peers and Piers*. Maritime Publications, 1999

Danielson, Richard. *Railway Ships and Packet Ports*. Twelveheads Press, 2007

Davison, Currie and Ogley. *Hampshire and Isle of Wight Weather*. Froglets Publications Ltd. 1993

Deayton, Alistair; Quinn, Iain and Murrel, Patrick. *MV Balmoral – The First 60 Years*. Amberley Publishing, 2009

Duckworth and Langmuir. *West Coast Steamers*. T Stephenson & Sons, 1966

Fairman, J R. *The Fawley Branch*. The Oakwood Press, 2002

Faulkner, John. The *Fisbourne Car Ferry* Wight Connection. Colourpoint Books, 2004.

Grimshaw, Geoffrey. *British Excursion Steamers 1920 – 1939*. Richard Tilling, 1945

Howarth, David & Stephen. *The Story of P&O*. The Peninsular and Oriental Steam Navigation Company, 1986

Holyoak, John. *Balmoral and the story of the Bristol Channel Steamers*. Waverley Excursions Ltd, 1992

Holyoak, John; Tedstone, Mike; McKendrick, Joe and Brown, Leslie. *Balmoral, Britains Classic Coastal Cruise Ship*. Waverley Excursions Ltd, 2003

Jordan, S. *Ferry Services of the London, Brighton & South Coast Railway*. The Oakwood Press, 1998

Mackett, John. *The Portsmouth – Ryde Passage*. The Ravensbourne Press, 1970

Marden, David. *A Further Look at Southampton's Quayside Railways*. Kestrel Railway Books, 2009

Mawson, Chris and Riding, Richard. *British Seaside Piers*. Ian Allen Publishing, 2008

Maund, T B. *Mersey Ferries, Vol 1 Woodside – Eastham*. Transport Publishing Co Ltd, 1991

Maycock, R J and Silsbury, R. *The Piers, Tramways and Railways at Ryde*. The Oakwood Press, 2005

Maycock, R J and Silsbury, R. *The Isle of Wight Central Railway*. The Oakwood Press, 2001

McCart, Neil. *Atlantic Liners of the Cunard Line*. Patrick Stephens Ltd, 1990

Monkhouse, F J. *A Survey of Southampton and Its Region*. British Association for the Advancement of Science, 1964

Moody, Bert. *150 Years of Southampton Docks*. Kingfisher Railway Productions, 1988

Nicholson, Tim. *Take the Strain*. The Alexandra Towing Company Ltd, 1990

O'Brien, Captain F T. *Early Solent Steamers*. David and Charles, 1973

Pannel, J P M. *Old Southampton Shores*. David and Charles, 1967

Paterson, J S. *The Golden Years of the Clyde Steamers (1889-1914)*. David and Charles, 1969

Rance, Adrian B. *Shipbuilding in Victorian Southampton*. Southampton University Industrial Archaeology Group, 1981

Shepherd, John. *The Liverpool and North Wales Steamship Company*. Ships in Focus Publications, 2006

Temple Patterson, A. *Southampton – A Biography*. Macmillan, 1970

Thornton, E C B. *South Coast Pleasure Steamers*. T Stephenson & Sons Ltd, 1962

Wilson, Roy. *Passenger Steamers of the Glasgow & South Western Railway*. Twelveheads Press, 1991

Woodley, Broomfield and Jemima. *Thorny's, an oral history of Vosper Thornycroft's Shipyard*. Southampton Oral History Unit, Southampton City Council, 2005

NOTES

Over the years this company has often been referred to as 'The Southampton Company' and 'The Isle of Wight Company'. For almost 75 years it has been locally known as Red Funnel and to avoid confusion it is referred to by this name throughout the book.

The shipbuilding and repair yards of John I Thornycroft Ltd feature often in these pages. Locally known as 'Thorny's', or 'Thornycrofts', I have generally referred to the firm simply as *Thornycroft's*.

When writing about Cowes I have referred to the town on the western side of river Medina as Cowes and the town on the east side as East Cowes. In Red Funnel timetables the destinations are now generally referred to as West Cowes and East Cowes.

SUBSCRIBERS

At the time of going to press, the following is an alphabetical list of persons who kindly helped to support this edition of Red Funnel 150 by subscribing for copies in advance of its publication. Orders for the book continue to arrive but to meet publishing deadlines it was not possible to include further names. The publisher and the author wish to thank everyone who has ordered copies of this special book and express the hope that they enjoy reading it as much as we have enjoyed researching, writing and producing it.

Anderson,	D.	Joliffe,	R.T.	Seaton,	C.
Beesley,	R.W.	Jones,	C.	Semple,	P.W.
Billings,	R.	Jones,	D.A.	Shaw,	G.
Bird,	N.	Jones,	D.K.	Shears,	C.T.
Bloxam,	P.F.	Jones,	J.	Sims,	R.J.
Boswell,	G.G.	Kearney,	R.J.	Smith,	C.J.
Bowden-Green,	J.	Kelly,	J.	Sparks,	H.
Bridges,	B.	Le Jeune,	B.	Spells,	J.
Brown,	D.	Lester,	D.H.J.	Stafford,	P.M.
Bungard,	R.	May,	J.	Stearn,	W.A.
Cade,	L.	McKendrick,	J.	Steeds,	P.
Cade,	P.R.	Mills,	H.H.	Stockdale,	N.M.
Chaplin,	D.	Mills,	R.	Sugden,	E.P.
Cheverton,	K.	Munn,	A.P.	Sunderland,	P.
Child,	G.J.	Ness,	C.J.	Sylvester,	T.
Cook,	J.	Palmer,	R.M.	Thomas,	J.
Coombes,	N.	Parsons,	D.	Thomas,	L.S.
Creswell,	T.	Perkins,	R.	Turner,	C.
Currie,	A.	Porter,	J.	Walker,	B.
Darby-Hoskin,	E.	Purcell,	R.S.	Wheeler,	G.E.
Davies,	P.L.	Purvis,	D.	Whettingsteel,	J.
Dixon,	R.	Robinson,	N.V.	Whittington,	J.J.
Donaldson,	J.	Rogers,	K.	Wilkin,	H.E.
Downs,	A.	Rowe,	D.	Williams,	G.S.
Dunn,	T.	Saunders,	K.C.	Willis,	N.W.
Eastham,	K.	Saunders,	R.P.F.	Wright,	F.C.
Eley,	R.				
Engert,	R.				
Ferguson,	G.C.				
Fitzpatrick,	W.S.				
Galley,	W.				
Garner-Richards,	P.				
Gladwell,	A.				
Glanville,	R.				
Gosling,	A.				
Grant,	I.				
Gray,	V.				
Haddleton,	D.S.				
Hall,	P.				
Harvey,	J.N.				
House,	J.				
Hoverd,	R.S.				
Howarth,	R.				
Huckett,	A.				
Jacobs,	G.A.				
Johnson,	A.				
Johnson,	D. J.				
Johnson,	P.A.				

Red Funnel's then flagship BALMORAL (I) approaching the old wooden pile pier at Weymouth in 1930 or earlier. BALMORAL still sports an all-white funnel. The pier was rebuilt and extended, providing better harbour railway facilities and berths for Weymouth's cross-Channel and pleasure steamers, in the years ending in 1933.
RED FUNNEL ARCHIVES

INDEX

INDEX

Approaching Ryde Pier on 26 July 1958, PRINCESS ELIZABETH is in her final summer season with Red Funnel. She was 31 years old when this photograph was taken and still had a few more years' service with other operators ahead of her. She remains afloat and in business to this day; permanently moored in Dunkirk Harbour PRINCESS ELIZABETH hosts business meetings, banquets, marriages and family gatherings for up to 300 people. RICHARD DANIELSON COLLECTION